PREPARING COMPANY ACCOUNTS

Practical guidelines for small and medium-sized companies

PREPARING COMPANY ACCOUNTS

Practical guidelines for small and medium-sized companies

Ray Mayes BA FCA

Buzzacott

Sixth Edition

Accountancy Books
Gloucester House
399 Silbury Boulevard
Central Milton Keynes
MK9 2HL

Tel: 01908 248000

© 1997 The Institute of Chartered Accountants in England and Wales

First Edition 1985
Second Edition 1990
Third Edition March 1993
Fourth Edition May 1993
Fifth Edition 1994
Sixth Edition 1997

All rights reserved.
UK statutory material in this publication is
acknowledged as Crown copyright.

Accounting Standards Board material
© 1996 Reproduced with the permission of the Accounting Standards Board Limited.

No part of this publication may be reproduced,
stored in a retrieval system, or transmitted in
any form or by any means electronic, mechanical,
recording or otherwise, without the prior permission
of the publisher.

Views expressed in this publication are the author's
and are not necessarily those of the Institute
or of his firm.

No responsibility for loss occasioned to any person
acting or refraining from action as a result of any
material in this publication can be accepted
by the author or publisher.

ISBN 1 85355 7331

British Library Cataloguing-in-Publication Data.
A catalogue record for this book is available from the British Library.

Typeset by RefineCatch Limited, Bungay, Suffolk
Printed in Great Britain by Headway Press, Reading

Contents

	page
Abbreviations	viii
Summary of implementation dates	ix

PART I GENERAL

1 Introduction — 3
  1.1 Purpose of the book — 3
  1.2 Company accounting problems — 4
  1.3 Companies Act 1985 — 4
  1.4 Companies Act 1989 — 4
  1.5 Statutory regulations affecting small companies — 5
  1.6 Recent changes for small companies — 5
  1.7 New special accounting provisions — 7
  1.8 The variety of small company accounts — 9

2 Company accounts provisions — 11
  2.1 Introduction — 11
  2.2 Accounts — 11
  2.3 True and fair view — 11
  2.4 Format of accounts — 11
  2.5 Accounting principles — 12
  2.6 Accounts disclosures — 13
  2.7 Directors' report — 13
  2.8 Audit reports — 14
  2.9 Dormant companies — 14
  2.10 Publication of non-statutory accounts — 14
  2.11 Group accounts — 15
  2.12 Approval and signature of accounts — 15

3 Accounts and accounting standards — 17
  3.1 Basic contents of financial statements — 17
  3.2 Primary statements — 17
  3.3 Accounting standards — 18
  3.4 Cash flow statements — 18
  3.5 The substance of transactions — 19
  3.6 Application of accounting standards to smaller companies — 19
  3.7 Small companies and the FRSSE — 19

4 Formats of accounts — 21
  4.1 The statutory formats — 21
  4.2 Format headings — 25
  4.3 Group accounts — 25
  4.4 Abbreviated accounts — 25
  4.5 The effect of FRS 3 — 25
  4.6 FRS 4 'Capital instruments' — 31

5 Guidelines and definitions — 33
  5.1 True and fair view — 33

Contents

5.2	Accounts	33
5.3	Profit and loss account	35
5.4	Balance sheet	39
5.5	Balance sheet: analysis of debtors and creditors	41
5.6	Capital instruments	43
5.7	Directors' report	44
5.8	Auditors' duty in connection with directors' report	45
5.9	Alternative bases of accounting	45
5.10	Groups: parent and subsidiary undertakings	46
5.11	The substance of transactions	47

PART II SMALLER COMPANIES

6 Small and medium-sized companies — 51
6.1	Classification of companies	51
6.2	Qualifying conditions	51
6.3	Parent companies	51
6.4	Decision chart to determine size qualification	52

7 Small company accounts — 55
7.1	Special provisions for small companies	55
7.2	New Schedule 8 substituted into Companies Act 1985	55
7.3	Less detailed balance sheet	56
7.4	Profit and loss account	56
7.5	Notes to the accounts	58
7.6	Directors' statements	58
7.7	Groups	59
7.8	Balance sheet format – small company balance sheet	59
7.9	Audit opinion: true and fair view	60
7.10	Disclosure concessions for small companies	60
7.11	Directors' report of a small company	62

8 Abbreviated accounts — 65
8.1	Filing accounts	65
8.2	Contents of abbreviated accounts	65
8.3	Directors' statements	66
8.4	Abbreviated balance sheet	67
8.5	Notes to abbreviated accounts	67
8.6	'Gross profit or loss'	69
8.7	Parent companies	69
8.8	Decision to prepare abbreviated accounts	69
8.9	Special auditors' report	69

9 Exemptions for small and medium-sized groups — 71
9.1	Group accounts	71
9.2	Exemptions	71
9.3	Small and medium-sized groups	71
9.4	Qualifying conditions: group exemptions	72
9.5	Auditors' report	72
9.6	Abbreviated group accounts	73
9.7	Decision chart to determine group accounts exemption	73

10 Small company audit exemption and accountants' reports — 75
10.1	Introduction: preparation of accounts irrespective of audit	75
10.2	Audit exemptions for certain categories of small company	75
10.3	Audit exemption not available	75
10.4	Right to require an audit	76
10.5	Determining audit exemption	76

10.6	Effect of audit exemption	76
10.7	Reports required on accounts of small companies	77
10.8	Audit exemption conditions	77
10.9	Statement by the directors	78
10.10	Accountants' report under s249A(2) Companies Act 1985	79
10.11	The reporting accountant	80
10.12	Audit exemption: abbreviated accounts	80

11 Financial Reporting Standard for Smaller Entities ('FRSSE') — 83
- 11.1 Introduction — 83
- 11.2 The FRSSE in outline — 83
- 11.3 FRS 3 and the FRSSE — 89
- 11.4 Related parties — 89
- 11.5 Foreign currency translation — 90

PART III EXAMPLE ACCOUNTS

12 Example accounts — 95
- 12.1 Accounts of Small Company Limited (pages 97–115) — 95
- 12.2 Abbreviated accounts of Small Company Limited (pages 116–123) — 95
- 12.3 Unaudited accounts of Dormant Small Company Limited (pages 124–125) — 96
- 12.4 Auditors' reports — 96

APPENDICES

Appendix A	Company accounts sections	129
Appendix B	Statutory formats of accounts – Companies Act 1985 Schedules 4 and 8	133
Appendix C	Special accounting provisions for small and medium-sized companies – Companies Act 1985 sections 246 to 249	147
Appendix D	Form and content of accounts prepared by small companies – Companies Act 1985 Schedule 8	153
Appendix E	Form and content of abbreviated accounts of small companies delivered to Registrar – Companies Act 1985 Schedule 8A	167
Appendix F	Exemptions from audit for certain categories of small company – Companies Act 1985 sections 249A to 249E	171
Appendix G	Dormant companies – Companies Act 1985 section 250	175
Appendix H	Disclosure of information: related undertakings – Companies Act 1985 Schedule 5	177
Appendix I	'Accounting Simplifications' and SI 1996 No. 189	181
Appendix J	Abbreviated accounts checklist	185
Appendix K	Selected reading	189

Index — 191

Abbreviations

ACT	Advance corporation tax
APB	Auditing Practices Board
ASB	Accounting Standards Board
CA 1985	Companies Act 1985 (as amended by CA 1989 and subsequent statutory instruments)
CA 1989	Companies Act 1989
DTI	Department of Trade and Industry
EEA	European Economic Area
ESOP	Employee share ownership plan
EU	European Union
FRS	Financial Reporting Standard
FRSSE	Financial Reporting Standard for Smaller Entities
FSA 1986	Financial Services Act 1986
NIC	National Insurance contribution
P & L account	Profit and loss account
PAYE	Pay as you earn
PN	APB Practice Note
s	section (unless otherwise stated, section references refer to CA 1985, as amended from time to time)
SAS	Statement of Auditing Standards
Sch	Schedule CA 1985 (for example, Sch 4.2(1) means Companies Act 1985 Schedule 4, paragraph 2(1))
SI	Statutory instrument
SI 1992 No. 2452	The Companies Act 1985 (Accounts of Small and Medium-sized Enterprises and Publication of Accounts in ECUs) Regulations 1992
SI 1994 No. 1935	The Companies Act 1985 (Audit Exemption) Regulations 1994
SI 1996 No. 189	The Companies Act 1985 (Miscellaneous Accounting Amendments) Regulations 1996
SI 1997 No. 220	The Companies Act 1985 (Accounts of Small and Medium-sized Companies and Minor Accounting Amendments) Regulations 1997
SI 1997 No. 570	The Company Accounts (Disclosure of Directors' Emoluments) Regulations 1997
SI 1997 No. 936	The Companies Act 1985 (Audit Exemption) (Amendment) Regulations 1997
SORP	Statement of Recommended Practice
SSAP	Statement of Standard Accounting Practice
SSRA	Statement of Standards for Reporting Accountants
UITF	ASB Urgent Issues Task Force
VAT	Value added tax

Summary of implementation dates

Implementation affects accounts for accounting periods ending on or after

SI 1996 No. 189	Miscellaneous Accounting Amendments	2 February 1996
SI 1997 No. 570	Disclosure of Directors' Emoluments	31 March 1997
SI 1997 No. 936	Audit Exemption	15 June 1997

Implementation affects accounts approved on or after

SI 1994 No. 1935	Small Companies Audit Exemption	11 August 1994
SI 1997 No. 220	Accounts of Small and Medium-sized Companies and Minor Accounting Amendments	1 March 1997

FRSSE implementation

This book has been prepared on the basis that provisions contained in the Draft FRSSE issued by the ASB in December 1996 are implemented as set out in the Exposure Draft.

The FRSSE is anticipated to be issued in summer 1997, at which time immediate adoption of the FRSSE (but not the Exposure Draft) will be permissible and encouraged. Until the effective date, accounting standards (FRSs, SSAPs and UITF Consensus Abstracts) must be considered in full and adopted where appropriate.

Reference should be made to the FRSSE itself, as finally adopted, for the detailed provisions.

Part I General

Chapter 1 Introduction

Preparing company accounts for small companies is not as easy as it seems at first sight.

Legislation over recent years, of both domestic and European origin, has resulted in a considerable standardisation of financial reporting for companies of all sizes. UK company law, nevertheless, is comprehensive and complex. Preparers of accounts have to contend with ever-increasing legislation and regulation.

Fortunately, for the small company, substantial progress has been made in simplifying the whole process of accounts production.

- Simplified small company accounts are now much less detailed than those of larger companies.
- The filing option of 'abbreviated accounts' affords a measure of further privacy and simplicity for small companies.
- A dedicated regime of statutory accounting and an accounting standard for small companies has lifted much of the 'fog' surrounding the preparation of accounts.
- Simplified external scrutiny and audit exemptions have provided the opportunity for some smaller companies to minimise the cost and effort involved in what many see as a 'statutory burden'. The scope of audit exemption has also been widened.

In an effort to make life easier, there are moves afoot to afford small companies the opportunity of preparing and filing their accounts using a somewhat mechanistic form of standard template or boilerplate approach. Many interested parties have reservations over this initiative.

Inevitably, the small company will always rely to varying degrees on the external support of the professional advisor – traditionally the auditor. Will a standard form of accounts, other than that already provided by existing legislation, really be the wholesale advantage its advocates maintain? Given the range of options of financial reporting for small companies, and despite recent simplifications, a standard template to cover all possible situations will be difficult to develop. Meanwhile, preparers of small company accounts will continue to turn to books such as this to save some of the heartache involved in finding their way thorough the labyrinth of legislation and professional standards.

1.1 Purpose of the book

This book is essentially concerned with the accounts of small companies, that is small and medium-sized companies as defined by the Companies Act 1985. The aim of the book is to illustrate and explain many of the company accounting requirements that affect such companies and the exemptions (both accounting and audit) that are available to them. The emphasis is on clarity and simplification, using charts and tables as a form of illustration.

This book includes the following:

- a summary of company accounts provisions – as they affect companies generally;
- guidelines and definitions – for accounting presentation and disclosure;
- an explanation of the company accounts' provisions for small and medium-sized companies – providing for both full statutory and abbreviated accounts;
- an explanation of the audit exemption available to certain small companies;
- an illustrative example of the accounts of a 'small company'.

Chapter 1   Introduction

Although certain statutory provisions affecting group accounts are inevitably covered, consolidated accounts and accounting for consolidations are generally not dealt with in detail.

The book is a quick and illustrative guide which simplifies the legislation and provides a ready explanation for anyone involved in the preparation of statutory accounts for the smaller company. It will be of particular help to company directors or financial managers of small or medium-sized private companies, as well as students and professional advisors. The book concentrates on those matters of practical relevance as far as accounts are concerned and does not purport to give comprehensive coverage of all the accounting provisions.

1.2   Company accounting problems

Recent company legislation has provided a measure of standardisation for company accounts, the codification of accounting rules and principles and, to some extent, the simplification of disclosure. Nevertheless, a great deal has been left to the accountancy profession to interpret in accordance with generally accepted accounting practice.

Increasingly, the accounts provisions of company law are being supplemented by guidance in the form of financial reporting standards issued by the Accounting Standard Board. Nevertheless, for many of the problems posed by the Companies Acts there may be no definitive answers. Interpretation may often be subjective; what is often required is a reasoned and reasonable approach to interpretation. In many instances there may be no alternative but to refer to the legislation itself.

1.3   Companies Act 1985

The Companies Act 1985 remains the principal and fundamental company law enactment. Reference should always be made to the Act, as amended by subsequent legislation including statutory instruments, in order to ensure that current and up-to-date legislation is being adhered to.

This book brings the legislation right up to date to April 1997.

In 1985, legislation was introduced to consolidate various company law enactments passed between 1948 and 1983. The Companies Act 1981 implemented the EC Fourth Directive on company accounts. It fundamentally amended the form and content of company accounts and increased the accounting requirements for all companies.

The Companies Act 1985 consolidates into one Act the bulk of company law and remains one of the largest enactments on the statute book, comprising over 750 sections and 27 schedules. However, the substance of law concerning company accounts, first introduced by the Companies Act 1981, remains unchanged.

From August 1994, certain small companies have been exempted from the statutory requirement to have an audit of their annual accounts. The scope for audit exemption has been widened from June 1997.

1.4   Companies Act 1989

The main purpose of the Companies Act 1989 was to implement the EC Seventh and Eighth Directives on consolidated accounts and the regulation of auditors respectively. Small and medium-sized groups were exempted from the need to prepare group accounts. The 1989 Act also included changes of company law simplifying company administration procedures for private companies, for example allowing business to be transacted by written resolution.

As it affected company accounts, the Companies Act 1989 added to and changed existing provisions by replacing, inserting or amending various sections of and schedules to the 1985 Act, in whole or in part.

1.5 Statutory regulations affecting small companies

1.5.1 Simplified small company accounts

A relaxation of the reporting requirements for small and medium-sized companies was introduced by regulations contained in SI 1992 No. 2452 The Companies Act 1985 (Accounts of Small and Medium-sized Enterprises and Publication of Accounts in ECUs) Regulations 1992. These regulations implemented an EC Directive amending earlier Directives (the Fourth and Seventh Directives) as concerns small and medium-sized companies, and introduced a package of further exemptions affecting small company accounts.

In essence, the regulations resulted in the following changes:

- the amount of information included and disclosed in the directors' report, balance sheet and notes in small company accounts was reduced significantly;
- companies are now allowed to publish and file their accounts in ECUs, in addition to the company's annual accounts.

1.5.2 Audit exemptions

SI 1994 No. 1935 The Companies Act 1985 (Audit Exemption) Regulations 1994 removed the audit requirements for certain small companies. The provisions have been subsequently amended by SI 1997 No. 936 The Companies Act 1985 (Audit Exemption) (Amendment) Regulations 1997.

In brief, the exemptions apply to companies with an annual turnover of under £350,000 and a balance sheet total of less than £1.4 million. Public companies, financial services companies and certain other categories are excluded from the audit exemption.

Except for charitable companies, where a company's turnover is under £350,000, statutory accounts may be prepared (and filed with the Registrar of Companies) unaudited without either an auditors' report or an accountants' report attached.

The old rules, whereby a company whose turnover exceeds £90,000 but is under £350,000 is exempt from the requirement for audit but must attach to its statutory accounts a report by an independent reporting accountant, will no longer apply.

The regulations do not alter the accounting provisions affecting small company accounts but simply the requirements or otherwise for audit.

The audit exemption provisions are dealt with in detail in Chapter **10**.

1.6 Recent changes for small companies

1.6.1 Accounting simplifications

Following DTI consultation in 1995, a considerable number of simplifications to accounting and audit requirements were introduced by SI 1996 No. 189 The Companies Act 1985 (Miscellaneous Accounting Amendments) Regulations 1996. The changes affected all limited companies generally, irrespective of size, and resulted in a relaxation from many accounting disclosures. The regulations came into effect (in most cases) for accounting years ending after 2 February 1996.

Chapter 1 Introduction

The accounting simplifications introduced by SI 1996 No. 189, most of which are of minor significance, are summarised in Appendix I.

1.6.2 Special provisions for small companies

Much of the complexity and consequent confusion in the preparation of small company accounts arose from the need to consider the basic requirements for all companies generally and then apply any exemptions that may have been applicable. SI 1997 No. 220 The Companies Act 1985 (Accounts of Small and Medium-sized Companies and Minor Accounting Amendments) Regulations 1997 in essence re-enacts the small companies accounts provisions on a 'stand-alone' basis so that all the relevant requirements are henceforth contained within specific sections and schedules (principally new Schedules 8 and 8A) of CA 1985.

The purpose of the regulations is to make it easier for small companies to identify which of the disclosure requirements apply to them without having to search through the whole range of provisions (principally Schedule 4) that apply to the generality of company. The regulations do not extend or alter the exemptions previously available but simplify them and make it easier to take advantage of them. The changes for medium-sized companies are more limited.

The changes brought about by SI 1997 No. 220, which came into effect in respect of annual accounts approved on or after 1 March 1997 or for financial years ending on or after 25 March 1997, are reflected in detail later in this book and are summarised in 1.7.

1.6.3 Financial Reporting Standard for Small Companies

Together with statutory rules and accounting principles, accounting standards are the bedrock upon which annual accounts are prepared. With recent Financial Reporting Standards becoming more detailed and complex and more exemptions being made for small entities, the need for a more succinct and relevant set of standards tailor-made for small companies has been recognised for some time.

For the smaller entity, the burden of considering and complying with the whole range of accounting standards has frequently outweighed the benefits of clearer financial reporting.

The ASB has responded to this situation by issuing a draft FRSSE – the Financial Reporting Standard for Smaller Entities. The FRSSE applies to all smaller entities (as defined) – not just companies – which prepare accounts showing a true and fair view and which choose to adopt the stand-alone document containing all the relevant standards. Additional reference may be required occasionally to existing SSAPs or FRSs (for example, on questions of accounting measurement or principles; additional guidance on true and fair view; or consolidation principles), but generally the FRSSE is intended to be the definitive source of guidance for those accounting standards for smaller entities – the 'vade-mecum' for the busy practitioner or company accountant.

The FRSSE is summarised in outline in Chapter 11.

The book has been prepared on the basis that the provisions of the draft FRSSE, issued in December 1996, are adopted. References are to the draft FRSSE.

1.6.4 Audit exemption – repeal of accountants' report conditions

Since August 1994, certain categories of small company have been exempted from the requirement to have an audit – either totally or alternatively with unaudited accounts subject to an accountants' report.

Audit exemption applied generally to companies with a turnover for a financial year not exceeding £350,000; those companies with a turnover between £90,001 and £350,000 and opting for unaudited accounts were required to have an accountants' report.

SI 1997 No. 936 The Companies Act 1985 (Audit Exemption) (Amendment) Regulations 1997 increases the turnover limit which a small company must not exceed in respect of a financial year if it is to be totally exempt from audit from £90,000 to £350,000. As a consequence of this increase, the requirement whereby relevant small companies had to obtain a report from a reporting accountant is repealed. The amendments apply to annual accounts for financial years ending on or after 15 June 1997.

The audit exemption rules for small charitable companies continue unchanged.

Amendments have also been made that enable a company which would otherwise be disqualified from claiming exemption from audit for a financial year because it was a parent company or subsidiary undertaking for any part of that year, to claim the exemption, provided that the group of which it was a member was a small group satisfying the conditions specified in the new provisions.

1.7 New special accounting provisions

1.7.1 Small Companies SI 1997 No. 220

SI 1997 No. 220 The Companies Act 1985 (Accounts of Small and Medium-sized Companies and Minor Accounting Amendments) Regulations 1997 amends provisions in Part VII of the Companies Act 1985 concerning the accounts of small and medium-sized companies as defined in section 247 of the CA 1985. The statutory instrument:

(a) substitutes a new
   - section 246 (special provisions for small companies), and
   - Schedule 8 (form and content of accounts prepared by small companies); and
(b) inserts a new Schedule 8A (form and content of abbreviated accounts of small companies delivered to registrar of companies).

The effect of these amendments is to set out in full the provisions governing the form and content of the accounts and reports prepared by small companies and delivered to the registrar, rather than, as previously, operating by affording exemptions from the full requirements of Schedule 4 to CA 1985. New section 246(8) simplifies the statements required on the balance sheets and in the directors' report of small companies. Otherwise there are no changes of substance.

A new section 246A (special provisions for medium-sized companies) brings together the (somewhat limited) special provisions applying to the accounts of medium-sized companies and simplifies the statement required on the balance sheet of such companies. Otherwise there are no changes of substance.

The provisions of CA 1985 are restated (without changes of substance) concerning:

- the circumstances in which the special provisions for small and medium-sized companies do not apply (new section 247A) (including 'ineligible' companies), and
- the preparation of group accounts by small companies (new section 248A).

A new section 247B restates the provisions previously contained in paragraph 24 of Schedule 8 to CA 1985 concerning the special auditors' report required when a small or medium-sized company delivers abbreviated accounts to the registrar of companies. There are two changes of substance:

(a) the auditors are no longer required to make a report to the directors as was formerly provided by paragraph 24(1) of old Schedule 8; and
(b) the special report of the auditors delivered to the registrar need no longer in all cases be accompanied by, or set out in full, the auditors' report under section 235. It need only do so where:

Chapter 1   Introduction

- the section 235 report was qualified, or
- the section 235 report contained a statement under section 237(2) (accounts, records or returns inadequate or accounts not agreeing with records and returns) or section 237(3) (failure to obtain necessary information and explanations).

Other minor amendments have been made to:

- section 250 (dormant companies) following SI 1996 No. 189; and
- paragraph 48(1)(b) of Schedule 4 CA 1985 (creditors), whereby disclosure should only be of amounts due after more than five years.

The new structure of the statutory provisions for small and medium-sized companies (that is, sections 246 to 249 and new Schedules 8 and 8A) are set out in Tables 1.1 and 1.2.

Table 1.1   Accounting provisions for small and medium-sized companies revised by SI 1997 No. 220

Sections 246 to 249

New s246 – substituted	Special provisions for small companies.	Provisions with which a small company must or may comply including provisions of new Schedule 8.
New s246A – inserted	Special provisions for medium-sized companies.	Provisions with which a medium-sized company must or may comply.
s247 – unchanged	Qualification of company as small or medium-sized.	Qualifying conditions and requirements.
New s247A – inserted	Cases in which special provisions do not apply.	E.g., public companies or ineligible companies etc.
New s247B – inserted	Special auditors' report.	Special auditors' report to accompany abbreviated accounts (for delivery to Registar of Companies).
s248 – unchanged	Exemption for small and medium-sized groups.	Where parent need not prepare group accounts.
New s248A – inserted	Group accounts prepared by small company.	Provisions with which the group accounts of a small company must or may comply.
s249 – unchanged	Qualification of group as small or medium-sized.	Qualification requirements.

Table 1.2   New Schedules 8 and 8A

New Schedule 8 substituted into CA 1985
Form and content of accounts prepared by small companies.

Part I	General rules and formats
Part II	Accounting principles and rules
Part III	Notes to the accounts
Part IV	Interpretation of schedule

New Schedule 8A substituted into CA 1985
Form and content of abbreviated accounts of small companies delivered to registrar

Part I	Balance sheet formats
Part II	Notes to the accounts

1.8 The variety of small company accounts

As will be seen later in this book, the variety and complexity of small company accounts can be bewildering. Accounts can vary according to the statutory requirements, size, criteria, etc. – depending on the circumstances. Table 1.3 sets out the matrix of options.

Table 1.3 Matrix of small company accounts

Type of accounts	\multicolumn{6}{c}{may be}					
	Audited with Audit report	Audit exempt no Audit report	Audit exempt with s249A(2) Accountants' report*	Audit exempt with no s249A(2) Accountants' report*	Audited with Special Audit report	Audit exempt No Special Audit or s249A(2) Accountants' report*
Full statutory accounts	●					
Full statutory accounts		●		●		
Full statutory accounts		●	●			
Small company accounts simplified	●					
Small company accounts simplified		●		●		
Small company accounts simplified		●	●			
Dormant accounts	●					
Dormant accounts		●				
Small company abbreviated accounts					●	
Small company abbreviated accounts			●			●

Full statutory accounts – Schedule 4 or less.
Small company accounts – Schedule 8.
Abbreviated accounts – Schedule 8A and sections 246(5) and (6).

* For audit exemption subsequent to SI 1997 No. 936, and the need or otherwise for an Accountants' Report under section 249A(2), see Chapter **10**.

Chapter 2 Company accounts provisions

2.1 Introduction

This chapter summarises the company accounts provisions of the Companies Act 1985. The Companies Act 1985, as amended, lays down provisions relating to:

- prescriptive formats of accounts;
- the content of accounts;
- principles and rules for determining amounts included in the accounts.

The chapter summarises accounts provisions of the Companies Act 1985, insofar as they relate to accounts ('individual accounts') that are prepared in accordance with the Companies Act 1985 section 226. 'Abbreviated' (modified statutory accounts) are considered separately in Chapter 8. Matters relating to groups of companies are generally not covered in detail.

2.2 Accounts

Full accounts prepared for shareholders must be prepared for all companies, irrespective of size. The full accounts of a 'small' company, however, may contain less detail. A company qualifying as 'small' or 'medium-sized' (see Chapter 6) may, in addition, prepare 'abbreviated' accounts for filing with the Registrar of Companies. *s226*

Depending on certain size criteria (see Chapter 10), small companies may be exempt from the requirement for audit. Dormant companies may also take advantage of audit exemption.

2.3 True and fair view

There is a fundamental requirement for full accounts (individual accounts or group accounts) to show a true and fair view. This applies irrespective of whether or not the accounts are subject to audit or independent reporting accountants' review. Any decision concerning the method of accounting or means of disclosing information must take this basic requirement into account. *s226 s227*

2.4 Format of accounts

The form and content of individual accounts is covered by Schedule 4 to the Act (companies generally) and Schedule 8 (small companies). The schedules prescribe the required formats from which companies may choose. Formats which are most commonly used are illustrated in Chapter 4. Schedule 4A deals with the rules for the form and content of group accounts.

Once a format has been adopted, the company must use the same format for subsequent years unless, in the directors' opinion, there are special reasons for changing; these must be disclosed in the year of change. *Sch 4.2 Sch 8.2*

Every balance sheet and profit and loss account must show the items listed in the adopted format if, of course, they apply either in the financial year or the preceding year. *Sch 4.1 Sch 8.1*

11

Chapter 2 Company accounts provisions

Adopting a particular format is not as restricting as it may seem, as there are a variety of options, for example:

s226
Sch 4.3
Sch 8.3
- departure is allowed if it is made to ensure a true and fair view (see above);
- certain headings may be combined;
- immaterial items may be disregarded;
- more information can be given if directors so wish;
- some information may be given in notes instead of on the face of the accounts.

Sch 4.3(2)
Sch 8.3(2)

> A company's accounts may include other items not listed in the various formats but there are three specific items which may not be treated as assets in a company's balance sheet:
>
> (a) preliminary expenses;
> (b) expenses of and commissions on any issue of shares or debentures; and
> (c) costs of research.

2.5 Accounting principles

Company accounts are required to be prepared in accordance with the principles set out in Schedule 4 (companies generally) and Schedule 8 (small companies). These principles are the fundamental accounting concepts that underlie accounts and are also incorporated within FRSs and SSAPs.

Sch 4.9–15
Sch 8.9–15
SSAP 2

The basic accounting principles are:

- *Going concern* – The company or reporting entity is to be presumed to be carrying on business as a going concern.
- *Consistency* – Accounting policies must be applied consistently within the same accounts and from one financial year to the next.
- *Prudence* – The amount of any item must be determined on a prudent basis and in particular:
  (i) only profits realised at the balance sheet date should be included in the profit and loss account, and
  (ii) all liabilities and losses arising in respect of the financial year (or preceding financial year) should be taken into account, including those liabilities and losses becoming apparent up to the date of approval of the accounts.
- *Accruals* – All income and charges relating to the financial year to which the accounts relate must be taken into account, without regard to the date of receipt or payment.
- *Individual determination* – In determining the aggregate amount of any item, the amount of each individual asset or liability that is taken into account should be determined separately.

Sch 4.5
Sch 8.5
FRS 5
- *Netting* – Amounts in respect of items representing assets or income must not be set off against amounts in respect of items representing liabilities or expenditure (as the case may be), or vice versa.

Sch 4.16–28
Sch 8.16–28

For fixed assets, stocks, investments and goodwill, rules regarding valuation, accounting and disclosure are laid down.

Historical cost principles are stated as the normal method of accounting but alternative bases (e.g., revaluation and current cost) are allowed provided that details and related historical cost figures are disclosed. The 'alternative accounting rules' are illustrated in **5.9**.

Sch 4.12(a)
Sch 8.12(a)
s262(3)

Only 'realised' profits can be included in the profit and loss account. 'Realised' profits are defined as profits which are treated as realised in accordance with generally accepted accounting principles (basically in accordance with SSAP 2).

2.6 Accounts disclosures

Schedule 4 (companies generally) and Schedule 8 (small companies) to the Companies Act 1985 set out the information required to be disclosed in a company's accounts, including that relating to the following heads:

Sch 4.35–58
Sch 8.35–51

- Disclosure of accounting policies.
- Share capital and debentures.
- Fixed assets.
- Investments.
- Reserves and provisions.
- Provision for taxation – deferred tax (Sch 4).
- Details of indebtedness (nature of security).
- Guarantees and other financial commitments.
- Interest (Sch 4).
- Tax (Sch 4).
- Turnover analysis.
- Staff details (Sch 4).

Schedule 8 ('The form and content of accounts prepared by small companies') is set out in Appendix **D**.

2.7 Directors' report

The directors of a company have to prepare an annual report (directors' report).

s234

Small companies are now permitted to omit much of the information otherwise required to be included in the directors' report (see **7.5**).

Companies, other than small companies, must provide the following details:

- *Principal activities* – 'The principal activities of the company and its subsidiary undertakings in the course of the year'.
- *Names of directors* – The names of directors at any time during the year.
- *Review of business* – 'A fair review of the development of the business and its subsidiary undertakings during the financial year and of their position at the end of it'.
- *Dividend* – Amount of dividend payment, if any, recommended.
- *Post balance sheet events* – Particulars of any important post balance sheet events affecting the company and its subsidiary undertakings.
- *Future developments* – Indication of likely future developments in the business of the company and its subsidiary undertakings.
- *Research and development* – Indication of research and development activities, if any, of the company and its subsidiary undertakings.
- *Land and buildings* – Any significant and substantial difference in market value of interests in land at the year end from balance sheet amount.
- *Directors' share interests* – Directors' interests in shares or debentures of the company or any other body corporate in the same group (i.e., its holding company or *corporate* undertaking). (These details may optionally be shown in the notes to the accounts, rather than in the directors' report.)
- *Directors' share options, etc.* – Options granted or exercised in group companies.
- *Acquisition of the company's own shares* – Details of acquisition of own shares.
- *Political and charitable gifts*.
- *Employment of disabled persons and employee involvement* – (Companies with 250 or more employees only).
- *Policy on payment of creditors* – (Public companies; not small or medium-sized companies).

s234

Sch 7

2.8 Audit reports

s235 Full statutory accounts (together with an audit or accountants' report, if appropriate), are required for shareholders for all companies. The availability or otherwise of audit exemption will determine whether the accounts should be accompanied by an auditors' report, an accountants' report or neither type of report. (See Chapter **10**.)

The auditors of a small company which has taken advantage of the special provisions in its full statutory accounts are no longer required to state specifically whether in their opinion the annual accounts have been properly prepared in accordance with the provisions 'applicable to small companies' (see **7.9**).

s235(3) The auditors must consider whether the information given in the directors' report is consistent with the accounts and, if not, must state that fact in their report. There is no requirement to state in what respect it is inconsistent.

s247B(2) Where abbreviated accounts are prepared (under the 'small' and 'medium-sized' company filing provisions), a special auditors' report is required stating that in the auditors' opinion:

- the company is entitled to deliver abbreviated accounts; and
- the abbreviated accounts have been properly prepared.

When the full statutory accounts are unaudited the abbreviated accounts should be accompanied by an accountants' report on the full accounts, only if it is required. (See **10.12**.)

2.9 Dormant companies

s250 Provided they comply with certain conditions, the Companies Act 1985 permits dormant companies not to appoint auditors.

SI 1992 No. 3003 The Act permits a company which:

(a) has been dormant since the end of the previous financial period;
(b) is entitled to prepare accounts applicable to 'small' companies, or would have been so entitled but for the fact that it was a member of an 'ineligible group'; and
(c) is not obliged to prepare group accounts;

to agree by special resolution not to appoint auditors (providing there is no specific requirement in the company's articles to appoint auditors).

Companies which take advantage of this provision may file 'small company' abbreviated accounts (an abbreviated balance sheet and notes), without an auditors' report but including a statement by the directors that the company was dormant throughout the financial year to which the accounts relate. (See example accounts in Chapter **12**.)

Section 250 is reproduced in Appendix **G**.

2.10 Publication of non-statutory accounts

s240 Where a company publishes non-statutory accounts (that is, abridged accounts giving less than full statutory accounts disclosure or other than as part of the company's statutory accounts), those accounts must state:

(a) that they are not the company's statutory accounts;
(b) whether statutory accounts (i.e., either full annual or abbreviated accounts) have been filed;

(c) whether the auditors have reported on the statutory accounts (under s235 CA 1985) or, if appropriate, whether the company's reporting accountant has made a report for the purposes of section 249A(2) on those accounts;
(d) whether the audit report or accountants' report (for the purposes of s249A(2)) was qualified, or modified, as the case may be.

The full audit report or accountants' report (as the case may be), however, is *not* to be published with non-statutory accounts.

Simplified accounting information, abridged accounts, announcements of company results to employees or the press, might be classified non-statutory accounts.

2.11 Group accounts

A parent company which has 'subsidiary undertakings' is required (with certain exceptions) to prepare group accounts in the form of consolidated accounts of the company and its subsidiary undertakings. Consolidation is not restricted to subsidiaries which are companies. *s227*

The Companies Act 1989 introduced new terminology and definitions are set out in **5.10**.

Group accounts are required to comply with the provisions of Schedule 4A to the Companies Act 1985 as to the form and content of consolidated accounts and additional information to be given. Schedule 4A provides, *inter alia*, for the following:

(a) elimination of group transactions;
(b) provisions for acquisition and merger accounting;
(c) treatment and disclosure of 'minority interests';
(d) non-consolidated subsidiary undertakings;
(e) joint ventures and associated undertakings;
(f) preparation 'as if' the group were a single company.

A subsidiary may be excluded from consolidation on the grounds of: *s229*

(a) immateriality;

and *must* be excluded in the following circumstances:

(b) severe long-term restrictions; *FRS 2*
(c) temporary control – holding with a view to subsequent resale; *FRS 2*
(d) where activities are 'so different' from those of other undertakings as to be incompatible with the obligation to give a true and fair view. *s229*

The statutory format amendments for group accounts are included in Appendix **B**.

The exemptions available for small and medium-sized groups are explained in Chapter **9**.

2.12 Approval and signature of accounts

The requirements for the approval and signature of the directors' report, the accounts and the auditors' report were amended by the Companies Act 1989 and SI 1992 No. 2452 and have been further amended by SI 1994 No. 1935.

A company's annual accounts must be approved by the board of directors and signed on behalf of the board by a director of the company. The signature must be on the company's individual balance sheet and the name of the signatory must be stated. Previously, the signature of *two* directors was normally required and although this is still permissible, it is no longer a statutory requirement. *s233*

Chapter 2   Company accounts provisions

s234A
The directors' report must also be approved by the board of directors and signed on their behalf by a director *or* the secretary of the company; the name of the signatory must be similarly stated.

s236
s249C
The auditors' or accountants' report must state the names of the auditors or reporting accountants (as the case may be) and be signed by them.

s246(7)
s246A(4)
The above requirements also apply to the approval and directors' signature of abbreviated accounts.

s246(8)
The balance sheet and directors' report of a small company which have been prepared in accordance with the special provisions for small companies must each contain a statement by the directors to that effect (see **7.6**).

Chapter 3 Accounts and accounting standards

3.1 Basic contents of financial statements

In its draft Statement of Principles for financial reporting, published in 1995, the Accounting Standards Board set out the concepts that underlie the preparation and presentation of financial statements. The ASB stated that the objective of financial statements is:

- 'to provide information about the financial position, performance and financial adaptability of an enterprise that is useful to a wide range of users for assessing the stewardship of management and for making economic decisions'.

To meet this objective, accounting information is normally presented in the form of a structured set of financial statements comprising:

- primary statements; and
- supporting notes, related to the primary statements.

Together these will form the true and fair view 'accounts' (as the term is used in this book).

3.2 Primary statements

Primary statements comprise: the profit and loss account; the statement of total recognised gains and losses (if necessary in addition to the profit and loss account); the balance sheet; and the cash flow statement. Notes to the financial statements amplify or explain items in the primary statements. The formats of the primary statements are determined as in Table 3.1.

A statement of total recognised gains and losses includes those items, being gains or losses that are recognised in the period, which do not pass through the profit and loss account. Gains, such as revaluation surpluses which are recognised but not necessarily realised in the period, are dealt with in the statement.

Table 3.1 Formats of the primary statements

Primary statement	Format
Profit and loss account	CA 1985 Schs 4 and 4A amplified by relevant FRSs
Statement of total recognised gains and losses	FRS 3 'Reporting financial performance'
Balance sheet	CA 1985 Schs 4 and 4A (Schs 8 and 8A small companies) amplified by relevant FRSs
Cash flow statement	FRS 1 'Cash flow statements'

3.3 Accounting standards

All companies preparing annual accounts must comply with 'generally accepted accounting principles' (GAAP) – these include the principles laid down in the Companies Act 1985 (principally Schedules 4 and/or 8, as appropriate) and also the Financial Reporting Standards (FRSs) and statements of standard accounting practice (SSAPs) adopted by the Accounting Standards Board. The requirement to adhere to GAAP, reinforced by the Companies Act 1989, derives from the basic principle that annual accounts should give 'a true and fair view'.

FRSs issued and SSAPs adopted by the Accounting Standards Board are 'accounting standards' for the purposes of the Companies Act 1985, which requires accounts, other than those prepared by small or medium-sized companies (as defined by the Act), to state whether they have been prepared in accordance with applicable accounting standards and to give particulars of any material departure from those standards and the reasons for it. References to accounting standards in the Act are contained in paragraph 36A of Schedule 4 (and, for banking and insurance companies, paragraph 18B of Schedule 9).

UITF abstracts are published consensus pronouncements of the Urgent Issues Task Force, a committee of the ASB, which deals with accounting issues and treatments requiring early authoritative interpretation. The pronouncements are made within the framework of the law and the principles established in accounting standards, and have a standing similar in authority to accounting standards. Once accepted by the ASB, an UITF abstract is to be regarded as accepted practice in the area in question and therefore effectively has the force of an accounting standard.

Accounting standards are applicable to financial statements of a reporting entity that are intended to give a true and fair view of its state of affairs at the balance sheet date and of its profit or loss (or income and expenditure) for the financial period ending on that date.

Accounting standards do not need to be applied to items judged to be immaterial.

s256
In preparing accounts giving a true and fair view, a company should therefore follow any applicable accounting standard (FRS or SSAP) unless there are good reasons for not doing so. In law, accounting standards are 'such standards as are, in accordance with their terms, relevant to the company's circumstances and to the accounts'.

Statutory exemption from disclosure overrides any analogous requirement prescribed by accounting standards. Two disclosure exemptions (taxation and operating leases) are the subject of comment in **7.10**.

A small company may choose to adopt the FRSSE instead of the whole range of FRSs and SSAPs which are more appropriate to larger entities.

3.4 Cash flow statements

FRS 1 'Cash flow statements' (revised with effect for accounts ending on or after 23 March 1997) requires, with exceptions, all entities producing true and fair view accounts to include a cash flow statement within the accounts drawn up in accordance with the FRS.

Small companies and other equivalent sized entities are exempt from the requirement to produce a cash flow statement. Wholly-owned subsidiary undertakings are also generally exempted.

Medium-sized and larger companies, and small ineligible companies (including, for example, a public, banking or insurance company or an authorised person under FSA 1986) are required to prepare cash flow statements in accordance with FRS 1.

The parent company of a small group, entitled to the exemption from preparing group accounts, is exempted from preparing a cash flow statement (whether its own individual statement or a consolidated one), whether or not group accounts are actually prepared.

3.5 The substance of transactions

FRS 5 'Reporting the substance of transactions' requires that financial statements should represent faithfully the commercial effects of the transactions and other events they purport to represent. Transactions should be accounted for in accordance with their substance and not merely their legal form.

FRS 5 was introduced to address the issue of 'off balance sheet financing' where complex arrangements were developed, the result of which was (invariably deliberately) that the legal form as reported in the accounts was not in accordance with the commercial effect of the arrangement.

The objective of the FRS is to ensure that the substance of an entity's transactions is reported fairly. The commercial effect of the entity's transactions, and any resulting assets, liabilities, gain or losses, should be faithfully represented in accounts.

3.6 Application of accounting standards to smaller companies

It is frequently recognised that the burden of complying with accounting standards falls more heavily upon the smaller company. While it is correct that the *principles* of accounting should apply equally to *all* companies, the application of certain accounting standards (particularly their disclosure requirements) is seen as inappropriate, cost-inefficient, immaterial or simply not applicable to small companies. There are therefore exemptions.

Table 3.2 gives an indication of the concessions that are available to small and medium-sized companies in the application of the various statements of standard accounting practice. Of particular significance is the exemption afforded to small (but not medium-sized) companies from the requirement to prepare a cash flow statement under FRS 1 'Cash flow statements'.

A small company applying Schedule 8 is exempt from the requirement of Schedule 4 paragraph 36A CA 1985 to state in its accounts whether they have been prepared in accordance with applicable accounting standards and to give particulars of and reasons for any material departure from those standards. This exemption relates only to disclosure – it does not diminish in any way the obligation of a small company to adopt and comply with appropriate accounting standards.

3.7 Small companies and the FRSSE

While the principles of accounting standards, explained above, apply to companies generally, small companies should have regard to the single Financial Reporting Standard covering all relevant accounting standards in one stand-alone document. The application of the FRSSE to the accounts of small companies is dealt with in Chapter 11.

Chapter 3 Accounts and accounting standards

Table 3.2 Accounting standards

This table shows the whole range of FRSs and SSAPs that could be applicable to small and medium-sized companies – exceptions and comments are made in the 'Application' column. A small company can choose to adopt the FRSSE, although many of the accounting principles and measurement criteria may still be relevant.

Statement	Accounting standard	Application
FRS 1	Cash flow statements	Not applicable to small companies and entities and most wholly-owned subsidiaries
FRS 2	Accounting for subsidiary undertakings	Applicable to parent undertakings preparing consolidated financial statements. However, a small or medium-sized parent undertaking exempted from preparing consolidated financial statements is required to provide disclosures in its individual accounts in accordance with CA 1985 Sch 5 and s231
FRS 3	Reporting financial performance	
FRS 4	Capital instruments	
FRS 5	Reporting the substance of transactions	Applicable for specific (generally more complex) transactions
FRS 6	Acquisitions and mergers	Applicable where appropriate for consolidated accounts
FRS 7	Fair values in acquisition accounting	Applicable where appropriate for acquisitions
FRS 8	Related party disclosures	Applicable but see FRSSE
SSAP 1	Accounting for associated companies	Where applicable
SSAP 2	Disclosure of accounting policies	
SSAP 3	Earnings per share	Not applicable
SSAP 4	Accounting for Government grants	
SSAP 5	Accounting for value added tax	
SSAP 8	Treatment of taxation under the imputation system in the accounts of companies	
SSAP 9	Stocks and work-in-progress	
SSAP 12	Accounting for depreciation	
SSAP 13	Accounting for research and development	Applicable but with disclosure exemptions
SSAP 15	Accounting for deferred taxation	
SSAP 17	Accounting for post balance sheet events	
SSAP 18	Accounting for contingencies	
SSAP 19	Accounting for investment properties	
SSAP 20	Foreign currency translation	
SSAP 21	Accounting for leases and hire-purchase contracts	
SSAP 22	Accounting for goodwill	
SSAP 24	Accounting for pension costs	
SSAP 25	Segmental reporting	Not generally applicable

Superseded SSAPs

SSAP 6	Extraordinary items and prior year adjustments	Superseded by FRS 3
SSAP 14	Group accounts	Superseded by FRS 2
SSAP 23	Accounting for acquisitions and mergers	Superseded by FRS 6

UITF abstracts

UITF 3	Treatment of goodwill on disposal of a business	
UITF 4	Presentation of long-term debtors in current assets	
UITF 5	Transfers from current assets to fixed assets	
UITF 6	Accounting for post-retirement benefits other than pensions	Rarely applicable
UITF 7	True and fair view override disclosures	
UITF 9	Accounting for operations in hyper-inflationary economies	Rarely applicable
UITF 10	Disclosure of directors' share options	
UITF 11	Capital instruments: issuer call options	Rarely applicable
UITF 12	Lessee accounting for reverse premiums and similar incentives	Applicable but see FRSSE
UITF 13	Accounting for ESOP trusts	Rarely applicable
UITF 14	Disclosure of changes in accounting policy	
UITF 15	Disclosure of substantial acquisitions	Rarely applicable
UITF 16	Income and expenses subject to non-standard rates of tax	Rarely applicable
UITF 17	Employee share schemes	Rarely applicable

Chapter 4 Formats of accounts

4.1 The statutory formats

The accounts formats from which a company may choose are given in Schedule 4 to the Companies Act 1985 and, for small companies, Schedule 8.

There is a choice of:

- *four* profit and loss account formats; and
- *two* balance sheet formats, both of which may be simplified for small companies.

Two profit and loss account formats and one of the balance sheet formats are in the 'vertical' styling in which most accounts are prepared. The two 'horizontal' styles of profit and loss account (Formats 3 and 4) and balance sheet (Format 2) are considered 'old-fashioned'. The statutory formats are reproduced in full in Appendix **B**.

4.1.1 Profit and loss account formats

In practice, care needs to be taken in the choice of formats and presentation of the profit and loss accounts. Set out in Table 4.3 is a comparison of the two formats, showing the differences in presentation and disclosure. It is particularly relevant to note:

- *gross profit or loss* is specifically disclosed only in Format 1 (but it may also be readily ascertained from Format 3);
- *depreciation* requires allocation over various cost headings in Formats 1 and 3 but needs only to be shown as one item in a Format 2 or 4 profit and loss account.

There are three items that *must* be shown on the *face* of the profit and loss account: *Sch 4.3(6)–(7)*
Sch 8.3(6)–(7)

- *profit or loss on ordinary activities before taxation* (an item not specified in the formats);
- *dividends:* aggregate amounts paid and proposed;
- *transfers to or from reserves:* including proposed transfers.

All other items in the profit and loss account formats (being represented by arabic numbers) could be combined and given in the notes to the accounts, provided the profit and loss account contains a summarised linking figure.

For small companies which are able and intend to file abbreviated accounts, the choice of profit and loss account formats may be of less consequence.

4.1.2 Balance sheet formats

The differences between the two balance sheet formats are illustrated in Tables 4.1 and 4.2.

A small company may adopt one of the simplified formats of balance sheet set out in Schedule 8 as illustrated in Table 7.2.

Chapter 4 Formats of accounts

Table 4.1 The two balance sheet formats compared

The items boxed need not be disclosed in Format 2. For illustrative purposes, the arabic number sub-headings (which are common to both formats) are not reproduced in this table but are set out in Table 4.2. Full balance sheet formats are given in Appendix **G**.

FORMAT 1	FORMAT 2
	ASSETS
A Called up share capital not paid	A Called up share capital not paid

B   Fixed assets
     I Intangible assets
     II Tangible assets
     III Investments
	B Fixed assets
	     I Intangible assets
	     II Tangible assets
	     III Investments

C   Current assets
     I Stocks
     II Debtors
     III Investments
     IV Cash at bank and in hand
	C Current assets
	     I Stocks
	     II Debtors
	     III Investments
	     IV Cash at bank and in hand

D Prepayments and accrued income	D Prepayments and accrued income
E Creditors: amounts falling due within one year	
⌐ F Net current assets (liabilities) ⌐ ⌐ G Total assets less current liabilities ⌐	- -

H Creditors: amounts falling due after more than one year	LIABILITIES
	A Capital and reserves
	     I Called up share capital
	     II Share premium account
	     III Revaluation reserve
	     IV Other reserves
	     V Profit and loss account
	
	[ ] Minority interests

I Provisions for liabilities and charges	B Provisions for liabilities and charges
J Accruals and deferred income	
[ ] Minority interests [*Alternative (1)*]	
- -	

K   Capital and reserves
     I Called up share capital
     II Share premium account
     III Revaluation reserve
     IV Other reserves
     V Profit and loss account
	C Creditors
	[*'Amounts falling due within one year' and 'amounts falling due after more than one year' should be shown separately, both in aggregate and for each of the constituent (arabic number) items of this heading.*]

[ ] Minority interests [*Alternative (2)*]	D Accruals and deferred income

The dotted line above in Format 1 illustrates the usual 'break-point' in the balance sheet, although in practice the balance sheet total could be 'struck' after item G. Format 2 requires balance sheet totals of ASSETS and LIABILITIES to be given.

Table 4.2 Arabic number sub-headings

INTANGIBLE ASSETS
1 Development costs
2 Concessions, patents, licences, trade marks and similar rights and assets
3 Goodwill
4 Payments on account

TANGIBLE ASSETS
1 Land and buildings
2 Plant and machinery
3 Fixtures, fittings, tools and equipment
4 Payments on account and assets in course of construction

INVESTMENTS
1 Shares in group undertakings
2 Loans to group undertakings
*3 Participating interests
4 Loans to undertakings in which the company has a participating interest
5 Other investments other than loans
6 Other loans
7 Own shares

STOCKS
1 Raw materials and consumables
2 Work-in-progress
3 Finished goods and goods for resale
4 Payments on account

DEBTORS
1 Trade debtors
2 Amounts owed by group undertakings
3 Amounts owed by undertakings in which the company has a participating interest
4 Other debtors
5 Called up share capital not paid
6 Prepayments and accrued income

INVESTMENTS
1 Shares in group undertakings
2 Own shares
3 Other investments

CASH AT BANK AND IN HAND

CREDITORS: AMOUNTS FALLING DUE WITHIN ONE YEAR
1 Debenture loans
2 Bank loans and overdrafts
3 Payments received on account
4 Trade creditors
5 Bills of exchange payable
6 Amounts owed to group undertakings
7 Amounts owed to undertakings in which the company has a participating interest
8 Other creditors including taxation and social security
9 Accruals and deferred income

CREDITORS: AMOUNTS FALLING DUE AFTER MORE THAN ONE YEAR
1 Debenture loans
2 Bank loans and overdrafts
3 Payments received on account
4 Trade creditors
5 Bills of exchange payable
6 Amounts owed to group undertakings
7 Amounts owed to undertakings in which the company has a participating interest
8 Other creditors including taxation and social security
9 Accruals and deferred income

PROVISIONS FOR LIABILITIES AND CHARGES
1 Pensions and similar obligations
2 Taxation, including deferred taxation
3 Other provisions

OTHER RESERVES
1 Capital redemption reserve fund
2 Reserve for own shares
3 Reserves provided for by the Articles of Association
4 Other reserves

* *For consolidated balance sheets, the Format heading is :* (a) *'Interests in associated undertakings';*
(b) *'Other participating interests'.*

Chapter 4   Formats of accounts

Table 4.3   Differences between profit and loss account formats

Items boxed show the differences in disclosure required by the formats. In other respects all formats require identical information, except that Formats 3 and 4 require separate totals of 'charges' and 'income'. Full profit and loss account formats are given in Appendix **B**.

Expenses classified by function
FORMAT 1
Format 3 requires the same information in a different presentation

1 Turnover

---
2 Cost of sales
3 Gross profit or loss
4 Distribution costs
5 Administrative expenses
---

6 Other operating income

Staff costs to be shown in Notes (Sch 4.56(4)) (not applicable for small companies)

Depreciation must be allocated over items 2, 4 and 5 (Sch 4.8 (note17)) and disclosed separately in Notes (Sch 4.19)

7 Income from shares in group undertakings
*8 Income from participating interests
9 Income from other fixed asset investments
10 Other interest receivable and similar income
11 Amounts written off investments
12 Interest payable and similar charges
13 Tax on profit or loss on ordinary activities
14 Profit or loss on ordinary activities after taxation

---
15 Extraordinary income
16 Extraordinary charges
17 Extraordinary profit or loss
18 Tax on extraordinary profit or loss
---

19 Other taxes not shown under the above items
20 Profit or loss for the financial year

Expenses classified by type
FORMAT 2
Format 4 requires the same information in a different presentation

1 Turnover

---
2 Change in stocks of finished goods and work-in-progress
3 Own work capitalised
---

4 Other operating income

---
5 (a) Raw materials and consumables
   (b) Other external charges

---
6 Staff costs:
   (a) Wages and salaries
   (b) Social security costs
   (c) Other pension costs
---

7 (a) Depreciation and other amounts written off tangible and intangible fixed assets

---
   (b) Exceptional amounts written off current assets
8 Other operating charges
---

9 Income from shares in group undertakings
*10 Income from participating interests
11 Income from other fixed asset investments
12 Other interest receivable and similar income
13 Amounts written off investments
14 Interest payable and similar charges
15 Tax on profit or loss on ordinary activities
16 Profit or loss on ordinary activities after taxation

---
17 Extraordinary income
18 Extraordinary charges
19 Extraordinary profit or loss
20 Tax on extraordinary profit or loss
---

21 Other taxes not shown under the above items
22 Profit or loss for the financial year

* For consolidated profit and loss accounts, the Format heading is: (a) 'Income from interests in associated undertakings';
(b) 'Income from other participating interests'.

Extraordinary items, although included within the statutory formats, are now viewed by FRS 3 'Reporting financial performance' as being extremely rare.

4.2 Format headings

Headings and sub-headings denoted in the formats by capital letters or roman numerals *must* be adopted in the accounts *exactly* as shown in the formats (i.e., in the order and under the headings and sub-headings given), unless there is no amount to be shown for the year or previous year.

Headings and sub-headings denoted by arabic numbers must be adapted (in arrangement and title) according to the circumstances or special nature of the business. Items denoted by arabic numbers may be combined to facilitate assessment, but if so, must be separately disclosed in the notes (unless combined on the grounds of immateriality in which case disclosure is not required).

Items may always be shown in greater detail than required by the formats and additional items may be included. Once adopted, the same format should be adopted consistently from year to year unless, in the opinion of the directors, there are special reasons for a change, in which case the change (and the reasons for it) should be disclosed.

The distinguishing letters and numbers in the formats are not required to be included in the accounts. Their purpose is simply to show the manner or position of disclosure.

4.3 Group accounts

The formats set out in Schedule 4 CA 1985 apply to group accounts with the amendments provided by Schedule 4A CA 1985 (Form and content of group accounts). Chapter **9** covers group accounts and the formats in relation to group accounts are shown in Appendix **B**. The main additions within the formats for groups relate to:

- minority interests;
- interests in associated undertakings;
- other participating interests.

4.4 Abbreviated accounts

The abbreviated balance sheet of a small company for delivery to the Registrar is set out in Schedule 8A and basically represents the headings denoted by capital letters and roman numerals in the full balance sheet formats.

The abbreviated balance sheet format is illustrated in Table 8.3.

4.5 The effect of FRS 3

FRS 3 'Reporting financial performance' introduced changes, in appropriate circumstances, to the format of the profit and loss account and a statement of total recognised gains and losses. Changes to the profit and loss account result from the requirement to analyse results between continuing operations (including the results of acquisitions) and the results of discontinued operations.

Small companies choosing to adopt the FRSSE (see Chapter 11) are relieved of many of the provisions of FRS 3.

Profits or losses on the sale or termination of an operation, costs of a fundamental reorganisation or restructuring, and profits or losses on the disposal of fixed assets also need to be identified. Analysis in accordance with the FRS is required to the level of operating profit, that is normally, profit before income from shares in group undertakings.

Chapter 4 Formats of accounts

4.5.1 Exceptional items
Exceptional items (other than those relating to reorganisations or reconstructions, sales or termination of an operation, and profits and losses on disposal of fixed assets) should be included under the statutory format headings to which they relate, with separate note disclosure where necessary.

4.5.2 Extraordinary items
Under FRS 3, the occurrence of extraordinary items (being unusual items outside ordinary activities) are viewed as being extremely rare. For all intents and purposes, therefore, extraordinary items have been abolished.

4.5.3 Supplementary notes
FRS 3 introduced the requirement to present *a note of historical cost profits and losses* (where there is a material difference between the result disclosed in a profit and loss account including revaluation gains and the result on an unmodified historical cost basis) and also *a reconciliation of movements in shareholders' funds*. Both these requirements can be dealt with as a note to the accounts.

The effect of FRS 3 on the format of the profit and loss account is illustrated in Table 4.4.

4.5.4 Illustrative examples
Illustrative examples based upon FRS 3 are reproduced in Table 4.5. The most appropriate form of disclosure will depend upon individual circumstances.

Following the introduction of the FRSSE (see Chapter 11), the examples in Table 4.5 will be mostly relevant to medium-sized and larger companies.

In the examples, which have been prepared using Format 1 as contained in Schedule 4 to the Companies Act 1985:

- the entity is a group of companies;
- the group has made acquisitions and disposals of operations during the year under review;
- there is no extraordinary item – the positioning of such an item on the face of the profit and loss account is shown, although in practice the caption would not appear if no extraordinary items existed.

The examples have been reproduced in £'000.

The effect of FRS 3

Table 4.4 The profit and loss account format under FRS 3

	1997 £	1996 £
TURNOVER		
Continuing operations	x	x
Acquisitions	x	x
	x	x
Discontinued operations	x	x
	x	x
Cost of sales (*Note 3*)	x	x
Gross profit (*Note 3*)	x	x
Net operating expenses		
Distribution costs	x	x
Administrative expenses	x	x
Other operating income	x	x
(*Note 1*)	x	x
OPERATING PROFIT		
Continuing operations	x	x
Acquisitions	x	x
	x	x
Discontinued operations	x	x
(*Note 2*)	x	x
Profits (losses) on sale or termination of an operation	x	x
Costs of a fundamental reorganisation or restructuring	x	x
Profits (losses) on the disposal of fixed assets	x	x
(*Note 2*)		
PROFIT ON ORDINARY ACTIVITIES BEFORE INTEREST	x	x

Note 1 The component headings of net operating expenses may be shown in the notes to the accounts and should disclose the analysis of these items between continuing operations, acquisitions and discontinued operations.
Note 2 Provisions in respect of such items should also be separately shown on the profit and loss account.
Note 3 The notes should disclose the analysis of these items between continuing operations, acquisitions and discontinued operations.

Chapter 4 Formats of accounts

Table 4.5 Illustrative formats based on FRS 3

Profit and loss account

	£'000	1997 £'000	1996 as restated £'000
TURNOVER			
Continuing operations	550		500
Acquisitions	50		
	600		
Discontinued operations	175		190
		775	690
Cost of sales		(620)	(555)
GROSS PROFIT		155	135
Net operating expenses		(104)	(83)
OPERATING PROFIT			
Continuing operations	50		40
Acquisitions	6		
	56		
Discontinued operations	(15)		12
Less: 1996 provision	10		
		51	52
Profit on sale of properties in continuing operations		9	6
Provision for loss on operations to be discontinued			(30)
Loss on disposal of discontinued operations	(17)		
Less: 1996 provision	20		
		3	
Profit on ordinary activities before interest		63	28
Interest payable		(18)	(15)
PROFIT ON ORDINARY ACTIVITIES BEFORE TAXATION		45	13
Tax on profit on ordinary activities		(14)	(4)
PROFIT ON ORDINARY ACTIVITIES AFTER TAXATION		31	9
Minority interests		(2)	(2)
[Profit before extraordinary items]		29	7
[Extraordinary items] (*included only to show positioning*)		—	—
PROFIT FOR FINANCIAL YEAR		29	7
Dividends		(8)	(1)
RETAINED PROFIT FOR THE FINANCIAL YEAR		21	6

The effect of FRS 3

Other primary statement

Statement of total recognised gains and losses

	1997	1996 as restated
	£'000	£'000
PROFIT FOR THE FINANCIAL YEAR	29	7
Unrealised surplus on revaluation of properties	4	6
Unrealised (loss)/gain on trade investment	(3)	7
	30	20
Currency translation differences on foreign currency net investments	(2)	5
TOTAL RECOGNISED GAINS AND LOSSES RELATING TO THE YEAR	28	25
Prior year adjustment (as explained in note [ ])	(10)	
TOTAL GAINS AND LOSSES RECOGNISED SINCE LAST ANNUAL REPORT	18	

If the reporting entity has no recognised gains and losses other than the profit or loss for the period, then a statement to that effect should be included immediately below the profit and loss account.

Note of historical cost profits and losses

	1997	1996 as restated
	£'000	£'000
REPORTED PROFIT ON ORDINARY ACTIVITIES BEFORE TAXATION	45	13
Realisation of property revaluation gains of previous years	9	10
Difference between a historical cost depreciation charge and the actual depreciation charge of the year calculated on the revalued amount	5	4
HISTORICAL COST PROFIT ON ORDINARY ACTIVITIES BEFORE TAXATION	59	27
Historical cost profit for the year retained after taxation, minority interests, extraordinary items and dividends	35	20

The note of historical cost profits and losses should be presented immediately following the profit and loss account or the statement of total recognised gains and losses.

The provision of a note of historical cost profits and losses is required in circumstances where there is a material difference between the result disclosed in the profit and loss account and the result on an unmodified historical cost basis.

Other notes

Reconciliation of movements in shareholders' funds

	1997	1996 as restated
	£'000	£'000
PROFIT FOR THE FINANCIAL YEAR	29	7
Dividends	(8)	(1)
	21	6
Other recognised gains and losses relating to the year (net)	(1)	18
New share capital subscribed	20	1
Goodwill written off	(25)	–
NET ADDITION TO SHAREHOLDERS' FUNDS	15	25
Opening shareholders' funds (originally £375,000 before deducting prior year adjustment of £10,000)	365	340
CLOSING SHAREHOLDERS' FUNDS	380	365

If the reconciliation of movements in shareholders' funds is included in the accounts as a primary statement, then it should be shown separately from the statement of total recognised gains and losses.

Note analysing operations

Analysis between continuing operations, acquisitions (as a component of continuing operations) and discontinued operations

	1997			1996 (as restated)		
	Continuing	Discontinued	Total	Continuing	Discontinued	Total
	£'000	£'000	£'000	£'000	£'000	£'000
Gross profit	145	10	155	115	20	135
Cost of sales	455	165	620	385	170	555
Net operating expenses						
Distribution costs	56	13	69	46	5	51
Administrative expenses	41	12	53	34	3	37
Other operating income	(8)	–	(8)	(5)	–	(5)
	89	25	114	75	8	83
Less 1996 provision	–	(10)	(10)			
	89	15	104			

The total figures for continuing operations in 1997 include the following amounts relating to acquisitions: costs of sales £40,000 and net operating expenses £4,000 (namely distribution costs £3,000, administrative expenses £3,000 and other operating income £2,000).

Gross profit arising from acquisitions amounted to £10,000 in 1997 (1996 – £4,000).

4.6 FRS 4 'Capital instruments'

FRS 4 'Capital instruments', which applies in material instances to all true and fair view accounts, deals with the means by which entities (including companies) raise finance and how the capital instruments used (for example, shares and debt liabilities) should be accounted for. Typical capital instruments include ordinary shares, preference shares, bank loans, options and warrants to subscribe for shares, and corporate bonds.

Many of the situations envisaged by FRS 4 may not be encountered by small companies and are not covered in the FRSSE.

All capital instruments must now be accounted for in the balance sheet within one of the categories: shareholders' funds, liabilities, or minority interests (consolidated accounts), and analysed and disclosed as in Table 4.4.

Table 4.6 Analysis of capital instruments

Item	Analysed between	
Shareholders' funds	Equity interests	Non-equity interests
Minority interests in subsidiaries	Equity interests in subsidiaries	Non-equity interests in subsidiaries
Liabilities	Convertible liabilities	Non-convertible liabilities

The most important disclosure and accounting requirements of FRS 4 can be summarised as follows:

- The total amount of shareholders' funds must be shown (i.e., identified) in the balance sheet.
- Shareholders' funds should be analysed between the amount attributable to equity interests and the amount attributable to non-equity interests. The amount of shareholders' funds attributable to equity interests is the difference between total shareholders' funds and the total amount attributable to non-equity interests. The amount attributable to non-equity interests is the aggregate of amounts relating to all classes of non-equity shares and warrants for non-equity shares.

The aggregate of shareholders' funds should be analysed as set out in Table 4.6 above.

- An analysis of the maturity of debt (i.e., loans due) should be presented showing amounts falling due:
  (a) in one year or less, or on demand;
  (b) between one and two years;
  (c) between two and five years; and
  (d) in five years or more.
- The finance costs of liabilities and non-equity shares should be allocated and charged to the profit and loss account at a constant rate over their lives based on the carrying account (i.e., amount outstanding). Direct issue costs (initial fees incurred in connection with raising the capital instrument) should be deducted from the gross proceeds of the instrument.

Before deciding whether or not to spread finance charges (within 'Interest and charges') in accordance with FRS 4, calculation will need to be made to assess the significance of the effect on profit and determine materiality.

- Liabilities must be shown within 'Creditors' and not as part of 'Capital and reserves' (as may

have happened, for example, with the disclosure of certain directors' loans which essentially constitute long-term capital to the business). (See Table 4.2 balance sheet format.)
- All finance costs, for example interest, should be charged in the profit and loss account (except in the case of investment companies). However, the capitalisation of interest etc., is not prohibited; finance costs which are regarded as part of the cost of an asset may be capitalised by way of simultaneous transfer from the profit and loss account. The gross interest charge and the amount capitalised are to be separately disclosed, together in the notes.
- Dividends in respect of non-equity shares are to be accounted for on an accruals basis, except where there are insufficient distributable profits and dividend rights are non-cumulative. This changes existing practice where most companies have not accrued for dividends on cumulative preference shares but have simply disclosed arrears in the notes to the accounts. This would now seem to be acceptable only where the likelihood of ultimate payment is remote. Dividends in respect of non-equity shares, therefore, have to be accounted for on an accruals basis and arrears of preference dividends must be provided for; in many cases, a prior year adjustment may be necessary to comply with FRS 4.

Chapter 5   Guidelines and definitions

Although the Companies Act 1985 provides a measure of standardisation for company accounts (in the form of prescriptive formats) and codification of accounting rules and principles, the Act provides only limited guidance in terms of definitions or interpretation.

In the light of this, most of the problems that have arisen in practice concern interpretation. How should expenses be analysed? How are headings and categories made up? How should they be presented?

Where there are no definitions or rules laid down by the Act or provided by Accounting Standards, it is necessary to:

- determine a reasonable interpretation of the requirement;
- ensure the proposed interpretation is sensible and appropriate to the business; and
- adopt the interpretation consistently from year to year.

This chapter gives guidelines on definitions, interpretation and analysis. Comment has not necessarily been made on every heading or term, but simply those headings that have tended to present difficulty in practice.

5.1   True and fair view

True and fair view accounts (not a statutory term but used in this book for convenience) are financial statements intended to give a true and fair view of the financial position and profit or loss (or income and expenditure) of an entity.

A 'true and fair view' (not specifically defined) is required to be given of the state of affairs of the company (and/or consolidated undertakings) as at the end of the financial year and of the profit or loss of the company (and/or consolidated undertakings so far as concerns members of the parent company) for the financial year.   *ss226–7*

Where compliance with the provisions of CA 1985 as to the matters to be included in 'annual accounts' ('individual accounts' or 'group accounts') or the notes would not be sufficient to give a true and fair view, the necessary additional information must be given in the accounts or in a note to them.

If in *special circumstances* such compliance is inconsistent with the requirement to show a 'true and fair view', the directors must depart from the relevant provision of CA 1985 to the extent necessary to show a 'true and fair view' and must explain such departure in a note to the accounts.   *UITF 7*

5.2   Accounts

Definitions of statutory terms concerning a company's accounts, prepared to show a 'true and fair view', are set out below.

5.2.1   Annual report
The 'Directors' Report' (s234 CA 1985) (relating to a company).   *s262*

Chapter 5 Guidelines and definitions

5.2.2 Annual accounts
s262
s226
Individual accounts – the accounts of a company prepared by the directors, for each financial year:

(a) comprising a balance sheet (as at the last day of the year), a profit and loss account, and notes to the accounts;
s261
(b) showing a 'true and fair view';
(c) complying with the provisions of Schedule 4 CA 1985 (as to form, content and additional note information).

s227 *Group accounts* – the accounts:

(a) prepared, in addition to 'individual accounts', by the directors of a parent company;
(b) comprising consolidated accounts (consolidated balance sheet and consolidated profit and loss account of the parent and its 'subsidiary undertakings');
(c) showing a 'true and fair view' of the consolidated undertakings as a whole (so far as concerns members of the parent company);
(d) complying with the provisions of Schedule 4A CA 1985 (as to form, content and additional note information).

Annual accounts of small companies – the individual or group accounts of small companies, as defined, prepared in accordance with the special provisions for small companies set out in
s246(2) section 246 Companies Act 1985.

Individual profit and loss account of parent company – the profit and loss account of a parent
s230 company:

(a) prepared in addition to, but omitted from, 'group accounts';
(b) omitting the supplemental information required by Schedule 4 CA 1985 (paras 52–57).

The fact of omission and the amount of the parent company's profit or loss for the year must be disclosed, and the individual profit and loss account of the parent company must be approved by the board of directors.

Notes to the accounts – notes forming part of the annual accounts (or annexed thereto), giving
s261 information required by any provision of CA 1985.

Income and expenditure account – the equivalent of a profit and loss account in the case of the
s262(2) undertaking not trading for profit.

5.2.3 Statutory accounts
The accounts that must be prepared for shareholders and/or filed with the Registrar of Companies. These will be either:

(a) annual accounts, together with the directors' report and auditors' report or independent
s242 accountants' report (if required); or
(b) abbreviated accounts, prepared in accordance with section 246(5) or (6) or 246A(3) CA 1985, together with (if appropriate) special auditors' report or accountants' report, and
s247B(1)(a) directors' statement.

5.2.4 Abbreviated accounts
The accounts prepared in accordance with special provisions for small or medium-sized companies, as the case may be, provided by sections 246 or 246A CA 1985 (as amended by SI 1997 No. 220). Companies which qualify as small in relation to a financial year are entitled to deliver to the Registrar of Companies accounts which include a balance sheet drawn up to comply with
s246(5) the requirements of Schedule 8A CA 1985.

Prior to the amendment of CA 1985 by CA 1989, such accounts were referred to in the legislation as 'modified accounts'. SI 1997 No. 220 defines the term 'abbreviated accounts'. *s247B(1)(a)*

5.3 Profit and loss account

The headings that have posed most difficulty as far as the allocation of costs and overheads are concerned are the Formats 1 and 3 headings of 'Cost of sales', 'Distribution costs' and 'Administrative expenses'. In practice, it has been found that expenses not conveniently or accurately falling under one of these headings have been attributed to additional, more appropriate, headings. A service or retail organisation, for example, may consider most of its overhead expenditure to be of a general nature rather than specifically 'distribution' or 'administrative'. Where the nature of the business is such that a more informative (and, perhaps, more detailed) analysis is considered appropriate, this approach should be adopted.

5.3.1 Formats 1 and 3

Costs and overheads may be attributed to the headings 'Cost of sales', 'Distribution costs' and 'Administrative expenses' on the lines set out below. There is no statutory interpretation of these items.

5.3.2 Cost of sales
- Opening less closing value of stocks and work-in-progress including stock provisions.
- Direct purchases and raw materials.
- Direct (manufacturing) costs.
- Cash discounts received.
- Plant and factory depreciation – depreciation must be allocated to this heading. *Sch 4.8 (Note 14)*
- Plant hire.
- Other external charges relating to production.
- Payroll costs of direct labour and subcontract work.
- Direct production overheads.
- Indirect production overheads (to the extent not related specifically to 'distribution' or 'administrative' functions).
- Property costs of factory buildings, e.g., rent and rates, repairs, insurance, etc.

5.3.3 Distribution costs (often amended to 'Selling and distribution costs')
- Payroll costs of the sales, marketing and distribution functions.
- Advertising, exhibitions, trade shows, etc.
- Travel and entertaining.
- Transport and delivery costs.
- Warehouse costs for distribution of finished goods. } including rent and rates, repairs, insurance, etc.
- Costs of maintaining sales outlets.
- Vehicle or other depreciation – depreciation must be allocated to this heading. *Sch 4.8 (Note 14)*
- Cash discounts on sales.
- Agents' commission payable.

5.3.4 Administrative expenses
- General management costs, including central functions, e.g., chief executive, accounting (to the extent not allocated elsewhere).
- Payroll costs of general administration.
- Property costs of administrative (as opposed to production) buildings, e.g., rent and rates, repairs, insurance, etc., and including depreciation – depreciation must be allocated to this heading. *Sch 4.8 (Note 14)*
- Bad debts.
- Legal and professional fees, audit and accountancy.

- Bank charges (but *not* bank 'interest payable').
- General administration costs, postage, stationery, etc.

5.3.5 Turnover

'The amounts derived from the provision of goods and services falling within the company's ordinary activities, after deduction of trade discounts, value added tax and any other taxes based on the amounts so derived'.

s262

Commission or rental income, for example, where forming part of the principal activity of the company, would be included in turnover. The heading 'Turnover' could in such cases be amended to a more appropriate title (e.g., 'Commission income' or 'Income from investment properties') in view of the 'special nature of the company's business'.

Sch 4.3(3)

For the purposes of analysis of turnover, if in the opinion of the directors the company's different classes of business or different geographical markets do not differ substantially from each other, they may be treated as one class or market.

Sch 4.55

Where such analysis would be seriously prejudicial to the interests of the company, the information need not be disclosed provided the fact of such non-disclosure is stated. There are special disclosure provisions for small companies (see **7.10.1** ('Turnover')).

5.3.6 Other operating income

'Other operating income' will include all other income not arising from turnover or the company's principal activities, except income dealt with elsewhere in the formats (e.g., dividends or interest, etc., receivable). It might include:

- Commissions. ⎫
- Rental income. ⎬ Where not main part of principal activities
- Profit on disposal of fixed assets.   Where material (otherwise reduce depreciation
- Foreign currency trading gains.   charge)

5.3.7 Own work capitalised (Formats 2 and 4)
(A credit to profit and loss account.)

The gross amount of items capitalised in the construction of a company's own tangible fixed assets, including direct labour, materials and overheads.

5.3.8 Other external charges (Formats 2 and 4)
- Other production-related costs.
- Other costs related directly to generating turnover.
- Subcontractors' costs and costs of self-employed consultants.

5.3.9 Other operating charges (Formats 2 and 4)
- Other overhead expenses, including audit and professional fees.
- Other charges relating to ordinary activities.
- Foreign currency trading losses.
- Cash discounts allowed.

In practice, the two headings 'Other external charges' and 'Other operating charges' have often been interpreted as alternatives; however defined, they should be used consistently.

5.3.10 Staff costs
'Staff costs' are wages and salaries, social security costs and other pension costs paid or payable to, or incurred by the company on behalf of, persons employed under contracts of service, i.e., employees of the company (including directors who are employees). This heading will not include subcontractors' costs or consultants, etc.

Sch 4.56

Social security costs: company (employers') contributions to any compulsory state, social security, National Insurance, or pension scheme.

Other pension costs: all other company contributions towards employee pensions (for example, company pension scheme).

The disclosure of the average number of employees within categories is to be determined by the directors 'having regard to the manner in which the company's activities are organised'. The number of employees included in this disclosure should be correlated with the amount disclosed for 'staff costs'.

Sch 4.56(5)

5.3.11 Income from shares in group undertakings
- Dividends received and receivable:
   (a) parent company – from subsidiary undertakings;
   (b) fellow subsidiary – from fellow group undertakings;
   (c) consolidated P & L account – from non-consolidated subsidiaries.
- Group's shares of earnings of non-consolidated (equity accounted) subsidiaries.

5.3.12 Income from participating interests
Individual company – income (e.g. dividends received and receivable) from shares in associated companies (SSAP 1), share of profits from partnerships, unincorporated associations.

Consolidated P & L account – group share of pre-tax profit (or loss) of associated companies.

5.3.13 Auditors' remuneration
Audit fee and related expenses charged in the accounts, including estimated money value of any benefits in kind (which should be disclosed).

s390A

5.3.14 Interest payable and similar charges
Bank loan and overdraft interest, interest on other loans, interest on finance leases, hire-purchase interest, commitment fees, factoring charges, group interest (less interest capitalised).

Foreign currency losses arising from financing. (Gains of a similar nature may be included under 'Other interest receivable and similar income'.)

The following definitions are based on the definitions contained in FRS 3 'Reporting financial performance'.

5.3.15 Ordinary activities
Any activities which are undertaken by a reporting entity as part of its business and such related activities in which the reporting entity engages in furtherance of, incidental to, or arising from, these activities.

Ordinary activities include the effects on the reporting entity of any event in the various environments in which it operates, including the political, regulatory, economic and geographical environments.

Chapter 5 Guidelines and definitions

Ordinary activities include the effect of any event irrespective of frequency or unusual nature.

5.3.16 Continuing operations
Operations other than 'discontinued operations'.

5.3.17 Acquisitions
Operations of the reporting entity that are acquired in the period.

5.3.18 Discontinued operations
Operations of the reporting entity that are sold or terminated and that satisfy *all* of the following conditions:

- The sale or termination is completed either in the period or before the earlier of three months after the commencement of the subsequent period and the date on which the financial statements are approved.
- If a termination, the former activities have ceased permanently.
- The sale or termination has a material effect on the nature and focus of the reporting entity's operations and represents a material reduction in its operating facilities resulting either from its withdrawal from a particular market (whether class of business or geographical) or from a material reduction in turnover in the reporting entity's continuing markets.
- The assets, liabilities, results of operations and activities are clearly distinguishable, physically, operationally and for financial reporting purposes.

5.3.19 Exceptional items
Material items which derive from events or transactions that fall within the ordinary activities of the reporting entity and which individually or, if a similar type, in aggregate, need to be disclosed by virtue of their size or incidence if the financial statements are to give a true and fair view.

Exceptional items should not be aggregated on the face of the profit and loss account but should each be included within its natural statutory format heading or relevant FRS 3 heading.

Exceptional items should be attributed to continuing or discontinued operations and should be disclosed with adequate description of the nature of the item.

The following exceptional items should be disclosed separately on the face of the profit and loss account:

- profits and losses on the sale or termination of an operation;
- costs of a fundamental reorganisation or restructuring having a material effect on the nature and focus of the reporting entity's operations;
- profits and losses on the disposal of fixed assets.

These items should be shown after operating profit and before interest, and included under the appropriate heading of continuing or discontinued operations.

5.3.20 Extraordinary items
Material items possessing a high degree of abnormality which arise from events or transactions that fall outside the ordinary activities of the reporting entity and which are not expected to recur. They do not include exceptional items nor do they include prior period items merely because they relate to a prior period.

Extraordinary items are extremely rare.

5.3.21 Prior period adjustments
Material adjustments applicable to prior periods arising from changes in accounting policies or from the correction of fundamental errors. They do not include normal adjustments or corrections of accounting estimates made in prior periods. Prior period adjustments should be accounted for by restating comparative figures and adjusting the opening balance of reserves.

5.3.22 Total recognised gains and losses
The total of all gains and losses of the reporting entity that are recognised in a period and are attributable to shareholders.

5.3.23 Profit or loss on disposal
The profit or loss on the disposal of an asset should be accounted for in the profit and loss account of the period in which the disposal occurs as the difference between the net sale proceeds and the net carrying amount, whether carried at historical cost (less any provisions made) or at a valuation. The profit or loss on disposal of a previously acquired business should include the attributable amount of purchased goodwill where it has previously been eliminated against reserves as a matter of accounting policy and has not previously been charged in the profit and loss account.

5.4 Balance sheet

Commentary on selected balance sheet headings, including guidelines on the analysis of debtors and creditors, is set out below.

5.4.1 Fixed assets
'Assets of a company which are intended for use on a continuing basis in the company's activities'. Assets not intended for such use are 'current assets'. *s262(1)*

'Fixed assets' include, on this definition, investments and intangibles in addition to tangible fixed assets.

Assets awaiting disposal: a fixed asset not in use at the balance sheet date and not intended to be used before disposal should be reclassified as a 'current asset'. (This does not apply to assets which it is intended to replace in the normal course of business.)

'Development costs' may be capitalised in 'special [undefined] circumstances'. Otherwise, 'costs of research' must not be treated as an asset. SSAP 13 provides the definition of these items lacking in CA 1985. *Sch 4.20*

'Preliminary expenses' and 'expenses of, and commission on, any issue of shares or debentures' may not be treated as assets. *Sch 4.3(2)*

5.4.2 Goodwill
'Amounts representing goodwill shall only be included to the extent that goodwill was acquired for valuable consideration' (Sch 4.8 (Note 3) or Sch 8.8 (Note 2)). Any goodwill valued and created by the company itself, therefore, cannot be capitalised and included in a company's balance sheet.

Chapter 5 Guidelines and definitions

Sch 4.21
Acquired goodwill should be systematically depreciated over a period (chosen by the directors) not exceeding the useful economic life of the goodwill. The period of write-off and the reasons for choosing that period must be disclosed.

The above considerations do not apply to goodwill arising on consolidation.

5.4.3 Tangible assets: headings
In practice, there is some latitude with the headings: for example, 'equipment' should not generally be included in 'plant and machinery' but may be aggregated with 'motor vehicles'. Strict interpretation would not allow, for example, 'plant and machinery' to be changed to 'plant and equipment', particularly in a company where the main activity is manufacturing. However, in a situation where 'equipment' is immaterial, this might acceptably be aggregated with plant and machinery under a heading 'plant, machinery and equipment'. Additional headings may be given but doing so increases the amount of disclosure required.

'Payments on account' and 'Assets in course of construction' have to be shown separately from other items but individually may be aggregated.

Grants relating to fixed assets should be accounted for by the deferred credit method, in which case the credit should be included under 'accruals and deferred income' and should *not* be deducted from fixed assets. Reducing the 'cost' of the asset by the grant would be considered to represent an 'offset', which is not permitted under CA 1985.

5.4.4 Cash at bank and in hand; bank loans and overdrafts
Bank balances and bank overdrafts, etc., should not be offset to show a net balance *unless* there is a legal right of set-off.

Cash is defined in FRS 1 (revised 1996) 'Cash flow statements' as 'cash in hand and deposits repayable on demand with any qualifying financial institution, less overdrafts from any qualifying financial institution repayable on demand. Deposits are repayable on demand if they can be withdrawn at any time without notice and without penalty or if a maturity or period of notice of not more than 24 hours or one working day has been agreed. Cash includes cash in hand and deposits denominated in foreign currencies.'

5.4.5 Current assets
s262(1) 'Assets not intended for use on a continuing basis in the company's activities'.

5.4.6 Participating interest
A 'participating interest' basically is an interest in an undertaking (other than one which is a group undertaking) which is held on a long-term basis (generally, an equity interest in excess of 20 per cent) for the purpose of securing a contribution to activities by the exercise of control or influence arising from that interest.

s260
FRS 2

The above definition of a 'participating interest' is wider than that of an 'associated company' in SSAP 1:

> 'An "associated company" is a company not being a subsidiary of the investing group or company in which the interest of the investing group or company is for the long-term and, having regard to the disposition of the other shareholdings, the investing group or company is in a position to exercise a significant influence over the company in which the investment is made.'

The statutory definitions of 'participating interest' and 'associated undertaking' are set out in **5.10**.

5.4.7 Stocks

The basis of arriving at the value of 'stocks' must be a reasonable approximation to actual cost (appropriate, in the opinion of the directors, to the circumstances of the company), e.g., FIFO (first in, first out), weighted average or other similar method.

Sch 4.27

The notes to the accounts must disclose any material difference between historical cost (purchase price or production cost) and the amount at which stock would have been disclosed if its value had been determined on the basis of replacement cost at the balance sheet date ('relevant alternative amount'). (Alternatively, 'relative alternative amount' may be determined in accordance with most recent price or cost before the balance sheet date, but only where this method gives a more appropriate standard of comparison in the opinion of the directors.)

Sch 4.27(3) –(5)

Differences, if applicable, must be separately determined for each of the sub-headings of stock, i.e., raw materials, work-in-progress, finished goods, etc. Where stock turns over reasonably quickly and where prices do not change significantly, the difference is unlikely to be material.

5.4.8 Provisions for liabilities and charges

'Any amount retained as reasonably necessary for the purpose of providing for any liability or loss which is either likely to be incurred, or certain to be incurred but uncertain as to amount or as to the date on which it will arise.'

Sch 4.89

5.4.9 Taxation

The two balance sheet format headings for 'Other creditors including taxation and social security' (Creditors) and 'Taxation, including deferred taxation' (Provision for liabilities and charges) may be contrasted as follows:

'Other creditors including taxation and social security' must be analysed between:

(a) other creditors – including proposed dividends (separately disclosed) and any other creditors; and
(b) taxation and social security – including corporation tax, VAT, ACT payable on proposed dividends, PAYE and social security payable, and excise duties.

'Taxation, including deferred taxation' will include any provision for deferred taxation (separately disclosed).

5.5 Balance sheet: analysis of debtors and creditors

The guidelines below indicate how certain of the 'debtors' and 'creditors' headings are made up. *Materiality* should be considered in any attempt to distinguish between the various categories, as excessive accuracy or refinement may not be necessary.

Sch 4.86

Amounts owing by group or any associated undertakings should be separately identified and disclosed.

Amounts falling due after more than one year should be separately analysed for each of the headings.

Chapter 5 Guidelines and definitions

5.5.1 Debtors

Trade debtors
Will generally comprise:

- sales ledger balances;
- purchase ledger debit balances;
- sales invoices/credit notes accrued;
- less: provision for bad debts.

Prepayments
Prepaid items and accrued income.

Deferred tax asset (ACT recoverable) (unless separately disclosed).

Other debtors
Debtors other than the above and debtors not otherwise separately disclosed.

5.5.2 Creditors

Trade creditors
Will generally comprise:

- bought ledger (or equivalent) balances;
- sales ledger credit balances;
- trade invoices (for purchases) accrued.

Generally, 'trade creditor' items will meet both of the following requirements:

- *expenditure has been incurred as part of the normal business activities of the company (e.g., purchase of goods, overhead expenditure, capital expenditure, etc.); and*
- *an invoice has been received dated as or before the year end; late invoices (i.e., received after year end but dated before it) should therefore be included in this heading.*

Taxation and social security
Includes VAT, NIC, PAYE and excise duties.

Current corporation tax and ACT payable on dividends are normally separately identified under a heading such as 'Corporation tax'.

Accruals
- Accrued items of overhead expenditure.
- Estimated accruals where invoice not received.
- Capital expenditure accruals.
- Bonuses, accrued remuneration.

Generally, 'accruals' items will meet both of the following requirements:

- *expenditure has been incurred before year end but the related invoice is not dated until after year end (or due payment date is after year end if no invoice will be received) (compare 'trade creditors'); and*
- *the amount and payment date of the item can be determined with reasonable certainty.*

Other creditors
Creditors, other than above:

- short-term loans;
- loans from directors (where not shown elsewhere).

Dividends
Normally shown as separate heading.

5.6 Capital instruments

The following definitions are based on those contained in FRS 4 'Capital instruments'.

5.6.1 Capital instruments
All instruments that are issued by reporting entities as a means of raising finance, including shares, debentures, loans and debt instruments, options and warrants that give the holder the right to subscribe for or obtain capital instruments. In the case of consolidated financial statements, the term includes capital instruments issued by subsidiaries except those that are held by another member of the group included in the consolidation.

5.6.2 Shareholders' funds
The aggregate of called up share capital and all reserves, excluding minority interests.

FRS 4 requires shareholders' funds to be analysed between the amount attributable to equity interests and the amount attributable to non-equity interests. The amount of shareholders' funds attributable to equity interests is the difference between total shareholders' funds and the total amount attributable to non-equity interests. The amount attributable to non-equity interests is the aggregate of amounts relating to all classes of non-equity shares and warrants for non-equity shares.

5.6.3 Share
Share in the share capital of the reporting company (or, in the context of consolidated financial statements, the holding company of a group), including stock.

5.6.4 Equity shares
Shares other than non-equity shares.

5.6.5 Non-equity shares (e.g., preference shares)
Shares possessing any of the following characteristics:

- Any of the rights of the shares to receive payments (whether in respect of dividends, in respect of redemption or otherwise) are for a limited amount that is not calculated by reference to the company's assets or profits or the dividends on any class of equity share.
- Any of the shares' rights to participate in a surplus in a winding-up are limited to a specific amount that is not calculated by reference to the company's assets or profits and such limitation had a commercial effect in practice at the time the shares were issued or, if later, at the time the limitation was introduced.
- The shares are redeemable either according to their terms or because the holder, or any party other than the issuer, can require their redemption.

5.6.6 Debt
Capital instruments that are classified as liabilities.

5.6.7 Liabilities
Liabilities are an entity's obligations to transfer economic benefits as a result of past transactions or events. (For example, to make cash payments or transfer other kinds of property).

Chapter 5 Guidelines and definitions

5.7 Directors' report

The minimal contents required for the directors' report of a small company are set out in **7.5**.

5.7.1 Drafting considerations
When drafting the directors' report for full shareholders' accounts, it is worth bearing in mind whether abbreviated accounts are going to be prepared.

In 'small company' abbreviated accounts, no directors' report is filed.

s234 The directors' report of a 'medium-sized company' is reproduced in full in abbreviated accounts and should be drafted with this in mind. Turnover or gross margin detail are not disclosed in abbreviated accounts and the directors' report of a medium-sized company should not therefore be drafted so as to provide such information.

5.7.2 Review of business
'A fair review of the development of the business of the company and its subsidiaries during the financial year ending with the balance sheet date, and of their position at the end of it.'

This review should at least comprise a brief commentary covering the following (having regard to the commercial aspects of disclosure):

- general state of affairs;
- comment on trading;
- comment on turnover and results (and comparisons with previous years);
- significant financial events affecting the company.

Some comment on the appropriateness of the 'going concern' concept may be necessary, for example, where reliance is made on the continuing support of bankers, loan creditors, or a holding company (parent undertaking in the case of subsidiaries).

5.7.3 Future developments
'An indication of likely future developments in the business of the company and of its subsidiary undertakings.'

Some comment on future developments is always required, but can be combined under the 'Review of business' heading.

5.7.4 Events since the end of the year
'Particulars of any important events affecting the company or any of its subsidiary undertakings which have occurred since the end of the year.'

Disclosure may duplicate or cross-refer to any note to the accounts concerning post balance sheet events. If there are no such events, no paragraph is required (refer to SSAP 17).

5.7.5 Research and development
'An indication of the activities (if any) of the company and its subsidiary undertakings in the field of research and development' (refer to SSAP 13).

5.8 Auditors' duty in connection with directors' report

The auditors are required to consider whether information given in the directors' report for the financial year is consistent with the annual accounts. If it is not, that fact is to be stated in the auditors' report. The directors' report is not, in other respects, subject to audit scrutiny.

s235(3)

Table 5.1 Alternative methods of valuation

Fixed assets (Sch 4.17–21)

Primary method of valuation:

Historical cost of purchase or production, less any provision for depreciation or diminution in value

	Alternative method of valuation ('Alternative accounting rules'):	
Intangible fixed assets, other than goodwill	Current cost	(Sch 4.31(1))
Tangible fixed assets	Market value (as at the date of their last valuation) or Current cost	(Sch 4.31(2))
Investments (fixed assets)	Market value (as at the date of their last valuation) or Directors' valuation (or any basis which the directors consider to be appropriate in the circumstances; the method of valuation and the reasons for adopting it must be disclosed)	(Sch 4.31(3))

Current assets (Sch 4.22–26)

Primary method of valuation:

Cost (purchase price or production cost – other than distribution costs) or net realisable value, if lower

	Alternative method of valuation ('Alternative accounting rules'):	
Investments (current assets)	Current cost	(Sch 4.31(4))
Stocks	Current cost	(Sch 4.31(5))

5.9 Alternative bases of accounting

The Companies Act 1985 permits two bases of accounting – historical cost accounting rules and alternative accounting rules. A company may choose whichever basis it wishes to follow and may use different bases within the same set of accounts; it is common practice, for example, to revalue properties or investments.

Companies may, therefore, prepare accounts:

- on the pure historical cost convention; or
- on the historical cost convention modified to include certain assets at valuation; or
- on the current cost convention.

Alternative methods of valuation permitted under the 'alternative accounting rules' are illustrated in Table 5.1.

Chapter 5 Guidelines and definitions

5.9.1 *Purchase price*

Sch 4.26

Includes any consideration, whether in cash or otherwise and also any incidental expenses (s262).

5.9.2 *Production cost*

Sch 4.26

The price of raw materials and consumables together with costs directly attributable to the production of the asset; a reasonable proportion of indirect costs (relating to the period of production); and interest on capital borrowed to finance the production of the asset (to the extent that it is accrued during the period of production).

5.9.3 *Revaluation reserve*

Sch 4.34

The difference between the amount of any item determined according to one of the alternative accounting rules and the amount at which it would be determined on the historical cost accounting rules should be debited or credited, as applicable, to a 'revaluation reserve'.

5.10 Groups: parent and subsidiary undertakings

The Companies Act 1989 introduced definitions for accounting purposes for a parent company and its subsidiaries. The principal definitions, which cover 'undertakings' and not just 'bodies corporate', are set out below.

s262 A *group* comprises a parent undertaking and its subsidiary undertakings.

An undertaking is a 'parent undertaking' in relation to another undertaking ('a subsidiary undertaking') if:

(a) it holds a majority of the voting rights in the undertaking; or
(b) it is a member of the undertaking and has the right to appoint or remove a majority of its board of directors; or
(c) it has the right to exercise a dominant influence over the undertaking:
   (i) by virtue of provisions contained in the undertaking's Memorandum or Articles; or
   (ii) by virtue of a control contract; or
(d) it is a member of the undertaking and controls alone, pursuant to an agreement with other shareholders or members, a majority of the voting rights in the undertaking.

s258

An undertaking is treated as a member of another undertaking:

(a) if any of its subsidiary undertakings is a member of that undertaking; or
(b) if any shares in that other undertaking are held by a person acting on behalf of the undertaking or any of its subsidiary undertakings.

An undertaking is also a parent undertaking in relation to another undertaking (a subsidiary undertaking) if it has a participating interest in the undertaking and:

(a) it actually exercises a dominant influence over it; or
(b) it and the subsidiary undertaking are managed on a unified basis.

s259 An *'undertaking'* means:

(a) a body corporate or partnership; or
(b) an unincorporated association carrying on a trade or business, with or without a view to profit.

'Fellow subsidiary undertakings' are undertakings which are subsidiary undertakings of the same parent undertaking but are not parent undertakings or subsidiary undertakings of each other. — *s259*

'Group undertaking' means an undertaking which is: — *s259*

(a) a parent undertaking or subsidiary undertaking of that undertaking; or
(b) a subsidiary undertaking of any parent undertaking of that undertaking.

A *'participating interest'* means an interest held by an undertaking in the shares of another undertaking, which it holds on a long-term basis, for the purpose of securing a contribution to its activities by the exercise of control or influence arising from or related to that interest. — *s260*

A holding of 20 per cent or more of the shares of an undertaking is presumed to be a participating interest unless the contrary is shown.

An interest in shares includes:

(a) an interest which is convertible into an interest in shares; and
(b) an option to acquire shares or any such interest.

An interest held on behalf of an undertaking shall be treated as held by it.

In the balance sheet and profit and loss formats set out in CA 1985 Schedules 4 and 8, 'participating interest' does not include an interest in a group undertaking.

An *'associated undertaking'* means an undertaking in which an undertaking, included in the consolidation, has a participating interest and over whose operating and financial policy it exercises a significant influence, and which is not:

(a) a subsidiary undertaking of the parent company; or
(b) a joint venture.

Where an undertaking holds 20 per cent or more of the voting rights in another undertaking, it is presumed to exercise such 'significant influence' over it unless the contrary is shown. — *Sch 4A.20*

A *'joint venture'* may be dealt with in group accounts by the method of proportional consolidation. A 'joint venture' is an undertaking, which (not being a body corporate or subsidiary undertaking of the parent company) is managed jointly by two or more undertakings, one of which is included in a consolidation. — *Sch 4A.19*

References to 'shares' are references to:

(a) allotted shares (for an undertaking with a share capital); or
(b) rights to share in the capital of the undertaking (for an undertaking with capital but no share capital); or
(c) interests:
    (i) conferring any right to share in the profits or liability to contribute to the losses of the undertaking; or
    (ii) giving rise to an obligation to contribute to the debts or expenses of the undertaking in the event of a winding up (undertaking without capital).

ss258–260
Sch 4A
Sch 10A
FRS 2

5.11 The substance of transactions

FRS 5 'Reporting the substance of transactions' requires that accounts should represent faithfully the commercial effects of the transactions and other events they purport to represent. This requires transactions to be accounted for in accordance with their substance and not merely their legal form, since the latter may not fully indicate the commercial effect of the arrangements entered into. It deals with the problems commonly referred to as 'off balance sheet financing', the most widely recognised effect of which is the omission of liabilities from the balance sheet.

The scope of FRS 5 extends to all kinds of transactions, subject only to certain specific exclusions.

FRS 5 should not change the accounting treatment and disclosure of the vast majority of transactions. Where transactions are straightforward and their substance and commercial effect are readily apparent, applying established accounting practices will usually be sufficient to ensure that such transactions are appropriately reported in the accounts. FRS 5 affects mainly those more complex transactions whose substance may not be readily apparent.

A reporting entity's accounts should report the substance of the transactions into which it has entered. In determining the substance of a transaction, all its aspects and implications should be identified and greater weight given to those more likely to have a commercial effect in practice. A series of transactions that achieves or is designed to achieve an overall commercial effect should be viewed as a whole.

Specific examples of complex transactions are given in application notes included in FRS 5. Those transactions may be summarised as follows:

- *Consignment stock* – Consignment stock is stock held by one party but legally owned by another, on terms that give the stockholder the right to sell the stock in the normal course of its business or, at its option, to return it unsold to the legal owner.
- *Sale and repurchase agreements* – Sale and repurchase agreements are arrangements under which assets are sold by one party to another on terms that provide for the seller to repurchase the asset in certain circumstances.
- *Factoring of debts* – Factoring of debts takes a variety of forms of obtaining finance, sales ledger administration services, or protection from bad debts.
- *Securitised assets* – Securitisation is a means by which providers of finance fund a specific block of assets rather than the general business of a company. Securitised assets have included household mortgages, credit card balances, hire purchase loans and trade debts and such non-monetary assets as property and stocks.
- *Loan transfers* – The transfer of interest-bearing loans to an entity other than a special purpose vehicle.
- *Quasi-subsidiaries* – Some arrangements give as much effective control over another entity as if that entity were a subsidiary. A 'quasi-subsidiary' of a reporting entity is a company, trust, partnership or other vehicle that, although not fulfilling the definition of a subsidiary, is directly or indirectly controlled by the reporting entity and gives rise to benefits for that entity that are in substance no different from those that would arise were the vehicle a subsidiary.

Part II Smaller companies

Chapter 6 Small and medium-sized companies

6.1 Classification of companies

Two classifications of companies – 'small' and 'medium-sized' – are entitled to certain special provisions with regard to the contents of the statutory accounts for filing with the Registrar of Companies.   *s246*

All companies are required to prepare full statutory accounts for shareholders but those for small companies may contain less detailed information. Small and medium-sized companies may also prepare 'abbreviated accounts' for filing. Where abbreviated accounts are prepared, therefore, two sets of accounts must be prepared – one for the shareholders and one for filing and public disclosure.

Certain categories of company, regardless of size, will not be entitled to any exemptions. These are: *s247A*

(a) public companies, or banking or insurance companies;
(b) 'authorised persons' under the Financial Services Act 1986; and
(c) members of an 'ineligible' group which includes a company set out in (a) or (b) above.

6.2 Qualifying conditions

Basically, a company is treated as small or medium-sized if it does not exceed more than one of the following criteria: *s247*

	Small	Medium-sized
Turnover	£2.8 m	£11.2 m
Balance sheet total	£1.4 m	£5.6 m
Average number of employees (on a monthly basis)	50	250

Turnover figures should be proportionately adjusted where the financial 'year' is not in fact 12 months.

'Balance sheet total' means gross assets before deduction of liabilities, accruals and provisions, i.e., the aggregate of headings A to D in Format 1 or the 'Assets' headings in Format 2.

As a general rule for a company to qualify as small or medium-sized, the criteria must be met for the current and previous year. If the criteria are not met for the following year, a company may continue to be treated as small or medium-sized, as appropriate, for that year. However, if the criteria are not met in the year after that, then the company must file accounts according to its size.

6.3 Parent companies

The size classification of a parent company is determined with regard to the aggregate qualifying criteria of the group taken as a whole (parent company and subsidiary undertakings), irrespective of the actual size qualification of the parent company itself (see Chapter 9).   *s247A(3)*

Chapter 6 Small and medium-sized companies

6.4 Decision chart to determine size qualification

The decision chart in Diagram 6.1 is designed to determine whether a company qualifies in any particular year to be treated as small or medium-sized, and hence whether it is entitled to special provisions in the preparation of its annual accounts, and whether it is entitled to prepare and file abbreviated accounts. The chart may also be used, as a separate consideration, to determine whether a company is entitled to small company audit exemption (see Chapter 10).

Terms, expressions, etc., used in the chart are explained as follows:

6.4.1 'Eligible company?'

s247A The following companies are not eligible and are not therefore entitled to prepare small company accounts or to file abbreviated accounts, irrespective of size:

- public companies;
- members of 'ineligible' (basically, public) groups;
- banking and insurance companies;
- authorised persons' under the Financial Services Act 1986.

s250(4)(d) A dormant company member of an ineligible group may prepare small company accounts.

6.4.2 'No abbreviated accounts'
The company is not entitled to file abbreviated accounts.

6.4.3 Years
Y   = current financial year
Y – 1 = preceding financial year
Y – 2 = financial year preceding Y – 1

6.4.4 'First financial year?'
In a company's first year of incorporation, it will qualify as small or medium-sized, as appropriate, provided it meets the qualifying conditions in its first financial year.

6.4.5 Qualifying conditions
In order to qualify as small or medium-sized, as the case may be, the qualifying conditions set out in **6.2** must be satisfied.

Note: Part B of the chart should only be used after following the logic route of Part A.

6.4.6 'Qualified as small (medium)?'
Did the company qualify as small (or medium-sized) in Y – 1?

6.4.7 'Large company'

s246 The company, being neither small nor medium-sized, is not entitled to prepare accounts in
s246A accordance with the relevant special provisions. The term 'large' is not used in the legislation.

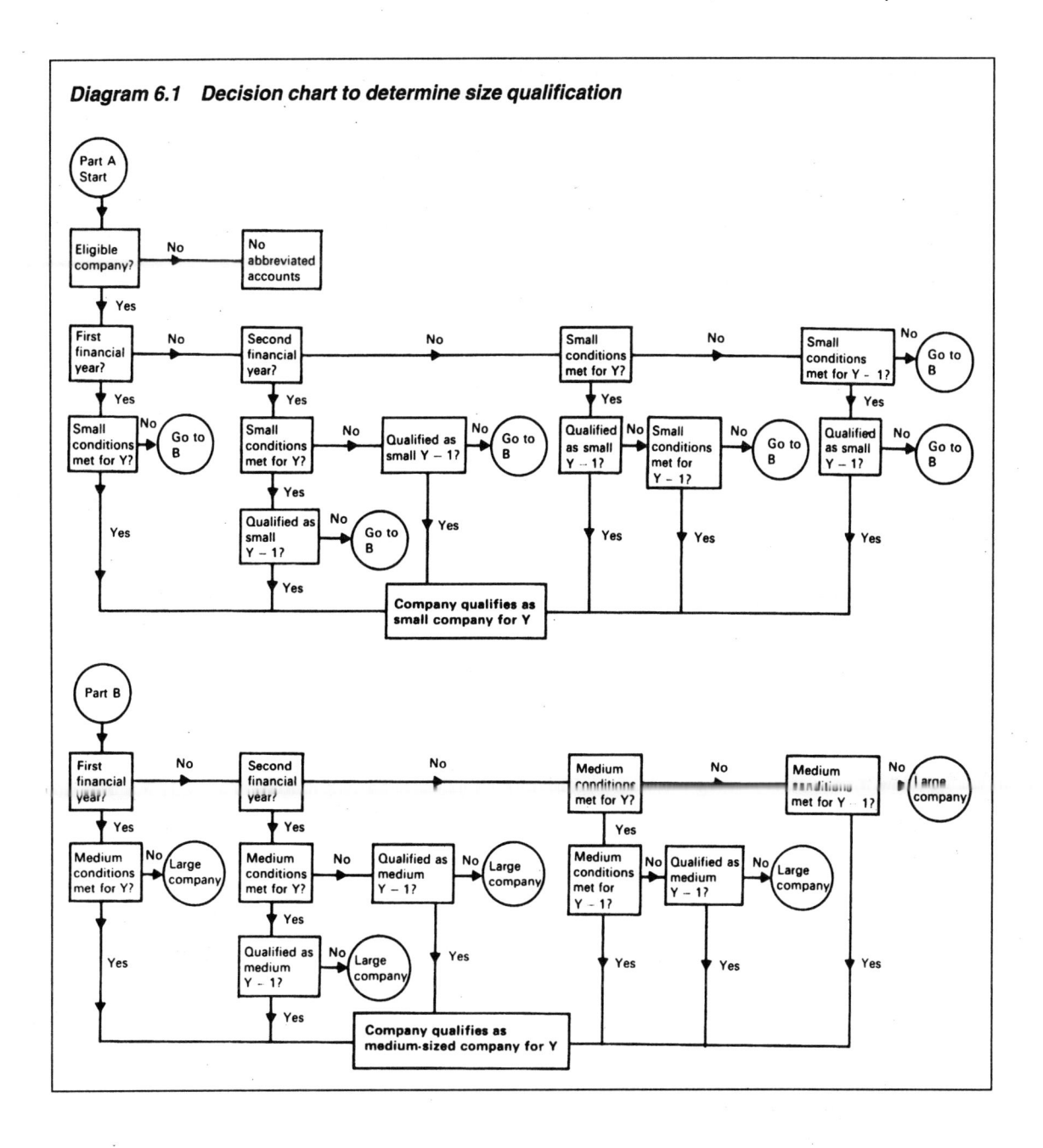

Decision chart to determine size qualification

Diagram 6.1 Decision chart to determine size qualification

Chapter 7   Small company accounts

7.1   Special provisions for small companies

A small company is entitled under the exemptions provided by CA 1985 section 246 (special provisions for small companies) to prepare:

- Annual accounts for shareholders – with a modified balance sheet and reduced disclosure requirements for the notes to the accounts and the directors' report.
- Abbreviated accounts for filing and delivery to the Registrar of Companies.

Small company accounts with modifications and reduced disclosure provided by section 246 and Schedule 8 are referred to as 'small company accounts' in this book. Other terms used in practice include 'simplified accounts', 'shorter format accounts' etc.

Certain small companies are exempt from the statutory requirement to have an audit of their annual accounts, as explained in Chapter 10.

Abbreviated accounts are explained in Chapter 8. A company wishing to file abbreviated accounts with the Registrar of Companies has to produce two sets of accounts: annual accounts for shareholders and abbreviated accounts.

CA 1985 section 246 and Schedule 8 together determine the minimum disclosure required in a small company's annual accounts. However, a small company does not have to take advantage of all the exemptions and modifications permitted if it does not wish to do so.

In terms of increasing amounts of disclosure, small company accounts may be prepared on the basis of complying with: *s246(2)*

- Schedule 8 – instead of Schedule 4 ('Small Company Accounts')
- Schedule 4 – in part (Small Company Accounts with additional disclosures)
- Schedule 4 – in whole ('Full Schedule 4 accounts')

In all cases the small company may take advantage of disclosure exemptions concerning financial years of subsidiaries, breakdown of aggregate directors' emoluments, details of the highest paid director's emoluments, numbers of directors exercising share options etc., and excess retirement benefits of directors and past directors.   *s246(3)*

SI 1997 No. 570

The special provisions for small companies apply not only to the individual accounts of such companies but also to the group accounts where a small company produces them.   *s248A*

7.2   New Schedule 8 substituted into Companies Act 1985

7.2.1   Form and content of accounts prepared by small companies
The new Schedule 8 to the Companies Act 1985 (inserted by SI 1997 No. 220), which sets out the provisions for the form and content of small company accounts is structured as in Table 7.1.

Chapter 7 Small company accounts

Table 7.1 New Schedule 8 to CA 1985

Part I General rules and formats

Section A   General rules

Section B   Required formats for accounts

- Balance sheet formats (Formats 1 and 2) and notes thereon
- Profit and loss account formats (Formats 1, 2, 3 and 4) and notes thereon

Part II Accounting principles and rules

Section A   Accounting principles

- Accounting principles
- Departure from accounting principles

Section B   Historical cost accounting rules

- Fixed assets
- Current assets
- Miscellaneous and supplementary provisions

Section C   Alternative accounting rules

- Alternative accounting rules
- Application of the depreciation rules
- Additional information to be provided in case of departure from historical cost accounting rules
- Revaluation reserve

Part III Notes to the accounts

Disclosure of accounting policies
Information supplementing the balance sheet
Information supplementing the profit and loss account
General

Part IV Interpretation of Schedule

Schedule 8 is reproduced in full in Appendix **D**.

7.3 Less detailed balance sheet

A small company may adopt a simplified format of balance sheet in its annual accounts. CA 1985 Schedule 8 (as revised) provides balance sheet formats that are less detailed than those in Schedule 4.

The individual balance sheet of a small company which adopts Format 1 would be as set out in Table 7.3. This amended format is also reproduced in Appendix **B**.

7.4 Profit and loss account

The choice of profit and loss account formats for a small company are set out in Schedule 8 (part I section B) and are reproduced in Appendix **B**. They are also illustrated in Table 7.2. The principles governing the formats are as set out in **4.1** and **4.2**.

Profit and loss account

Table 7.2 Small company profit and loss account formats (Schedule 8)

Items boxed show the differences in disclosure required by the formats. In other respects all formats require identical information, except that Formats 3 and 4 require separate totals of 'charges' and 'income'. Full profit and loss account formats are given in Appendix **B**.

Expenses classified by function	**Expenses classified by type**
FORMAT 1	FORMAT 2
Format 3 requires the same information in a different presentation	*Format 4 requires the same information in a different presentation*

Format 1:
1. Turnover

> 2. Cost of sales
> 3. Gross profit or loss
> 4. Distribution costs
> 5. Administrative expenses

6. Other operating income

> *Staff costs disclosure – not applicable for small companies*

Depreciation must be allocated over items 2, 4 and 5 (Sch 8.8 (note 11)) and disclosed separately in Notes (Sch 8.19)

7. Income from shares in group undertakings
8. Income from participating interests
9. Income from other fixed asset investments
10. Other interest receivable and similar income
11. Amounts written off investments
12. Interest payable and similar charges
13. Tax on profit or loss on ordinary activities
14. Profit or loss on ordinary activities after taxation

> 15. Extraordinary income
> 16. Extraordinary charges
> 17. Extraordinary profit or loss
> 18. Tax on extraordinary profit or loss

19. Other taxes not shown under the above items
20. Profit or loss for the financial year

Format 2:
1. Turnover

> 2. Change in stocks of finished goods and work-in-progress
> 3. Own work capitalised

4. Other operating income

> 5. (a) Raw materials and consumables
>   (b) Other external charges

6. Staff costs:
   (a) Wages and salaries
   (b) Social security costs
   (c) Other pension costs

> 7. (a) Depreciation and other amounts written off tangible and intangible fixed assets
>   (b) Exceptional amounts written off current assets
> 8. Other operating charges

9. Income from shares in group undertakings
10. Income from participating interests
11. Income from other fixed asset investments
12. Other interest receivable and similar income
13. Amounts written off investments
14. Interest payable and similar charges
15. Tax on profit or loss on ordinary activities
16. Profit or loss on ordinary activities after taxation

> 17. Extraordinary income
> 18. Extraordinary charges
> 19. Extraordinary profit or loss
> 20. Tax on extraordinary profit or loss

21. Other taxes not shown under the above items
22. Profit or loss for the financial year

Extraordinary items, although included within the statutory formats, are now viewed by FRS 3 'Reporting financial performance' as being extremely rare.

Chapter 7   Small company accounts

7.5   Notes to the accounts

A small company must set out in the notes the information specified in Schedule 8 (CA 1985 Sch 8 paras 35–51) covering the following:

Sch 8.36
- *Disclosure of accounting policies*

Information supplementing the balance sheet

Sch 8.38–39
- *Share capital and debentures*
  Authorised capital; redeemable shares; share allotments

Sch 8.40–41
- *Fixed assets*
  Movements; revaluation; depreciation

Sch 8.42
- *Investments*
  Listed investments; market valuation

Sch 8.43
- *Reserves and provisions*
  Movements and transfers

Sch 8.44–45
- *Details of indebtedness*
  Creditors > 5 years; security; arrears of cumulative dividends

Sch 8.46
- *Guarantees and other financial commitments*
  Charges on assets; contingent liabilities; capital commitments not provided for; pension commitments; and financial commitments

Information supplementing the profit and loss account

Sch 8.49
- *Turnover*
  Percentage attributable to geographical market

Sch 8.50
- *Miscellaneous*
  Effect of prior year adjustments and exceptional transactions, and particulars of extraordinary charges or income

General

Sch 8.51
- *Basis of translation of foreign currencies*
- *Comparative figures*

Those disclosure requirements from which a small company is excepted are set out in **7.10.1**, which shows the items that are no longer required to be set out in the individual accounts of a small company.

7.6   Directors' statements

s246(8)
A company which qualifies as a small company in relation to a financial year and takes advantage of the special provisions with respect to the preparation of annual accounts and/or directors' report must include the following statements in its accounts, where appropriate:

7.6.1   Balance sheet
The balance sheet must contain (above the signature of a director required by section 233):

- a statement that the accounts have been prepared in accordance with the special provisions of Part VII of Companies Act 1985 relating to small companies.

7.6.2   Directors' report
The directors' report must contain (immediately above the signature of a director or secretary required by section 234A):

- a statement that the report has been prepared in accordance with special provisions of Part VII of Companies Act 1985 relating to small companies.

7.7 Groups

Where a small company has prepared individual accounts for a financial year in accordance with the special provisions provided by CA 1985 section 246 (introduced by SI 1997 No. 220) and prepares group accounts for the same year, it may prepare group accounts in accordance with those provisions.

s248A

7.8 Balance sheet format – small company balance sheet

The balance sheet format of a small company which adopts balance sheet Format 1 would be as in Table 7.3.

Table 7.3 Small company balance sheet (Schedule 8)

CALLED UP SHARE CAPITAL NOT PAID

FIXED ASSETS
Intangible assets
    Goodwill
    Other intangible assets

Tangible assets
    Land and buildings
    Plant and machinery, etc.

Investments *(Note 1)*
    Shares in group undertakings and participating interests
    Loans to group undertakings and undertakings in which the company has a participating interest
    Other investments other than loans
    Others

CURRENT ASSETS
Stocks
    Stocks
    Payments on account

Debtors *(Note 2)*
    Trade debtors
    Amounts owed by group undertakings and undertakings in which the company has a participating interest
    Others

Investments
    Shares in group undertakings
    Other investments

Cash at bank and in hand

PREPAYMENTS AND ACCRUED INCOME

CREDITORS: amounts falling due within one year
    Bank loans and overdrafts
    Trade creditors
    Amounts owed to group undertakings and undertakings in which the company has a participating interest
    Other creditors

NET CURRENT ASSETS (LIABILITIES)

TOTAL ASSETS LESS CURRENT LIABILITIES

> **CREDITORS: amounts falling due after more than one year** (Note 3)
>   Bank loans and overdrafts
>   Trade creditors
>   Amounts owed to group undertakings and undertakings in which the company has a participating interest
>   Other creditors
>
> **PROVISIONS FOR LIABILITIES AND CHARGES**
>
> **ACCRUALS AND DEFERRED INCOME**
>
> **CAPITAL AND RESERVES**
> **Called up share capital**
> **Share premium account**
> **Revaluation reserve**
> **Other reserves**
> **Profit and loss account**
>
> Note 1 Where a small company prepares small group accounts, in a consolidated balance sheet the format for 'Investments' is:
>   1 shares in group undertakings;
>   2 interests in associated undertakings;
>   3 other participating interests;
>   4 loans to group undertakings and undertakings in which a participating interest is held;
>   5 other investments other than loans; and
>   6 others.
>
> Note 2 A small company must disclose the aggregate total of 'debtors falling due after more than one year' but such disclosure (*if the amount is not material*) may be in the notes to the accounts rather than in the balance sheet.
>
> Note 3 Where a small company adopts balance sheet Format 2, if it discloses in the notes to its accounts the aggregate amounts included under 'Creditors' which fall due within one year and which fall due after one year respectively, it is not required to disclose the amounts falling due within one year and after one year separately for each item under 'Creditors'.

Appendix **B** reproduces balance sheet Formats 1 and 2 provided by CA 1985 Schedule 8.

7.9 Audit opinion: true and fair view

Where advantage is taken of any of the special provisions provided by section 246 of or Schedule 8 to the Companies Act 1985, the annual accounts of a small company nevertheless continue to be deemed to give a true and fair view as required by the Act. The auditors of a small company subject to audit are responsibile for considering whether the accounts give a true and fair view.

s249C(2)

s249C(4)

In the circumstances where a small company is exempted from audit and an independent accountants' report is required, the reporting accountant in his report is required to state only whether, having regard to the information in the accounting records, the accounts have been drawn up in a manner consistent with the provisions of the Act.

7.10 Disclosure concessions for small companies

7.10.1 *Notes to small company accounts – information that may be omitted*

For the purposes of comparison, the following table shows the information that would otherwise be required by CA 1985 Schedule 4 (for example, for medium-sized and large companies) that may be omitted in the individual annual accounts of a small company.

Table 7.4 Disclosure concessions for small companies

Stocks and fungible assets (including investments)
Difference (where material) between the replacement cost of such assets and the amount at which they are included in the balance sheet. — *Sch 4.27(3)*

Contingent rights to the allotment of shares
Options to subscribe for shares. — *Sch 4.40*

Issues of debentures during the financial year — *Sch 4.41*

Land and buildings
The amounts ascribable to freehold, long leasehold and short leasehold tenure. — *Sch 4.44*

Provision for taxation
Deferred taxation and other provision for taxation to be separately stated. — *Sch 4.47*

Indebtedness (creditors) falling due for payment after more than five years
The terms of payment or repayment and the rate of interest payable on the debt. — *Sch 4.48(2)*

Note: A small company may provide the aggregate total of such indebtedness rather than a total for each item of creditors. — *Sch 4.48(1)*

Secured creditors
The nature of the security given in respect of secured creditors. — *Sch 4.48(4)(b)*

Loans provided by way of financial assistance by the company for the purchase of its own shares
Aggregate amount outstanding. — *Sch 4.51(2)*

Dividend and amount recommended for distribution (Sch 4.51(3) – repealed by SI 1996 No. 189)

The following items of income and expenditure
- Interest on bank loans and overdrafts and on other loans (except loans from group undertakings). — *Sch 4.53(2)*

and

- Amounts set aside for the redemption of share capital and loans.
- Income from listed investments.
- Net rents from land (where rent comprises substantial part of company's revenue).
- Hire of plant and machinery.

(Sch 4.53(3)–(6) – repealed by SI 1996 No. 189).

Taxation
Particulars of tax including special circumstances affecting liability, amount and analysis of tax charge and [basis of computations – Sch 4.54(1) repealed by SI 1996 No. 189]. — *Sch 4.54*

Turnover
Particulars analysed by class of business and geographical market. — *Sch 4.55*

Note: a small company which supplies geographical markets outside the United Kingdom is required to state the percentage of the company's turnover that is, in the opinion of the directors, attributable to those markets during the financial year.

Staff particulars of persons employed by the company
Including aggregate amounts of wages and salaries, social security costs and other pension costs, and also details of average numbers employed by category. — *Sch 4.56*

Amounts attributable to dealings with or interests in group undertakings
Where the company is a parent company or subsidiary undertaking (Sch 4.59 – repealed by SI 1996 No. 189).

Chapter 7 Small company accounts

	Related undertakings (companies not required to prepare group accounts)
Sch 5.4	Financial years of subsidiary undertakings with non-coterminous year ends.
	Valuation of investment of the company in subsidiary undertakings by the equity method (Sch 5.5(2) – repealed by SI 1996 No. 189).
Sch 6.7	Excess retirement benefits of directors and past directors
	Directors' emoluments
Sch 6.2–5	Details of the emoluments of the highest paid director.

7.10.2 Disclosure requirements for small companies concerning directors' emoluments

SI 1997 No. 570 The Companies Act 1985 (Disclosure of Directors' Emoluments) Regulations 1997 has changed the disclosure requirements for all companies concerning directors' emoluments. For small companies, the requirements are as set out in Table 7.5.

s246(3)

Table 7.5 Small Companies – directors' emoluments

A small company *is* required to disclose the aggregate amounts of:

Sch 6.1
- directors' emoluments, being the total of the aggregates of:
  (a) directors' emoluments (including salaries, fees, bonuses, expense allowances and estimated non-cash benefits receivable) (Sch 6.1(3) as amended by SI 1997 No. 570);
  (b) amounts receivable under long-term incentive schemes;
  (c) company contributions paid to money purchase pension schemes;

Sch 6.8
- compensation to directors or past directors for loss of office;

Sch 6.9
- sums paid to third parties in respect of directors' services.

7.11 Directors' report of a small company

The directors' report of a small company need not give any of the information specified in CA 1985 s246(4).

The directors' report of a small company is only required to provide the following information:

- names of directors;
- principal activities;
- directors' share interests;
- directors' share options;
- political and charitable gifts (exceeding £200).

Table 7.6 compares the contents of a small company directors' report with the requirements for other companies, including medium-sized companies.

For a small company to take advantage of the exemptions provided by section 246(4) CA 1985 with respect to the preparation of a directors' report, the report must contain a statement to that effect. (Section 246(8) – reproduced in full in Appendix C.) This is explained in **7.6**.

Directors' report of a small company

Table 7.6   Contents of directors' report

'Small companies'	Companies other than 'small companies'
Section 234	Section 234
Names of directors during the financial year.	Names of directors during the financial year.
Principal activities of the company and its subsidiary undertakings and any significant changes during the year.	Principal activities of the company and its subsidiary undertakings and any significant changes during the year.
	A fair review of the development of the business and its subsidiary undertakings during the financial year and of their position at the end of it. Amount of dividend payment, if any, recommended. Amount of transfer to reserves, if any, proposed by the directors.
Schedule 7	Schedule 7
	Asset values – any significant and substantial difference in market value of interests in land at the year end from balance sheet amount.
Directors' interests in shares or debentures of the company or body corporate in the same group (i.e., its holding company or corporate undertaking). *Option to show details in the notes to the accounts, rather than in the directors' report.* (State if nil.)	Directors' interests in shares or debentures of the company or body corporate in the same group (i.e., its holding company or corporate undertaking). *Option to show details in the notes to the accounts, rather than in the directors' report.* (State if nil.)
Directors' share options, etc. (rights to subscribe for shares or debentures) in group companies granted or exercised. (State if nil.)	Directors' share options, etc. (rights to subscribe for shares or debentures) in group companies granted or exercised. (State if nil.)
Political and charitable gifts exceeding £200 (not applicable for wholly-owned subsidiaries).	Political and charitable gifts exceeding £200 (not applicable for wholly-owned subsidiaries).
	Particulars of any important post balance sheet events affecting the company and its subsidiary undertakings. Indication of likely future developments in the business of the company and its subsidiary undertakings. Indication of research and development activities (if any), of the company and its subsidiary undertakings. Indication of the existence of branches outside UK (unless company is unlimited company).
Particulars of any purchase by the company of its own shares.	Particulars of any purchase by the company of its own shares.

Chapter 7 Small company accounts

Contents of directors' report – *continued*

'Small companies'	**Companies other than 'small companies'**
Schedule 7	Schedule 7
Statement of policy of the company concerning the employment of disabled persons. (*Small companies with 250 or more employees only – an unlikely situation.*)	Statement of policy of the company concerning the employment of disabled persons. (*Companies with 250 or more employees only.*)
	Statement of arrangements adopted concerning employee involvement. (*Companies with 250 or more employees only.*) Statement of policy and practice on the payment of creditors. (*Public company and large subsidiaries only.*)

Chapter 8 Abbreviated accounts

8.1 Filing accounts

A company, classified as small or medium-sized, is permitted to deliver 'abbreviated accounts', in place of full statutory accounts ('individual accounts'), to the Registrar of Companies. Accounts abbreviated in such a way are statutory accounts and are then filed as 'annual accounts' with the Registrar of Companies in accordance with the Companies Act 1985 section 242, as amended.   *s246(5)*   *s246A(3)*

Abbreviated accounts are accounts prepared in accordance with: *s247B(1)*

Small company
- s246(5) – abbreviated Sch 8A Balance Sheet
- s246(6) – disclosure exemptions within
    - full annual accounts Sch 4 or Sch 8   (s242(1))
    - small company abbreviated accounts   (s246(5)(c))
    being exemptions from disclosure of:
    financial years of subsidiaries   Sch 5.4
    shares held by subsidiaries   Sch 5.6
    directors' emoluments, pensions etc.   Sch 6 Part 1
    auditors' remuneration   s390A(3)

Medium-sized company
- s246A(3) – disclosure exemptions from medium-sized company profit and loss account

Some 44 per cent of all annual accounts filed with the Registrar of Companies are abbreviated accounts.

Table 8.1 Annual accounts registered at Companies House by type 1995–96		
Great Britain in total		
	000s	%
Full individual accounts	301.5	38.6
Abbreviated accounts		
Small company	336.9	43.2
Medium-sized company	4.1	0.5
Group accounts	14.5	1.9
Dormant company accounts	123.3	15.8
Interim/initial accounts	0.4	0.0
	780.7	100.0
Source: DTI Report *Companies in 1995–96* (HMSO)		

8.2 Contents of abbreviated accounts

Abbreviated accounts are not required to give a true and fair view; they are a form of accounts containing less information and disclosure than the annual accounts for shareholders and basically comprise:

Chapter 8 Abbreviated accounts

Sch 8A *Small company* – 'an abbreviated balance sheet', being an abbreviated version of the full balance sheet, and certain notes.

s246A *Medium-sized company* – full statutory accounts *except* that analysis of turnover and derivative of gross profit or loss may be omitted.

Sch 8A
s246A Abbreviated accounts will usually comprise the points shown in Table 8.2.

Table 8.2 Abbreviated accounts

	Small company	Medium-sized company
Directors' report	No report	Full report
Profit and loss account	No profit and loss account	Profit and loss account may commence with 'gross profit or loss'
Balance sheet	Abbreviated balance sheet Sch 8A format	Full balance sheet
	Debtors and creditors falling due after more than one year	
Cash flow and other primary statements	Not required	Full statements required
Notes	Limited information only Sch 8A disclosures	Full notes, except particulars of turnover omitted
	No information on directors' or employees' emoluments	
Auditors' report	Special report	Special report
Accountants' report*	Special report – report on full accounts reproduced	Not available

* as appropriate

Abbreviated accounts, in practice, can be prepared on the basis of minimal or selective departures from full Schedule 4 annual accounts. For example, the s247B(1) definition of 'abbreviated accounts' means that accounts prepared in accordance with the full requirements of Schedule 4 except for an exemption afforded by s246(6) (see **8.1** above) can represent abbreviated accounts for filing purposes.

8.3 Directors' statements

s246(8)
s246A(4) Abbreviated accounts must include a statement in a prominent position on the balance sheet (above the signature of the director) that:

- the accounts have been prepared in accordance with the special provisions relating to small or medium-sized companies, as the case may be.

The requirement can be illustrated as follows:

> 'The [abbreviated] accounts have been prepared in accordance with the special provisions of Part VII of Companies Act 1985 relating to small [medium-sized] companies.'

Accounts that are subject to audit exemption are also required to have additional statements as explained in Chapter **10** and illustrated in Example 10.1.

8.4 Abbreviated balance sheet

The abbreviated balance sheet formats provided by Schedule 8A CA 1985 are set out in Table 8.3. Schedule 8A is reproduced in full in Appendix **B**.

Table 8.3 Form and content of abbreviated accounts of small companies delivered to Registrar

BALANCE SHEET FORMATS

A small company may deliver to the registrar a copy of the balance sheet showing the items listed in either of the balance sheet formats set out below in the order and under the headings and sub-headings given in the format adopted, but in other respects corresponding to the full balance sheet.

Balance Sheet Formats

Format 1

A. Called up share capital not paid
B. Fixed assets
   I Intangible assets
   II Tangible assets
   III Investments
C. Current assets
   I Stocks
   II Debtors
   III Investments
   IV Cash at bank and in hand
D. Prepayments and accrued income
E. Creditors: amounts falling due within one year
F. Net current assets (liabilities)
G. Total assets less current liabilities
H. Creditors: amounts falling due after more than one year
I. Provisions for liabilities and charges
J. Accruals and deferred income
K. Capitals and reserves
   I Called up share capital
   II Share premium account
   III Revaluation reserve
   IV Other reserves
   V Profit and loss account

Format 2

ASSETS
A. Called up share capital not paid
B. Fixed assets
   I Intangible assets
   II Tangible assets
   III Investments
C. Current assets
   I Stocks
   II Debtors
   III Investments
   IV Cash at bank and in hand
D. Prepayments and accrued income

LIABILITIES
A. Capitals and reserves
   I Called up share capital
   II Share premium account
   III Revaluation reserve
   IV Other reserves
   V Profit and loss account
B. Provisions for liabilities and charges
C. Creditors
D. Accruals and deferred income

8.5 Notes to abbreviated accounts

The notes forming part of abbreviated accounts of a small company are only required to include the provisions set out in Table 8.4. *Sch 8A*

Chapter 8 Abbreviated accounts

Table 8.4 Notes to abbreviated accounts

	Schedule 8A paragraph	Illustrated in example abbreviated accounts by
Accounting policies	4	Note 1
Share capital and redeemable shares	5	Note 5
Particulars of share allotments	6	Note 5
Fixed assets movements and depreciation [for letter or roman number format headings only]	7	Note 2
Debtors: amounts falling due after more than one year (aggregate)	2(1)	Note 3
Creditors: amounts falling due within one year or after more than one year for each category of creditors (Format 2)	2(2)	—
Particulars of creditors:		Note 4
Debts falling due after five years	8(1)	
Secured debts	8(2)	
Basis of translation of foreign currencies	9(1)	Note 1
Comparative figures	9(2)–(3)	Accounts
	Schedule 5 paragraph	
Subsidiary undertakings	1–3	Note 2
Other significant (20% or more) undertakings	7–9	—
Parent undertakings and ultimate parent company	11–12	—
	Schedule 6 paragraph	
Loans, quasi-loans and other transactions with directors	15–30	Note 6

Table 8.5 Profit and loss account items combined as 'Gross profit or loss'

Format 1	Format 2	Format 3	Format 4
1 Turnover	1 Turnover	B1 Turnover	B1 Turnover
2 Cost of sales		A1 Cost of sales	
	2 Change in stocks of finished goods and work-in-progress		A1 Reduction in stocks of finished goods and work-in-progress
			B2 Increase in stocks of finished goods and work-in-progress
3 Gross profit or loss			
	3 Own work capitalised		B3 Own work capitalised
6 Other operating income	4 Other operating income	B2 Other operating income	B4 Other operating income
	5 (a) Raw materials and consumables (b) Other external charges		A2 (a) Raw materials and consumables (b) Other external charges

References are to item numbers in the statutory formats of CA 1985 Schedule 4.

8.6 'Gross profit or loss'

8.6.1 Medium-sized company abbreviated profit and loss account

A medium-sized company may prepare abbreviated accounts in which the profit and loss account includes items combined as 'Gross profit or loss' as in Table 8.5. *s246A(3)*

The resultant figure of 'gross profit or loss', it will be appreciated, will depend on which format is adopted and also is not what might normally be understood by the term, for example, because of the inclusion of 'other operating income' and also the exclusion (in Formats 2 and 4) of staff costs and depreciation charges.

8.7 Parent companies

As noted in Chapter **9** there is no statutory provision to file abbreviated group accounts. A parent company which files its own abbreviated individual accounts includes within those accounts considerable disclosure relating to subsidiaries and other significant holdings in undertakings (see Appendices **H** and **J**). A parent company wishing to produce group accounts will need to prepare these as 'non-statutory' accounts in addition to its own statutory individual abbreviated accounts.

8.8 Decision to prepare abbreviated accounts

The decision whether or not to take advantage of the exemptions to prepare abbreviated accounts will be a commercial one. As full statutory accounts have to be prepared in any case for shareholders, the directors of small or medium-sized companies will have regard to:

(a) the additional costs involved in the preparation of an additional set of accounts; and
(b) the sensitivity or confidentiality of financial information for public display.

A decision can only be reached after a comparison is made of full and limited disclosure and after the relative costs and benefits have been considered. For small companies, a further consideration will be the fact that the annual accounts of a small company can, in any case, now be prepared with less detailed information than for larger companies.

8.9 Special auditors' report *s247B*

Abbreviated accounts delivered to the Registrar of Companies (other than those of audit-exempt or dormant companies) must be accompanied by a special report of the auditors under s247B(2). APB guidance has been provided in APB Bulletin 1997/1 (May 1997) 'The special auditors' report on abbreviated accounts in Great Britain' and is reflected in the example abbreviated accounts in **12.2**.

The auditors are required to state that in their opinion: *s247B(2)*

- the company is entitled to deliver abbreviated accounts in accordance with the relevant provisions; and
- the abbreviated accounts to be delivered are properly prepared in accordance with the relevant provisions.

The legislation does not envisage a qualified opinion; if the auditor cannot give the positive statements of opinion required as above, the directors are not entitled to deliver abbreviated accounts.

Chapter 8 Abbreviated accounts

s247B(3) The special auditors' report no longer needs to include the full auditors' report under s235, reproduced in full, except where:

- the s235 report was qualified; or
- the s235 report contained a statement under s237(2) (accounts, records or returns inadequate or accounts not agreeing with records or returns) or s237(3) (failure to obtain necessary information and explanations).

In Bulletin 1997/1, the APB also recommends, where the s235 is unqualified but contains an explanatory paragraph regarding a fundamental uncertainty (for example, concerning the going concern basis), the special auditors' report should also include the explanatory paragraph, within a section entitled 'other information'. The auditor should include whatever information is considered important for a proper understanding of the report.

Chapter 9 Exemptions for small and medium-sized groups

9.1 Group accounts

Group accounts are required where, at the end of a financial year, a company is a parent company having subsidiary undertakings. The group accounts are in addition to individual accounts for the year and are to be prepared in the form of consolidated accounts. s227

Group accounts must comply with the provisions of Schedule 4A to CA 1985, a schedule inserted by CA 1989 ('Form and Content of Group Accounts').

Where a small company has prepared individual accounts for a financial year in accordance with the special provisions for small companies provided by CA 1985 section 246 and prepares group accounts for the same year, it may prepare group accounts in accordance with those provisions. s248A

9.2 Exemptions

Certain parent companies are exempt from the requirement to prepare group accounts. Basically, these are: s228

(a) A parent company, being itself a wholly-owned subsidiary undertaking.
(b) A parent company, being itself a 50 per cent (or more than 50 per cent) subsidiary undertaking where group accounts are not requested by at least half of the minority shareholders.

(In both (a) and (b), the company must be included in larger EU group (consolidated) accounts and must be non-listed.)

(c) A parent company, being the parent undertaking of a 'small' or 'medium-sized' group. s248

A parent company not producing group accounts is required to provide details on its 'related undertakings' (subsidiary and associated undertakings) in its own individual accounts – the information required is set out in Appendix H. s231
Sch 5

9.3 Small and medium-sized groups

The Companies Act 1989 introduced the exemption for 'small' and 'medium-sized' companies from the requirement to prepare group accounts.

Certain categories of group (termed 'ineligible') regardless of size are not entitled to the exemptions to prepare group accounts if any of the group members are: s248

(a) public companies, or banking or insurance companies; or
(b) authorised persons under the Financial Services Act 1986.

Chapter 9 Exemptions for small and medium-sized groups

9.4 Qualifying conditions: group exemptions

s249 Basically, a group is exempt from producing group (consolidated) accounts as a small or medium-sized group if it does not exceed more than one of the following criteria on one or other of the following two bases:

Criteria	*Net basis*	*Gross basis*
Turnover	£11.2m	£13.44m
Balance sheet total	£5.6m	£6.72m
Average number of employees (on a monthly basis)	250	250

(The bases may be mixed)

These criteria are criteria for *both* small and medium-sized groups because a small group by definition is within the criteria for a medium-sized group. CA 1985 section 249 gives the small group criteria as:

- Turnover – not more than £2.8 million net (or £3.36 million gross).
- Balance sheet total – not more than £1.4 million net (or £1.68 million gross).
- Average number of employees – not more than 50 employees.

Figures are aggregated from individual statutory accounts for the relevant financial year of companies within the group. In each case:

- Turnover figures should be proportionately adjusted where the financial 'year' is not in fact 12 months.
- 'Balance sheet total' means gross assets before deduction of liabilities, accruals and provisions, i.e., the aggregate of headings A to D in Format 1 or the 'Assets' headings in Format 2.

The alternative bases for turnover and balance sheet totals (as qualifying conditions for exemption) are:

- *'Net' basis* – Aggregate figures arrived at with the set-offs and consolidation adjustments (elimination of group transactions, etc.) required by Schedule 4A CA 1985.
- *'Gross' basis* – Aggregate figures arrived at without such set-offs and consolidation adjustments.

CA 1985 Schedule 4A consolidation adjustments include:

(a) Elimination of intra-group transactions and assets and liabilities.
(b) Elimination of intra-group unrealised profits or losses.
(c) Adjustments to effect uniform accounting policies within the group.

As a general rule, for a group to qualify as exempt, the criteria must be met for the current and previous year. If the criteria are not met for the following year, a group may continue to be exempt for that year. However, if the criteria are not met in the year after that, group accounts must then be prepared.

9.5 Auditors' report

s248 A parent company of a small or medium-sized group was previously not entitled to the exemption from preparing group accounts unless the company's auditors provide a report stating that in their opinion the company was so entitled. Following SI 1996 No. 189, this is no longer required.

s237(4A) If the directors take advantage of the section 248 exemption from the need to prepare group accounts, the auditors are now required to refer to the exemption only if in their opinion the directors were not entitled to do so. The auditors' statement of non-entitlement to the section 248 exemption would be made in the audit report under section 235.

9.6 Abbreviated group accounts

There is no provision to prepare and submit abbreviated group accounts. Either full consolidated (small company or medium-sized company) accounts of the group are filed at Companies House or no group accounts are filed if the group qualifies as exempt.

9.7 Decision chart to determine group accounts exemption

A parent company need not prepare group accounts for a financial year in relation to which the group headed by that company qualifies as a small or medium-sized group and is not an ineligible group.   *s248*

Whether a parent company is exempted from preparing group accounts can be illustrated broadly as in Table 9.1.

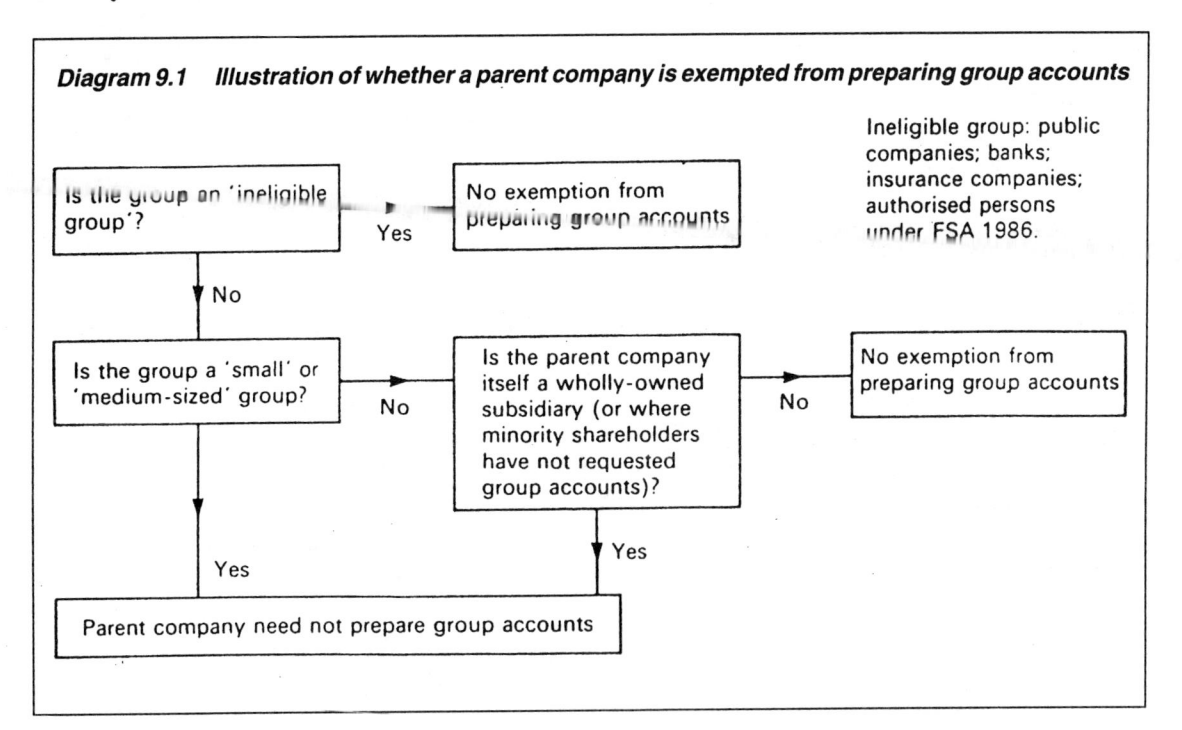

Diagram 9.1 *Illustration of whether a parent company is exempted from preparing group accounts*

[Decision flowchart:
- Is the group an 'ineligible group'? → Yes → No exemption from preparing group accounts (Ineligible group: public companies; banks; insurance companies; authorised persons under FSA 1986.)
- No → Is the group a 'small' or 'medium-sized' group?
  - Yes → Parent company need not prepare group accounts
  - No → Is the parent company itself a wholly-owned subsidiary (or where minority shareholders have not requested group accounts)?
    - Yes → Parent company need not prepare group accounts
    - No → No exemption from preparing group accounts]

Notwithstanding the above, a parent company may prepare group accounts for its own management accounting purposes and not submit them to the Registrar of Companies but file instead its own individual statutory accounts with appropriate disclosures. If group accounts are not prepared because the group accounts exemptions are met, the company may, if it wishes, file abbreviated accounts provided it qualifies as a small or medium-sized company.

Chapter 10 Small company audit exemption and accountants' reports

10.1 Introduction: preparation of accounts irrespective of audit

Generally speaking, company law requires the directors of *all* companies to prepare annual (statutory) accounts irrespective of the requirement or otherwise for the need for these accounts to be audited. Statutory accounts for shareholders should: *s226*

- Give a true and fair view.
- Comply (to the appropriate extent) with Companies Act 1985 Schedule 4 (or Schedule 8 for small companies) as to form, content and information provided.

For each financial year, the directors must (with exceptions) lay the annual accounts, directors' report and auditors' report ('accounts and reports') before the company in general meeting. However, a private company may elect by elective resolution to dispense with this requirement, in which case copies of the accounts and reports should be sent to the members, debenture holders and anyone entitled to receive notices of general meetings.   *s241*
s253

s238

For each financial year, the directors must also deliver ('file') a copy of the accounts and reports to the Registrar of Companies. The period allowed for filing is 10 months for a private company or seven months for a public company, after the end of the financial year (relevant 'accounting reference date'). (For a newly incorporated company, the periods are from the first anniversary of incorporation or within three months of the year end, whichever is the later.) A company which is small or medium-sized may file abbreviated accounts instead of full acounts.   *s242*

s244

s246(5)
s246A(3)

The directors of an unlimited company are not required to deliver accounts and reports to the Registrar (provided certain conditions are met).   *s254*

10.2 Audit exemptions for certain categories of small company

SI 1994 No. 1935 The Companies Act 1985 (Audit Exemption) Regulations 1994 introduced certain categories of small company as exempt from audit. Other than for charitable companies, the threshold for audit exemption has subsequently been extended to £350,000 turnover for annual accounts ending on or after 15 June 1997 by SI 1997 No. 936 The Companies Act 1985 (Audit Exemption) (Amendment) Regulations 1997.

10.3 Audit exemption not available

Audit exemption is not available to any company which was at any time during the year any of the following: *s249B(1)*

- a public company;
- a parent or a subsidiary undertaking;
- an authorised person or an appointed representative under the Financial Services Act 1986;
- a banking or insurance company;

75

Chapter 10 Small company audit exemption and accountants' reports

- an insurance broker enrolled by the Insurance Brokers Registration Council;
- a special register body, being a trade union or employers' association under the Trade Union and Labour Relations (Consolidation) Act 1992.

10.4 Right to require an audit

s249B(2) Any member or members holding not less than 10 per cent in aggregate in the nominal value of the company's issued share capital of a company (or any class of it) or (if the company does not have a share capital) not less than 10 per cent in number of the members of the company, may require an audit of the company's accounts. To do so, the member or members must deposit a notice in writing at the company's registered office during the financial year but not later than one month before the end of the year. The company is then not entitled to audit exemption for the year to which the notice relates.

s249B(3)

There is no requirement for a company to advise members of their rights to require an audit (or the manner in which it may be exercised) nor, for example, of their rights to audit when the accounting year end is changed.

10.5 Determining audit exemption

Table 10.1 summarises the position to demonstrate:

- when an audit is required, which accounts may be prepared (and for whom), and
- whether accounts should be filed at Companies House.

The table applies to a company:

- which qualifies as a Small Company (in accordance with section 247 CA 1985), and
- the 'balance sheet total' (CA 1985 section 247) of which does not exceed £1.4m;
- which is NOT:
  (a) a public company;
  (b) a banking or insurance company or insurance broker;
  (c) an authorised person or appointed representative under the Financial Services Act 1986; or
  (d) a 'special register body' – trade union or employers' association;
- which, if a parent company or a subsidiary undertaking, is not the member of a small ineligible group.

It assumes that audit exemption has not otherwise been vetoed by shareholders holding 10 per cent or more of any class of share capital (or 10 per cent of the members) or is precluded in accordance with the Articles of Association.

Notwithstanding the availability of exemption, an audit may nevertheless be voluntarily carried out.

10.6 Effect of audit exemption

For those small companies (other than charitable companies) which are able to take advantage of the exemption, the position broadly is as follows in respect of annual accounts ending on or after 15 June 1997.

Turnover	Effect of exemption
Not more than £350,000	• No audit is required
	• No report of an independent reporting accountant is required
SI 1997 No. 936 More than £350,000	• Audited accounts are required

Audit exemption conditions

The audit exemption conditions are explained in full in **10.8**.

To be entitled to audit exemption for the year, a small company must:

- Meet the relevant 'exemption conditions' (s249A).
- Have a 'balance sheet total' of not more than £1.4 million (s249A(3)/(4)).
- Provide within its balance sheet a directors' statement (s249B(4)).
- Not be one of the 'exemption unavailable' categories (s249B(1)).
- Not have received notice from 10 per cent or more of members requiring an audit (s249B(2)).

Table 10.1 Small Companies – summary of accounts and the need for audit

Turnover (Charities: Gross Income)	Small Company – full Sch 8 accounts (s246) available?	Small Company – abbreviated accounts available?	Audit required?	Reporting Accountant's report (s249A(2)) required? (1)	Accounts filing with Registrar of Companies (Companies House) required? (1)	Full accounts to be submitted to shareholders? (2)
Small Companies other than Charities						
Not more than £90,000	Yes	Yes	No	No	Yes	Yes
£90,001–£350,000	Yes	Yes	No	No(4)	Yes	Yes
£350,001–£2.8m	Yes	Yes	Yes	N/A	Yes	Yes
£2.8m–£11.2m	No	No(3)	Yes	N/A	Yes	Yes
Incorporated Charities						
Not more than £90,000	Yes	Yes	No	No	Yes	Yes
£90,001–£250,000	Yes	Yes	No	Yes	Yes	Yes
£250,001–£2.8m	Yes	Yes	Yes	N/A	Yes	Yes
£2.8m–£11.2m	No	No(3)	Yes	N/A	Yes	Yes

Note 1 Full or abbreviated statutory accounts, except for unincorporated companies (where filing is not required).
Note 2 Accounts should be laid before the members/shareholders in general meeting or sent to them where an elective resolution is in force (s252 CA 1985).
Note 3 Medium-sized company abbreviated accounts available.
Note 4 Yes – in respect of annual accounts ending on or before 15 June 1997.

10.7 Reports required on accounts of small companies

Type of Report	*Type of Accounts*
Auditors' report (s235)	Full accounts – Audited
Special auditors' report (s247B)	Abbreviated accounts – Audited
Accountant's Report (s249A(2)) [s249C]	Full accounts *and* abbreviated accounts – Audit exemption s249A(4) (Report conditions met) (Same report used for both types of accounts)
No report (audit or accountants')	Full accounts or abbreviated accounts – Audit exemption s249A(3) (Total exemption)

10.8 Audit exemption conditions

10.8.1 *Exemptions from audit*
Subject to the exceptions noted above in **10.3**, a company which meets the 'total exemption conditions' in respect of a financial year will be exempt from the requirement to have its accounts audited in respect of that year.

s249A(1)

Chapter 10 Small company audit exemption and accountants' reports

However, charitable companies which meet 'report conditions' in respect of a financial year will be exempt from the requirement to have their accounts for that year audited provided the directors cause a report, made to the company's members, to be prepared in respect of the company's individual accounts for that year, in accordance with section 249C.

s249A(2)

SI 1997 No. 936 The 'total exemption conditions' are met by a company in respect of a financial year (ending on or after 15 June 1997) if:

- it qualifies as a small company in relation to that year for the purposes of section 246;
- *s249A(3)* its turnover in that year is not more than £350,000 (£90,000 charitable companies); and
- *s249A(3A)* its balance sheet total for that year is not more than £1.4 million.

The 'report conditions' are met by a charitable company in respect of a financial year if:

- it qualifies as a small company in relation to that year for the purposes of section 246;
- its turnover in that year is more than £90,000 but not more than £250,000; and
- *s249A(4)* its balance sheet total for that year is not more than £1.4 million.

For companies that are charities, reference to 'turnover' should be substituted with the term 'gross income', the upper limit of which is £250,000 rather than £350,000 when determining audit exemption 'report conditions' for such companies. 'Gross income' means the company's income from all sources, as shown in its income and expenditure account.

s249A(5)

'Balance sheet total' is defined by section 247(5) (see **6.2**). 'Turnover' is defined in **5.3.5**. The maximum turnover or gross income figures above are to be proportionately adjusted where the company's financial 'year' is not, in fact, 12 months.

s249A(6)

Entitlement to exemption is determined on a year-by-year basis – where balance sheet total or turnover thresholds are exceeded, this may result in a company ceasing to retain entitlement for a further year.

10.9 Statement by the directors

Companies taking advantage of the audit exemptions must include in their balance sheet a statement by the directors to the effect that:

s249B(4)

- for the year in question the company was entitled to exemption from audit under section 249A(1) [*total exemption*] or 249A(2) [*exemption with accountant's report*] [*as the case may be*];
- no notice by a member or members requesting an audit pursuant to section 249B(2), in respect of the year, has been deposited;
- the directors acknowledge their responsibilities for:
  (a) ensuring that the company keeps accounting records which comply with section 221, and
  (b) preparing accounts which give a true and fair view of the state of affairs of the company as at the end of the financial year and of its profit or loss for the financial year in accordance with the requirements of section 226, and which otherwise comply with the requirements of the Act relating to accounts, so far as applicable to the company.

The directors' statement is to appear in the balance sheet of a small company taking advantage of audit exemption, above the signature required by section 233, or where the company has taken advantage of the special provisions for small companies ('small company accounts'), above the statements required by section 246(8). (See **7.6** and **8.3**.)

s249B(5) Examples of a form of directors' statement are illustrated in Example 10.1.

> **Example 10.1 Small company audit exemption directors' statements: balance sheet**
>
> For the financial year ended [30 September 1997], the company was entitled to exemption from audit under section 249(1) [*total exemption*] [or 249A(2)] [*exemption with accountants' report – charitable company*], [*as the case may be*] Companies Act 1985; and no notice has been deposited under section 249B(2) [*member or members requesting an audit*]. The directors acknowledge their responsibilities for ensuring that the company keeps accounting records which comply with section 221 [of the Act] and preparing accounts which give a true and fair view of the state of affairs of the company as at the end of the year and of its profit or loss for the financial year in accordance with the requirements of section 226 and which otherwise comply with the requirements of the Companies Act 1985, so far as applicable to the company. [*Note 1*]
>
> The [abbreviated] accounts have been prepared in accordance with the special provisions of Part VII of Companies Act 1985 relating to small [medium-sized] companies. [*Note 2*]
>
> Note: [Words in italics are explanatory only]
>
> *The above statements are applicable as follows:*
>
> *(1) applicable, where audit exemption applies, in*
>   *(a) full balance sheets*
>   *(b) Sch 8 balance sheets*
>   *(c) abbreviated balance sheets;*
> *(2) applicable where small company accounts (on the basis of Sch 8) are adopted, for both audited or audit-exempt accounts; also applicable where abbreviated accounts are prepared, for both audited or audit-exempt accounts.*

10.10 Accountants' report under s249A(2) Companies Act 1985

The report required, for the purposes of section 249A(2), is to be prepared by a 'reporting accountant'. *s249C(1)*

It has to state whether in the opinion of the reporting accountant:

- the accounts of the company for the financial year in question are in agreement with the accounting records kept by the company under section 221; and
- having regard only to, and on the basis of, the information contained in those accounting records, those accounts have been drawn up in a manner consistent with the provisions of the Act specified in section 249C(6), so far as applicable to the company. *s249C(2)*

The provisions of the Companies Act 1985 specified in section 249C(6) are as follows:

- *Form and content of company accounts* – section 226(3), Schedule 4 and Schedule 8;
- *Related/subsidiary undertakings* – section 231 and paragraphs 7 to 9A and 13(1), (3) and (4) of Schedule 5; and
- *Directors' emoluments and other benefits* – section 232 and Schedule 6 where appropriate as modified by section 246(2) and (3) (small company provisions). *s239C(6)*

The report also has to state that in the opinion of the reporting accountant (having regard only to, and on the basis of, the information contained in the accounting records kept by the company under section 221) the company satisified the requirements for exemption from audit of the accounts for the year specified in section 249A(4) and did not, at any time within that year, fall within any of the categories of companies not entitled to exemption specified in section 249B(1). *s239C(3)*

The illustrative example of an accountants' report, expressing an affirmative opinion on all relevant matters, provided in the APB SSRA 'Audit exemption reports', is set out in Example 10.2.

> **Example 10.2 Accountants' report to the shareholders on the unaudited accounts of Small Company (Charity) Limited**
>
> We report on the accounts for the year ended [   ] set out on pages [   ] to [   ].
>
> *Respective responsibilities of directors and reporting accountants*
> As described on page [   ], the company's directors are responsible for the preparation of the accounts, and they consider that the company is exempt from an audit. It is our responsibility to carry out procedures designed to enable us to report our opinion.
>
> *Basis of opinion*
> Our work was conducted in accordance with the Statement of Standards for Reporting Accountants and so our procedures consisted of comparing the accounts with the accounting records kept by the company, and making such limited enquiries of the officers of the company as we considered necessary for the purposes of this report. These procedures provide only the assurance expressed in our opinion.
>
> *Opinion*
> In our opinion:
>
> (a) the accounts are in agreement with the accounting records kept by the company under section 221 of the Companies Act 1985;
> (b) having regard to, and on the basis of, the information contained in those accounting records:
>   (i) the accounts have been drawn up in a manner consistent with the accounting requirements specified in section 249C(6) of the Act; and
>   (ii) the company satisfied the conditions for exemption from an audit of the accounts for the year specified in section 249A(4) of the Act and did not, at any time within that year, fall within any of the categories of companies not entitled to the exemption specified in section 249B(1).
>
> ....
> TRUE & FAIRVIEW
> Reporting Accountants
>
> 17 Queens Place,
> LONDON EC4P 3BC   3 October 1997

10.11 The reporting accountant

Generally a reporting accountant for the purposes of audit exemption has to be a member of one of the accounting bodies recognised in section 249D(1) and be either engaged in public practice or be eligible as a company auditor or independent reporting accountant. (Section 249D is reproduced in Appendix **F**.)

s249D(1)

The recognised accounting bodies are:

- the three Institutes of Chartered Accountants (England and Wales, Scotland and Ireland);
- the Association of Chartered Certified Accountants;
- the Association of Authorised Public Accountants;
- the Association of Accounting Technicians;
- the Association of International Accountants; and
- the Chartered Institute of Management Accountants.

s249D(3)

10.12 Audit exemption: abbreviated accounts

A company which has taken advantage of audit exemption in preparing full shareholders' accounts may prepare abbreviated accounts for filing with the Registrar of Companies. This is explained in Chapter 8.

For a company which has met the 'total exemption' conditions, no auditors' report or accountants' report is required to be attached to the accounts, whether they are full or abbreviated accounts.

A company which meets the 'report conditions' (being a charitable company, in respect of annual accounts ending on or after 15 June 1997) must, with its full (individual) accounts submit a report by an independent accountant for the purposes of section 249A(2) to accord with the provisions of section 249C. Its abbreviated accounts are not required to have a special auditors' report nor any comparable 'special reporting accountants' report'.   *s247B*

However, the directors are nevertheless required to file the section 249A(2) accountants'-report prepared on the full individual accounts), but not necessarily together with (or bound in with) the audit-exempt abbreviated accounts. The most convenient approach to deal with this requirement is to include within the 'package' containing the abbreviated accounts the accountants' report suitably preceded by a rubric to distinguish the accounts upon which the report has been made from the abbreviated accounts to which they are attached. The text of such a rubric could be on the following lines: *s242(1)*
   s249E(2)(b)

> 'The following reproduces the text of the Accountants' Report prepared for the purposes of section 249A(2) Companies Act 1985 in respect of the company's annual accounts, from which the abbreviated accounts (set out on pages [   ] to [   ]) have been prepared.'

Chapter 11 Financial Reporting Standard for Smaller Entities ('FRSSE')

11.1 Introduction

The new Financial Reporting Standard for Smaller Entities ('FRSSE'), anticipated to be adopted by the ASB during summer 1997, prescribes the basis for preparing and presenting the accounts of small entities (as defined in the standard – basically on the same criteria as 'small companies').

A small company preparing true and fair view accounts which chooses to adopt the FRSSE is exempt from all other SSAPs, FRSs and UITF Consensus Abstracts (except those relevant to the production of consolidated accounts, that is SSAP 1, SSAP 22, FRSs 2, 5, 6 and 7 and UITF 3). A small company may choose not to adopt the FRSSE in which case the SSAPs, FRSs and UITF Abstracts apply in full where appropriate or not otherwise specifically exempted.

The FRSSE presents, in one self-contained FRS, definitions, accounting treatments and measurement criteria that are consistent with existing accounting standards but in a simplified version. Some disclosure requirements are also simplified or excluded.

The FRSSE does not apply to:

- Large or medium-sized companies or groups
- Public companies (or subsidiaries of public groups)
- Banks or insurance companies
- Authorised persons under FSA 1986

A small company which chooses to adopt the FRSSE may do so as soon as it wishes, in advance of the effective date stated in the FRSSE.

Paragraph references in this chapter are based upon the draft FRSSE issued in December 1996.

This chapter presents a summary of the FRSSE.

11.1.1 True and fair view
Accounts drawn up in compliance with the FRSSE and the requirements, for example, of new Schedule 8 CA 1985 may be deemed to be true and fair as required by the Companies Act 1985, provided full and appropriate disclosures of the transactions are made.

11.2 The FRSSE in outline

The outline summary in Table 11.1 does not constitute a complete checklist of the FRSSE requirements.

Chapter 11 Financial Reporting Standard for Smaller Entities ('FRSSE')

Table 11.1 The FRSSE in outline

	FRSSE paragraph	Principal derivation
Objective To provide useful and relevant information about the financial position, performance and stewardship of a small entity.	1	
Scope True and fair view accounts of: • small companies under companies legislation • small unincorporated entities (on same criteria).	2	
True and fair view Requirement to present a true and fair view, having regard to the substance of any transaction or arrangement.	3	
Any true and fair view override should be stated clearly and unambiguously, with disclosures.	7–8	UITF 7
Accounting principles and policies Presumption: basic accounting concepts have been adopted.	6	SSAP 2
Material or critical accounting policies adopted should be disclosed in notes. Explanations to be as clear, fair and brief as possible.		
Profit and loss account All gains and losses recognised in the accounts for the financial period should be included in: • the profit and loss account, or • the statement of total recognised gains and losses.	9	FRS 3
Exceptional items	10–11	FRS 3
Determination of profit or loss on disposal of assets	12	
Extraordinary items	13	
Prior period adjustments	14	
Changes in disclosure in accounting policy – a restatement for a change in policy should include an indication of the effect; where the effect is immaterial, this should be stated.	15	
Statement of total recognised gains and losses (See Tables 4.5 and 11.2).	16	
A primary statement should be presented, with the same prominence as the profit and loss account, showing the total of recognised gains and losses and its components. The components should be the gains and losses that are recognised in the period insofar as they are attributable to shareholders. Where the only recognised gains and losses are the results included in the profit and loss account no separate statement to this effect need be made.		
Foreign currency translation • Method of translation and determination of gains and losses • Denomination of foreign equity investments financed by foreign currency borrowings • Groups and foreign enterprises.	 17–20 21 22–27	SSAP 20

The FRSSE in outline

	FRSSE paragraph	Principal derivation

Taxation
- UK corporation tax, including disclosure of special circumstances affecting the overall tax charge — 28–29 — SSAP 8
- Deferred tax, computed on the liability method, should be accounted for to the extent that it is probable a liability or asset will crystallise. Generally computation and disclosure as per SSAP 15 — 30–44 — SSAP 15
- ACT and dividends (outgoing or incoming). — 45–47

Goodwill — 48–55 — SSAP 22

Purchased goodwill (difference between fair value of consideration given and the aggregate of fair values of separable net assets acquired) should not be carried in the balance sheet (of a company or group) as a permanent item but should normally be eliminated from the accounts either:

- normally by immediate write off upon acquisition against reserves, or
- by amortisation on a systematic basis though the profit and loss account over its useful economic life.

No amount should be attributed to non-purchased goodwill. Produced goodwill should not be revalued.

Investment properties (except charities) — 56–60 — SSAP 19

Investment properties should be included in the balance sheet at their open market value and should not be subject to periodic charges for depreciation except for properties held on lease which should be depreciated over the period when the unexpired term is 20 years or less. Changes in market value should be taken to the statement of total recognised gains and losses unless a deficit (or its reversal) on an individual property is expected to be permanent in which case it should be charged (or credited) to the profit and loss account of the period.

Depreciation of fixed assets (other than investment properties, goodwill, development costs and investments) — 61–73 — SSAP 12

Provision for depreciation of fixed assets having a finite useful economic life should be made by allocating the cost (or revalued amount) less estimated residual value of the assets as fairly as possible to the periods expected to benefit from their use. The depreciation methods used should be the ones that are the most appropriate having regard to the types of asset and their use in the business.

Disclosures include the depreciation methods used; the useful economic lives or the depreciation rates used; total depreciation charged for the period; and the gross amount of depreciable assets and the related accumulated depreciation.

Government grants — 74–77 — SSAP 4

Government grants should be recognised in the profit and loss account so as to match them with the expenditure towards which they are intended to contribute. A government grant should not be recognised in the profit and loss account until the conditions for its receipt have been complied with and there is reasonable assurance that the grant will be received. To the extent that the grant is made as a contribution towards expenditure on a fixed asset, the amount of a grant so deferred should be treated as deferred income; a UK company may not deduct such grants from the purchase price or production costs of fixed assets.

Research and development — 78–84 — SSAP 13

The cost of fixed assets acquired or constructed in order to provide facilities for research and development activities over a number of accounting periods

Chapter 11   Financial Reporting Standard for Smaller Entities ('FRSSE')

	FRSSE paragraph	Principal derivation

should be capitalised and written off over their useful lives through the profit and loss account.

Expenditure on pure and applied research should be written off in the year of expenditure through the profit and loss account.

In certain circumstances development expenditure may be deferred to the extent that its recovery can reasonably be regarded as assured; otherwise development expenditure should be written off in the year of expenditure except in certain defined circumstances when it may be deferred to future periods.

If development costs are deferred to future periods, they should be amortised.

Stocks and long-term contracts   85–88   SSAP 9

The amounts at which stocks are stated in the financial statements should be the total of the lower of cost and net realisable value of the separate items of stock or of groups of similar items.

Long-term contracts should be assessed on a contract-by-contract basis and reflected in the profit and loss account by recording turnover and related costs as contract activity progresses. Turnover is ascertained in a manner appropriate to the stage of completion of the contract, the business and the industry in which it operates.

Where it is considered that the outcome of a long-term contract can be assessed with reasonable certainty before its conclusion, the prudently calculated attributable profit should be recognised in the profit and loss account as the difference between the reported turnover and related costs for that contract.

Debt factoring   89–91   FRS 5

Debts or liability in respect of proceeds received from the factor should not be reflected in the balance sheet (where there is no obligation to repay the factor).

Where significant benefits and risks relating to factored debts are retained, such debts are to be shown gross after providing for bad debts, credit protection charges and any accrued interest.

Leases (HP and leasing)

Lessees   92–97   SSAP 21

A finance lease should be recorded in the balance sheet of a lessee as an asset and as an obligation to pay future rentals. At the inception of the lease the sum to be recorded both as an asset and as a liability should normally be the fair value of the asset unless present value of minimum lease payments is a more realistic estimate.

An asset leased under a finance lease should be depreciated over the shorter of the lease term or its useful life. However, in the case of a hire purchase contract that has the characteristics of a finance lease the asset should be depreciated over its useful life.

Rentals payable under operating leases and finance charges payable under finance leases should be charged on a straight-line basis over the lease term even if the payments are not made on such a basis, unless another systematic and rational basis is more appropriate.

Incentives to sign a lease, in whatever form they may take, should be spread by the lessee on a straight-line basis over the lease term or, if shorter than the full lease term, over the period to the review date on which the rent is first expected to be adjusted to the prevailing market rate.   UITF 12

The FRSSE in outline

	FRSSE paragraph	Principal derivation

Lessors — 98–100

The total gross earnings under finance leases and rental income from operating leases should be recognised on a systematic and rational basis. This will normally be a constant periodic rate of return on the lessor's net investment.

The amount due from the lessee under a finance lease should be recorded in the balance sheet of a lessor as a debtor at the amount of the net investment in the lease after making provisions for items such as bad and doubtful rentals receivable.

An asset held for use in operating leases by a lessor should be recorded as a fixed asset and depreciated over its useful life.

Other transactions (e.g., sale and leaseback) and disclosures. — 101–107

Pensions — 108–117, SSAP 24

The accounting objective is that the employer should recognise the expected cost of providing pensions and other post-retirement benefits on a systematic and rational basis over the period during which it derives benefit from the employees' services.

For a defined contribution scheme, the charge against profits should be the amount of contributions payable to the pension scheme in respect of the accounting period.

For defined benefit schemes, the pension cost should be calculated using actuarial valuation methods.

Capital instruments — 118–121, FRS 4

Capital instruments other than shares should be classified as liabilities if they contain an obligation to transfer economic benefits (including a contingent obligation to transfer economic benefits). Capital instruments that do not contain an obligation to transfer economic benefits should be reported within shareholders' funds.

The finance costs of debt should be allocated to periods over the term of the debt at a constant rate on the carrying amount. All finance costs should be charged in the profit and loss account.

Where the entitlement to dividends in respect of shares is calculated by reference to time, the dividends should be accounted for on an accruals basis except in those circumstances (for example, where profits are insufficient to justify a dividend and dividend rights are non-cumulative) where ultimate payment is remote. All dividends should be reported as appropriations of profit in the profit and loss account.

Contingencies — 122–128, SSAP 18

In addition to amounts accrued under the accounting principle of prudence, a material contingent loss should be accrued in financial statements where it is probable that a future event will confirm a loss that can be estimated with reasonable accuracy at the date on which the financial statements are approved by the board of directors.

A material contingent loss not accrued should be disclosed except where the possibility of loss is remote.

Contingent gains should not be accrued in financial statements. A material contingent gain should be disclosed in financial statements only if it is probable that the gain will be realised.

Chapter 11 Financial Reporting Standard for Smaller Entities ('FRSSE')

	FRSSE paragraph	Principal derivation
Post balance sheet events Financial statements should be prepared on the basis of conditions existing at the balance sheet date.	129–134	SSAP 17
A material post balance sheet event requires changes in the amounts to be included in financial statements where either it is an adjusting event, or it indicates that application of the going concern concept to the whole or a material part of the entity is not appropriate.		
A material post balance sheet event should be disclosed where either it is a non-adjusting event of such materiality that its non-disclosure would affect the ability of the users of financial statements to reach a proper understanding of the financial position; or it is the reversal or maturity after the year end of a transaction entered into before the year end, the substance of which was primarily to alter the appearance of the entity's balance sheet.		
Related parties Financial statements should disclose material transactions undertaken by the reporting entity with a related party. Disclosure should be made irrespective of whether a price is charged. The materiality of a related party transaction should be judged not only in terms of its significance to the reporting entity, but also in relation to the other related party.	135–139	FRS 8
Personal guarantees given by directors in respect of borrowings by the reporting entity should be disclosed in the notes to the financial statements.		
Consolidated financial statements Where the reporting entity is preparing consolidated financial statements, it should regard as standard the accounting practices and disclosure requirements set out in:	140	

FRS 2   Accounting for Subsidiary Undertakings
FRS 6   Acquisitions and mergers
FRS 7   Fair values in acquisition accounting

and, as they apply in respect of consolidated accounts:

FRS 5   Reporting the substance of transactions
SSAP 1   Accounting for associated companies
SSAP 22   Accounting for goodwill
UITF 3   Treatment of goodwill on disposal of a business.

11.3 FRS 3 and the FRSSE

Table 11.2 indicates those requirements of FRS 3 that have been continued into the FRSSE.

Table 11.2 FRS 3 and the FRSSE

FRS 3 para	FRSSE para	
13	9/16	Primary statement of total recognised gains and losses (no separate statement required if gains and losses all recognised in profit and loss account).
19–20	10–11	Exceptional items: include as charge or credit within statutory headings (with separate disclosure if prominence required for true and fair view) (see **4.5.1**).
19		No reference to continuing or discontinued operations.
21	12	Profit or loss on disposal accounted for in period of disposal (net sales proceeds less net carrying amount).
22	13	Extraordinary items (see **4.5.2**).
29	14	Prior period adjustments.
62	15	Disclosure of changes in accounting policy (as per UITF 14(3)) – restatement on basis of new policies and indication of effect of change (state if immaterial).
23	29	Disclosure of special circumstances affecting overall tax charge (but no specific requirement to disclose tax on exceptional items).
5–6	167/169	Definitions of 'exceptional items', 'extraordinary items', 'ordinary activities' and 'prior period adjustments', 'total recognised gains and losses' (see **4.5**).

11.4 Related parties

The FRSSE requires the disclosure of:

- information on related party transactions;
- the name of the controlling party (if any), whether or not any transactions between the parties have taken place; and
- personal guarantees given by directors in respect of borrowings by the reporting entity.

Aggregated disclosures are allowed subject to certain restrictions.

Related party disclosures within accounts should identify material transactions undertaken by the reporting entity with a related party. Disclosure should be made irrespective of whether a price is charged.

Two or more parties are related parties when at any time during the financial period:

- one party has direct or indirect control of the other party; or
- the parties are subject to common control from the same source; or
- one party has influence over the financial and operating policies of the other party to an extent that the other party might be inhibited from pursuing at all times its own separate interests; or

- the parties, in entering a transaction, are subject to influence from the same source to such an extent that one of the parties to the transaction has subordinated its own separate interests.

The disclosures should include:

- the names of the transacting related parties;
- a description of the relationship between the parties;
- a description of the transactions;
- the amounts involved;
- any other elements of the transactions necessary for an understanding of the accounts;
- the amounts due to or from related parties at the balance sheet date and provisions for doubtful debts due from such parties at that date; and
- amounts written off in the period in respect of debts due to or from related parties.

No disclosure is required in consolidated accounts of intragroup transactions and balances eliminated on consolidation. A parent undertaking is not required to provide related party disclosures in its own accounts when those accounts are presented with consolidated accounts of the group.

The materiality of a related party transaction should be judged not only in terms of its significance to the reporting entity, but also in relation to the other related party.

Transactions with related parties may be disclosed on an aggregated basis (aggregation of similar transactions by type of related party) unless disclosure of an individual transaction, or connected transactions, is necessary for an understanding of the impact of the transactions on the accounts of the reporting entity or is required by law.

Disclosure is not required of emoluments in respect of services as an employee of the reporting entity. Nor is disclosure required of the relationship and transactions between the reporting entity and the following parties simply as a result of their role as:

- providers of finance in the course of their business;
- utility companies;
- government departments and their sponsored bodies;
- a customer, supplier, franchiser, distributor or general agent with whom an entity transacts a significant volume of business.

When the reporting entity is controlled by another party, there should be disclosure of:

- the related party relationship
- the name of the controlling party and, if different, that of the ultimate controlling party. If the controlling party or ultimate controlling party of the reporting entity is not known, that fact should be disclosed. (These disclosures are irrespective of whether any transactions have taken place between the controlling parties and the reporting entity.)

11.5 Foreign currency translation

Each asset, liability, revenue or cost arising from a transaction denominated in a foreign currency should be translated into the local currency at the exchange rate in operation on the date on which the transaction occurred; if the rates do not fluctuate significantly, an average rate for a period may be used as an approximation. Where the transaction is to be settled at a contracted rate, that rate should be used.

Where a trading transaction is covered by a related or matching forward contract, the rate of exchange specified in that contract may be used.

Except for the treatment of foreign equity investments financed by foreign currency borrowings, no subsequent translations should normally be made once non-monetary assets have been translated and recorded.

At each balance sheet date, monetary assets and liabilities denominated in a foreign currency should be translated by using the closing rate or, where appropriate, the rates of exchange fixed under the terms of the relevant transactions.

All exchange gains or losses on settled transactions and unsettled monetary items should be reported as part of the profit or loss for the year from ordinary activities (unless they result from transactions which themselves would fall to be treated as extraordinary items, in which case the exchange gains or losses should be included as part of such items).

Where a company has used foreign currency borrowings to finance, or to provide a hedge against, its foreign equity investments and the conditions set out in the FRSSE apply, the equity investments may be denominated in the appropriate foreign currencies and the carrying amounts translated at the end of each accounting period at closing rates for inclusion in the investing company's financial statements. Where investments are treated in this way, any exchange differences arising should be taken to reserves and the exchange gains or losses on the foreign currency borrowings should then be offset, as a reserve movement, against these exchange differences.

Part III Example accounts

Chapter 12   Example accounts

The example accounts do not represent a comprehensive checklist of the statutory disclosure requirements nor do they purport to be definitive or exhaustive. The intention is to illustrate the more common situations. Other presentations may be equally acceptable, provided that they adhere to the rules set out in the Companies Act 1985 and relevant financial reporting standards.

The accounts are, of course, entirely fictional. Text in *italics* in the example accounts represents commentary and explanation or alternative presentation.

Depending on whether audit exemption is available, the accounts will contain an appropriate auditors' report, or an independent accountants' report, or no accountants' report (in the case of total exemption). Alternative reports are illustrated, to be adopted according to the circumstances.

In the example accounts, tinted or boxed items indicate the following:

- Grey tint – text that may be omitted or is relevant, as the case may be, only in the circumstances where the FRSSE is adopted.
- Other boxed items – text that is optional or may be omitted according to the circumstances.

12.1   Accounts of Small Company Limited

The illustrative example accounts of Small Company Limited illustrate the accounts of a small company (as defined in Chapter 6) producing accounts for a financial period ending on or after 31 March 1997.

Pages 4–13 (see pp103–112) comprise the full statutory accounts of the company (a small company) prepared in accordance with Companies Act 1985, **and taking full advantage of special provisions (Schedule 8 and section 246) with respect to the preparation of annual accounts of small companies**. In practice, a small company may exceed the basic minimum disclosure as is considered desirable.

The form of both the profit and loss account and the balance sheet are presented in Format 1.

The company has chosen to adopt the FRSSE.

Pages 14–16 (see pp113–115), indicated as 'For management information only', do not form part of the statutory accounts but are illustrative of a detailed profit and loss account, together with summaries, that might be prepared for management accounting purposes.

12.2   Abbreviated accounts of Small Company Limited

Pages 2–5 (see pp120–123) comprise the abbreviated accounts of the company prepared for filing with the Registrar of Companies in accordance with Companies Act 1985 sections 246(5) and (6) and a balance sheet complying with Schedule 8A.

The accounts are based upon the above full statutory individual accounts of the small company.

12.3 Unaudited accounts of Dormant Small Company Limited

The accounts illustrate the unaudited accounts of a dormant small company (see pp124–125).

12.4 Auditors' reports

The APB Statement of Auditing Standards 'Auditors' reports on financial statements' (SAS 600) introduced the form of report by auditors to be adopted with respect to true and fair view accounts. The report required by SAS 600 is intended to clarify the respective responsibilities of auditors and directors; it distinguishes between responsibilities of the directors for the preparation of accounts and the reporting responsibilities of the auditors. Where the accounts or accompanying information (for example, the directors' report) does not include an adequate statement of directors' responsibilities, the auditors should include a description of those responsibilities in their report. The example accounts include an illustrative statement of directors' responsibilities which is contained in the directors' report on **page 1** (see p100).

SAS 600, although generally prescriptive as to the form and content of the auditors' report, does permit some flexibility when using the format and wording of the example reports contained in the Statement. The use of the term 'accounts', for example, in preference to 'financial statements' accords with the Companies Act 1985 and is essentially a question of personal choice and is permissible, provided the term is adequately defined (see example accounts on the index page preceding **page 1** (see p99).

The special auditors' report required in connection with abbreviated accounts is no longer required to reproduce the full text of the auditors' report on the annual accounts, except in the circumstances of a qualification or explanatory paragraph regarding a fundamental uncertainty. This is illustrated on **page 1** of the abbreviated accounts (see p117) and explained further in **8.9**.

It should be noted that the illustrative auditors' reports contain no references to 'cash flows' (company exempt from the requirements of FRS 1 and choosing to adopt the FRSSE) and 'total recognised gains' (a statement of which may be required under the FRSSE or FRS 3). The opinion paragraph of an auditors' report is required to refer only to the state of affairs and profit or loss for the year.

SAS 600 applies in the conduct of *audits* and is therefore not appropriate in the circumstances of unaudited accounts; a directors' responsibility statement on the lines set out on **page 1** (see p100) is not therefore required in such circumstances (but balance sheet statements (**page 5** (see p104)) would, nevertheless, be necessary).

Small Company Limited annual report and accounts

**Registered number:
01715561200
England and Wales**

SMALL COMPANY LIMITED
ANNUAL REPORT AND ACCOUNTS
30 SEPTEMBER 1997

Small company – definition

As a basic rule, a company is treated as a small company if it does not exceed more than two of the following criteria:

Turnover	£2.8 m
Balance sheet total	£1.4 m
Average number of employees	50

See **6.1** for the detailed definition.

The qualifications for a small or medium-sized company are specified in CA 1985 section 247 and (for a group) section 249.

Annual report and accounts – These comprise: (a) the directors' report ('annual report'); (b) the company's annual accounts ('individual accounts') together with notes to the accounts; and (c) the auditors' report or, where the accounts are unaudited, the independent accountants' report, if necessary. Advantage has been taken of the special provisions available under CA 1985 s246 and Sch 8 as a small company. Collectively these are the full statutory accounts.

Registered number – Any document delivered to the Registrar of Companies must state in a prominent position the registered number of the company to which it relates (CA 1985 s706(2)).

Small Company Limited annual report and accounts

SMALL COMPANY LIMITED

Directors Teresa L Bramshaw – Chairman
James Longslade – Managing director
Charles TG Favell
William D Norley

Secretary Charles TG Favell

Registered office 10 Crockford Street
London SW19 7JP

Registered number 01715561200 England and Wales

Auditors True & Fairview
Chartered Accountants
17 Queen's Place
London EC4P 3BC

ANNUAL REPORT AND ACCOUNTS – 30 SEPTEMBER 1997

Pages

1–2	Report of the directors
3	Auditors' report [*audited accounts only*]
	or
3	*Accountants' report [unaudited accounts, where relevant]*
	Accounts, comprising:
4	Profit and loss account
5	Balance sheet
6	*Statement of total recognised gains and losses*
7–13	Notes to the accounts

The following pages do not form part of the statutory accounts:

14–15	Detailed profit and loss account
16	Profit and loss account summaries

Directors and advisers etc. – Although it is common practice to give the information on this page, there is no requirement to do so, and the page may be omitted.

Chapter 12 Example accounts

SMALL COMPANY LIMITED
REPORT OF THE DIRECTORS

Page 1

The directors present their annual report with the accounts of the company for the year ended 30 September 1997.

Principal activity

The principal activity of the company in the year under review was the manufacture and distribution of office equipment and components.

The company's subsidiary company, Smallsub Limited, provides office design and consultancy services.

Directors

The directors in office in the year and their beneficial interests in the company's issued ordinary share capital were as follows:

	30 September 1997	1 October 1996
J Longslade	30,000	20,000
TL Bramshaw	21,000	14,000
CTG Favell (appointed 1 May 1997)	3,000	3,000*
WD Norley	300	200

DV Bolderwood (retired on 31 October 1996)

* At date of appointment

The directors have no interest in the shares of any other group company, including rights to subscribe for shares.

CTG Favell, who was appointed to the board since the last annual general meeting, retires and offers himself for re-election. In accordance with the Articles of Association, TL Bramshaw retires by rotation and offers herself for re-election.

Directors' responsibilities

Company law requires the directors to prepare accounts for each financial year which give a true and fair view of the state of affairs of the company and of the profit or loss of the company for that period. In preparing those accounts, the directors are required to:

- select suitable accounting policies and then apply them consistently;
- make judgements and estimates that are reasonable and prudent;
- *follow applicable accounting standards, subject to any material departures disclosed and explained in the accounts;*
- prepare the accounts on the going concern basis unless it is inappropriate to presume that the company will continue in business.

The directors are responsible for keeping proper accounting records which disclose with reasonable accuracy at any time the financial position of the company and to enable them to ensure that the accounts comply with the Companies Act 1985. They are also responsible for safeguarding the assets of the company and hence for taking reasonable steps for the prevention and detection of fraud and other irregularities.

Small Company Limited annual report and accounts

SMALL COMPANY LIMITED
REPORT OF THE DIRECTORS
(*continued*)

Page 2

Political and charitable contributions
During the year the company made a political contribution of £250 to the Conservative Party and various charitable contributions totalling £3,000.

Auditors

The auditors, True & Fairview, will be proposed for reappointment in accordance with Section 385 of the Companies Act 1985.

or: The Auditors, True & Fairview, are deemed to be reappointed in accordance with Section 386 of the Companies Act 1985.

The above report has been prepared in accordance with the special provisions of Part VII of the Companies Act 1985 relating to small companies.

CA 1985 s246(8)

Signed on behalf of
the board of directors

CA 1985 s234A

C. Favell
....
CTG FAVELL
Director [*or Secretary*]

Approved by the board: 28 February 1998

Directors' responsibilities – *The APB SAS 600 'Auditors' reports on financial statements' requires the financial statements or accompanying information (for example, the directors' report) to include an adequate statement of directors' responsibilities. (See* **12.4**.*) Where the accounts omit such a statement of responsibilities, the auditors' report must include one instead.*

Where the accounts are unaudited (i.e., audit-exempt), the independent accountants' report, where required, should include a statement that the directors are responsible for the preparation of the accounts.

It is nevertheless considered best practice (although not statutorily required) to include a statement of directors' responsibilities on the above lines in the directors' report.

A small company preparing accounts under Sch 8 is no longer required to state in its accounts whether they have been prepared in accordance with applicable accounting standards (Sch 4.36A). Applicable accounting standards (for example, the FRSSE) do, of course, have to be followed (and disclosed, where material) and this fact has, therefore, been explained in the above statement of responsibilities.

Auditors – *There is no requirement to disclose the appointment or reappointment of auditors, although it is common practice to do so. Similarly no reference to 'independent accountants' need be made.*

Chapter 12 Example accounts

AUDITORS' REPORT TO THE SHAREHOLDERS OF SMALL COMPANY LIMITED

Page 3

We have audited the accounts on pages 4 to 13 which have been prepared in accordance with the accounting policies set out on pages 7 and 8.

Respective responsibilities of directors and auditors
As described on page 1, the company's directors are responsible for the preparation of accounts. It is our responsibility to form an independent opinion, based on our audit, on those accounts and to report our opinion to you.

Basis of opinion
We conducted our audit in accordance with Auditing Standards issued by the Auditing Practices Board. An audit includes examination, on a test basis, of evidence relevant to the amounts and disclosures in the accounts. It also includes an assessment of the significant estimates and judgements made by the directors in the preparation of the accounts, and of whether the accounting policies are appropriate to the company's circumstances, consistently applied and adequately disclosed.

We planned and performed our audit so as to obtain all the information and explanations which we considered necessary in order to provide us with sufficient evidence to give reasonable assurance that the accounts are free from material misstatement, whether caused by fraud or other irregularity or error. In forming our opinion we also evaluated the overall adequacy of the presentation of information in the accounts.

Opinion
In our opinion the accounts give a true and fair view of the state of the company's affairs as at 30 September 1997 and of its profit (*loss*) for the year then ended and have been properly prepared in accordance with the Companies Act 1985.

True & Fairview

TRUE & FAIRVIEW
Chartered Accountants and Registered Auditors

17 Queens Place
London EC4P 3BC   3 March 1998

(1) **Report to the shareholders** – *The auditors' report is made to the members of the company, who are normally the shareholders.*

(2) **Audit opinion: small companies** – *there is no longer any requirement to state in the opinion paragraph that the accounts have been properly prepared 'in accordance with **the special provisions** of the Companies Act 1985 **applicable to small companies'**. (See **2.8**)*

SAS 600 gives guidance on the application of the 'true and fair view' to small companies and provides illustrative wording for an audit report (in Appendix 2 Example 5). The phrase '... applicable to small companies' may continue to be used until such time as it is formally withdrawn by the APB.

(3) **Cash flows** – *Where a cash flow statement under FRS 1 (or the FRSSE) is not required, and not presented, in the accounts, the auditors' report is only required to refer explicitly to 'the state of affairs' and 'profit or loss', and no reference is required to 'cash flows'.*

(4) **Signature of auditors' report** – *CA 1985 s236.*

(5) **Reappointment of auditors** – *Auditors are reappointed under the Companies Act 1985, as amended, in accordance with the following sections:*

  (a) *Section 385 – where company has not elected to dispense with laying of accounts.*
  (b) *Section 385A – where company has elected (under CA 1985 s252) to dispense with laying of accounts and reports before the company in general meeting.*
  (c) *Section 386 – where company has elected to dispense with the obligation to appoint auditors annually. (Elective resolutions in accordance with CA 1985 s379A.)*

Dormant companies may, by special resolution, exempt themselves from the obligation to appoint auditors (CA 1985 s250).

(6) **Accountants' report** – *The form of an accountants' report for the purposes of s249A(2) CA 1985 (audit exempt charity) is given in Example 10.2.*

Small Company Limited annual report and accounts

SMALL COMPANY LIMITED
PROFIT AND LOSS ACCOUNT
FOR THE YEAR ENDED 30 SEPTEMBER 1997

Page 4

	Notes	1997 £	1996 £
Turnover – Continuing operations	2	1,558,080	950,700
Cost of sales		(891,586)	(577,211)
Gross profit		666,494	373,489
Distribution costs		(258,536)	(180,641)
Administrative expenses		(270,243)	(205,193)
Operating profit (loss) – Continuing operations	3	137,715	(12,345)
Loss on disposal of fixed assets		(724)	—
Income from investments		15,000	1,000
Interest payable		(20,654)	(9,200)
Profit (loss) on ordinary activities before taxation		131,337	(20,545)
Taxation		(34,100)	5,720
Profit (loss) for the financial year after taxation		97,237	(14,825)
Dividends paid or proposed (including non-equity)	4	(17,500)	(700)
Retained profit (loss) for the financial year		79,737	(15,525)
Retained profit at 1 October 1996		131,920	147,445
Retained profit at 30 September 1997		£211,657	£131,920

Alternative disclosures
Not required if FRSSE adopted.

Continuing operations
All of the company's activities [operations] in the above two financial years derived from continuing operations.
or: Turnover and operating profit derive wholly from continuing operations.

Total recognised gains and losses
The company has no recognised gains or losses other than the profit or loss for the period [above two financial years].

The above statements are only to be used where applicable.

Statement of total recognised gains and losses – *this could be presented on this page beneath the profit and loss account (see **example accounts page 6** (see p105)).*

Taxation – *the full format heading is 'Tax on profit or loss on ordinary activities'.*

Chapter 12   Example accounts

SMALL COMPANY LIMITED
BALANCE SHEET – 30 SEPTEMBER 1997

	Notes	1997 £	1996 £
Fixed assets			
Intangible assets	5	22,065	18,846
Tangible assets	6	310,544	282,548
Investments	7	1,000	11,500
		333,609	312,894
Current assets			
Stocks		195,667	156,750
Debtors	8	251,531	146,237
Cash at bank and in hand		2,708	5,463
		449,906	308,450
Creditors: amounts falling due within one year	9	(233,191)	(251,924)
Net current assets		216,715	56,526
Total assets less current liabilities		550,324	369,420
Creditors: amounts falling due after more than one year	10	(66,667)	(10,500)
Net assets		£483,657	£358,920
Capital and reserves			
Called up share capital	11	75,000	50,000
Share premium account		10,000	10,000
Revaluation reserve	12	187,000	167,000
Profit and loss account		211,657	131,920
Shareholders' funds (including non-equity interests)	13	£483,657	£358,920

> *Audit exemption only*
> For the financial year ended 30 September 1997, the company was entitled to exemption from audit under section 249A(1) [*total exemption*] [or 249A(2)] [*exemption with accountant's report*], [*as the case may be*] Companies Act 1985; and no notice has been deposited under section 249B(2) [*member or members requesting an audit*]. The directors acknowledge their responsibilities for ensuring that the company keeps accounting records which comply with section 221 [of the Act] and preparing accounts which give a true and fair view of the state of affairs of the company as at the end of the year and of its profit or loss for the financial year in accordance with the requirements of section 226 and which otherwise comply with the requirements of the Companies Act 1985, so far as applicable to the company.

The accounts have been prepared in accordance with the special provisions of Part VII of the Companies Act 1985 relating to small companies *[and in accordance with the Financial Reporting Standard for Smaller Entities]*.

Signed on behalf of
the board of directors

....
CTG FAVELL
Director

Approved by the board: 28 February 1998

Approval of accounts – A company's annual accounts must be approved by the board of directors and be signed on behalf of the board by a director of the company (previously two directors) (CA 1985 s233(1)).

Small Company Limited annual report and accounts

SMALL COMPANY LIMITED   Page 6
STATEMENT OF TOTAL RECOGNISED GAINS AND LOSSES
FOR THE YEAR ENDED 30 SEPTEMBER 1997

	1997 £	1996 £
Profit (loss) for the financial year after taxation	97,237	(14,825)
Unrealised surplus on revaluation of property	20,000	—
Total recognised gains relating to the year	£117,237	(£14,825)

Note of historical cost profits and losses
The difference between the results as disclosed in the profit and loss account and the result on an unmodified historical cost basis is not material.

Statement of total recognised gains and losses – This statement, showing the total of recognised gains and losses and its components, should be presented as a primary statement with the same prominence as the other primary statements, i.e., profit and loss account and balance sheet. The gains and losses are those recognised in the period insofar as they are attributable to shareholders. The statement could be presented in the **example accounts page 4** *(see p102) beneath the profit and loss account:*

Where the 'profit (loss) for the financial year after taxation' represents the entire total recognised gains or losses relating to the year (where, for example, there are no other unrealised surpluses or losses), a separate 'statement of total recognised gains and losses' is not required. However, unless the company adopts the FRSSE, the profit and loss account on **page 4** *(see p103) should include a statement on the following lines, immediately below the profit and loss account:*

'The company has no recognised gains and losses other than the profit and loss for the period.'

Note of historical cost profits and losses – A note of historical cost profits and losses should be presented immediately following the profit and loss account or the statement of total recognised gains and losses. A note is required in circumstances where there is a material difference between the result disclosed in the profit and loss account and the result on an unmodified basis (see Table 4.5), for example where a company charges a significant amount of depreciation on a revalued fixed asset.

105

SMALL COMPANY LIMITED
NOTES TO THE ACCOUNTS – 30 SEPTEMBER 1997

1 Accounting policies

Basis of accounting
The accounts have been prepared under the historical cost convention as modified by the revaluation of certain fixed assets [and in accordance with the Financial Reporting Standard for Smaller Entities].

Consolidation
The company and its subsidiary comprise a small group. The company has therefore taken advantage of the exemption provided by section 248 of the Companies Act 1985 not to prepare group accounts.

Cash flow
The accounts do not include a cash flow statement because the company, as a small reporting entity, is exempt from the requirement to prepare such a statement under Financial Reporting Standard 1 'Cash flow statements'.

Turnover
Turnover represents net invoiced sales of goods, excluding VAT.

Tangible fixed assets
Depreciation is provided, after taking account of any grants receivable, at the following annual rates in order to write off each asset over its estimated useful life:

Freehold buildings   –   2% on cost or revalued amounts
Plant and machinery –   15% on cost
Fixtures and fittings – 10% on cost
Motor vehicles   –   25% on cost

No depreciation is provided on freehold land.

Stocks
Stocks and work-in-progress are valued at the lower of cost and net realisable value, after making due allowance for obsolete and slow moving items. Cost includes all direct expenditure and an appropriate proportion of fixed and variable overheads.

Deferred taxation
Provision is made at current rates for taxation deferred in respect of all material timing differences except to the extent that, in the opinion of the directors, there is reasonable probability that the liability will not arise in the foreseeable future.

Research and development
Expenditure on research and development is written off in the year in which it is incurred.

Foreign currencies
Assets and liabilities in foreign currencies are translated into sterling at the rates of exchange ruling at the balance sheet date. Transactions in foreign currencies are translated into sterling at the rate of exchange ruling at the date of the transaction. Exchange differences are taken into account in arriving at the operating profit.

Disclosure of accounting policies
The FRSSE requires a note to the accounts to disclose those accounting policies followed for dealing with items that are judged material or critical in determining profit or loss for the year and in stating the financial position. The explanations should be clear, fair and as brief as possible.

Although the disclosure of certain accounting policies are indicated above (by boxing) as not required by the FRSSE, disclosure may nevertheless be appropriate either to show a true and fair view or because the policies are considered to be 'material or critical' in presenting the accounts.

In the absence of any specifically disclosed statement of accounting policy, the presumption is that the accounting principles set out in the FRSSE have been observed in the preparation of the accounts.

SMALL COMPANY LIMITED
NOTES TO THE ACCOUNTS – 30 SEPTEMBER 1997

> **Leased assets**
> Rentals applicable to operating leases where substantially all of the benefits and risks of ownership remain with the lessor are charged against profit as incurred.
>
> Assets held under finance leases and hire purchase contracts are capitalised and depreciated over their useful lives. The corresponding lease or hire purchase obligation is treated in the balance sheet as a liability. The interest element of rental obligations is charged to profit and loss account over the period of the lease at a constant proportion of the outstanding balance of capital repayments.
>
> **Pension costs**
> Contributions in respect of the company's defined contribution pension scheme are charged to the profit and loss account for the year in which they are payable to the scheme.

2 Turnover
Turnover attributable to geographical markets outside the United Kingdom amounted to 23% (1996 – 19%).

3 Operating profit (loss)
The operating profit (1996 – loss) is stated after charging:

	1997 £	1996 £
Depreciation of tangible fixed assets	44,496	42,178
Amortisation of intangible fixed assets	6,847	5,100
Operating lease charges	4,100	3,600
Auditors' remuneration	5,200	5,700
Exceptional development expenditure	62,000	—
Pension costs	18,100	13,200
Directors' emoluments	£77,031	£62,254

4 Dividends

	1997 £	1996 £
Non-equity preference dividend – paid	700	700
Dividend on ordinary shares – proposed (25.85p per share)	16,800	—
	£17,500	£700

Directors' emoluments
*A small company's individual accounts may give the aggregate in total of (a) directors' emoluments (for services as director or management of the company or any subsidiary), (b) amounts receivable under long-term incentive schemes, and (c) company pension contributions to money purchase schemes (s246(3) following SI 1997 No. 570). (See **7.10.2**.)*

SMALL COMPANY LIMITED
NOTES TO THE ACCOUNTS – 30 SEPTEMBER 1997

Page 9

5 Intangible fixed assets

	Goodwill £	Other intangible assets £	Total £
Cost			
At 1 October 1996	15,000	13,127	28,127
Additions	—	10,264	10,264
Disposals	—	(3,000)	(3,000)
At 30 September 1997	15,000	20,391	35,391
Amortisation			
At 1 October 1996	7,500	1,781	9,281
On disposals	—	(2,802)	(2,802)
Charge for the year	2,000	4,847	6,847
At 30 September 1997	9,500	3,826	13,326
Net book values			
At 30 September 1997	£5,500	£16,565	£22,065
At 30 September 1996	£7,500	£11,346	£18,846

6 Tangible fixed assets

	Land and buildings £	Plant and machinery etc. £	Total £
Cost or valuation			
At 1 October 1996	283,500	266,914	550,414
Additions	—	55,893	55,893
Revaluation	20,000	—	20,000
Disposals	(2,500)	(9,213)	(11,713)
At 30 September 1997	301,000	313,594	614,594
Cost	31,000	313,594	344,594
Valuation – 1997	270,000	—	270,000
	301,000	313,594	614,594
Depreciation			
At 1 October 1996	31,340	236,526	267,866
On disposals	—	(8,312)	(8,312)
Charge for year	3,160	41,336	44,496
At 30 September 1997	34,500	269,550	304,050
Net book values			
At 30 September 1997	£266,500	£44,044	£310,544
At 30 September 1996	£252,160	£30,388	£282,548

SMALL COMPANY LIMITED
NOTES TO THE ACCOUNTS – 30 SEPTEMBER 1997

6 Tangible fixed assets (continued)

The net book value of plant and machinery includes £5,000 (1996 – nil) in respect of assets held under finance leases. The amount of depreciation in respect of such assets amounted to £850 for the year (1996 – nil).

Land and buildings were revalued during the year by A. Surveyor FRICS on the basis of open market value. The cost or valuation of freehold buildings on which depreciation is charged amounted to £131,000 (1996 – £131,000).

The historical cost of freehold land and buildings included above at a valuation of £270,000 was £83,000 (1996 – £85,500) and the aggregate depreciation thereon would have been £28,200 (1996 – £27,300).

7 Investments

	Subsidiary undertaking £	Listed investments £	Total £
Cost			
At 1 October 1996	1,000	10,500	11,500
Disposals	—	(10,500)	(10,500)
At 30 September 1997	£1,000	£ —	£1,000

Subsidiary undertaking
The company's investment in its subsidiary company represents the cost of acquisition of the whole of the ordinary share capital of Smallsub Limited, which provides office design and consultancy services.

At 30 September 1997, the aggregate of the share capital and reserves of Smallsub Limited amounted to £56,300 and the profit for the year to that date was £3,560.

Listed investments
Listed investments comprise investments listed on The London Stock Exchange, the market value of which at 30 September 1996 amounted to £11,100.

8 Debtors

	1997 £	1996 £
Trade debtors	190,579	111,150
Others	60,952	35,087
	£251,531	£146,237

Other debtors include an amount of £4,000 (1996 – £nil) falling due after more than one year.

Chapter 12 Example accounts

SMALL COMPANY LIMITED
NOTES TO THE ACCOUNTS – 30 SEPTEMBER 1997

9 Creditors: amounts falling due within one year

	1997 £	1996 £
Bank loans and overdrafts (secured)	38,790	74,920
Obligations under finance leases	3,000	—
Debt due within one year	41,790	74,920
Trade creditors	94,506	125,390
Other creditors	96,895	51,614
	£233,191	£251,924

10 Creditors: amounts falling due after more than one year

	1997 £	1996 £
Bank loans and overdraft	62,500	—
Obligations under finance leases	2,000	—
Debt due after more than one year	64,500	
Other creditors	2,167	10,500
	£66,667	£10,500
Debt due after more than one year		
– repayable between 1–5 years	52,000	—
– repayable in 5 years or more	12,500	—
	£64,500	—

The bank loan, the aggregate total of which amounts to £75,000, is repayable in annual instalments of £12,500 commencing 31 March 1997.

11 Called up share capital

	1997 £	1996 £
Authorised		
50,000 *10% (now 7% plus tax credit)*		
7% preference shares of £1 each	50,000	50,000
100,000 ordinary shares of £1 each	100,000	100,000
	£150,000	£150,000
Allotted, called up and fully paid		
10,000 7% preference shares of £1 each	10,000	10,000
65,000 (1996 – 40,000) ordinary shares of £1 each	65,000	40,000
	£75,000	£50,000

During the year 25,000 ordinary shares of £1 each were allotted and fully paid for cash at par.

SMALL COMPANY LIMITED
NOTES TO THE ACCOUNTS – 30 SEPTEMBER 1997

12 Revaluation reserve

	£
At 1 October 1996	167,000
Surplus on revaluation or property (note 6)	20,000
At 30 September 1997	£187,000

13 Shareholders' fund

(a) Analysis of shareholders' funds

	1997	1996
Non-equity (7% preference shares)	10,000	10,000
Equity	473,657	348,920
Total shareholders' funds	£483,657	£358,920

Non-equity interests

Shareholders' funds attributable to non-equity interests comprise 10,000 7% preference shares of £1 each at par value. Dividends are payable annually at 7% net of tax credit and are cumulative. The shares are redeemable (at par value) on 30 September 2007; have a priority over ordinary shares, in the event of an earlier winding up (to the extent of their par value and the arrears (if any) of dividends); and have no vote, provided dividends are not in arrears.

(b) Reconciliation of movements on shareholders' funds

	1997 £	1996 £
Profit (loss) for the financial year after taxation	97,237	(14,825)
Dividends	(17,500)	(700)
	79,737	(15,525)
Other recognised gains relating to the year	20,000	—
New share capital subscribed	25,000	—
	124,737	(15,525)
Opening shareholders' funds at 1 October 1996	358,920	374,445
Closing shareholders' funds at 30 September 1997	£483,657	£358,920

14 Contingent liability

A writ for damages amounting to £120,000 has been served on the company, alleging supply of faulty goods. The directors have obtained legal advice and are contesting the claim, which they consider is without foundation. No provision has been made in these accounts in respect of the claim.

SMALL COMPANY LIMITED
NOTES TO THE ACCOUNTS – 30 SEPTEMBER 1997

15 Commitments

Capital commitments
At 30 September 1997, capital expenditure commitments were as follows:

	1997	1996
Contracted but not provided for in the accounts	£20,000	£ —

Pension commitments
The company operates a defined contribution pension scheme on behalf of its directors and certain employees. The assets of the scheme are held separately from those of the company in an independently administered fund. Contributions are paid based upon the recommendations of a qualified actuary. The annual commitment under this scheme is for contributions of £21,300 (1996 – £18,100).

Lease commitments – operating leases
At 30 September 1997, the company had annual commitments of £4,000 (1996 – £3,400) under non-cancellable operating leases which expire within two to five years.

Other financial commitments
At 30 September 1997, the company had entered into a joint venture agreement to commence in 1998, the initial contribution to which will be £50,000.

16 Related party transactions

Loan to director
During the year James Longslade was granted a short-term loan to facilitate the purchase of a house. Indebtedness on the loan was as follows:

Liability at 1 October 1996 £	Maximum liability during the year £	Liability at 30 September 1997 £
—	15,000	15,000

The loan is repayable on 31 August 1998. Interest, at the rate of 6% per annum, is payable upon repayment and at 30 September 1997 no interest was due and unpaid.

Material interests of directors
During the year the company purchased goods to the value of £312,100 (1996 – £197,000) from Medium Company (London) Limited, a company in which Teresa Bramshaw and James Longslade are materially interested as shareholders. The purchases were made on a normal trading basis.

17 Post balance sheet events

On 5 January 1998 the company acquired the goodwill and net assets of Automated Office Technology Products for a consideration of £50,000 which has been financed by a secured bank loan, repayable over five years.

Small Company Limited annual report and accounts

FOR MANAGEMENT INFORMATION ONLY

SMALL COMPANY LIMITED
DETAILED PROFIT AND LOSS ACCOUNT
FOR THE YEAR ENDED 30 SEPTEMBER 1997

Page 14

	1997 £	1997 £	1996 £	1996 £
Sales		1,558,080		950,700
Cost of sales				
Stocks 1 October 1996	156,750		133,281	
Purchases	519,166		345,210	
	675,916		478,491	
Less: stocks 30 September 1997	195,667		156,750	
	480,249		321,741	
Production wages	266,519		177,500	
Depreciation	38,717		35,270	
Hire of plant and machinery (operating leases)	4,100		3,600	
Other production expenses (including research and development)	102,001		39,100	
	411,337		255,470	
Cost of sales		891,586		577,211
Gross profit (42.8% – 1996: 39.3%)		666,494		373,489
Distribution costs				
Distribution				
Carriage	50,104		29,606	
Motor expenses	30,402		20,204	
Lorry and warehouse	18,702		7,648	
Depreciation	3,508		3,648	
	102,716		61,106	
Selling and marketing				
Salaries	84,588		73,440	
Advertising	18,900		17,225	
Travel and motor expenses	29,111		19,120	
Entertaining	23,221		9,750	
	155,820		119,535	
	258,536		180,641	
Totals carried forward	258,536	666,494	180,641	373,489

This page does not form part of the statutory accounts.

FOR MANAGEMENT INFORMATION ONLY

SMALL COMPANY LIMITED
DETAILED PROFIT AND LOSS ACCOUNT
FOR THE YEAR ENDED 30 SEPTEMBER 1997
(*continued*)

	1997 £	1997 £	1996 £	1996 £
Totals brought forward	258,536	666,494	180,641	373,489
Administrative expenses				
Establishment expenses				
Rent and rates	55,270		41,777	
Light, heat and power	18,100		12,120	
Insurance	15,900		10,091	
Repairs	12,012		6,171	
Depreciation	5,030		4,611	
	106,312		74,770	
Administration costs				
Salaries and payroll	35,457		33,520	
Directors' remuneration	57,031		52,254	
Pension costs	18,100		13,200	
Postage and telephone	8,211		5,100	
Printing and stationery	12,100		8,275	
Depreciation	4,088		3,749	
General administration	9,834		1,200	
Audit and accountancy	5,200		5,700	
Legal and professional	600		—	
Bank charges	500		305	
Bad debts	12,810		7,120	
	163,931		130,423	
	270,243		205,193	
		528,779		385,834
Operating profit (loss)		137,715		(12,345)
Loss on disposal of fixed assets		(724)		—
Income from investments		15,000		1,000
Interest payable				
Bank loan	(12,100)		—	
Bank overdraft	(8,554)		(9,200)	
		(20,654)		(9,200)
Profit (loss) on ordinary activities before taxation		£131,337		£(20,545)

This page does not form part of the statutory accounts.

Small Company Limited annual report and accounts

FOR MANAGEMENT INFORMATION ONLY

SMALL COMPANY LIMITED
PROFIT AND LOSS ACCOUNT SUMMARIES
FOR THE YEAR ENDED 30 SEPTEMBER 1997

Page 16

Summaries of items disclosed in the statutory profit and loss account

	1997 £	1996 £
Depreciation		
Production – cost of sales	31,870	30,170
Amortisation – cost of sales	6,847	5,100
	38,717	35,270
Distribution	3,508	3,648
Establishment expenses	5,030	4,611
Administration costs	4,088	3,749
	£51,343	£47,278
Staff costs*		
Production wages	266,519	177,500
Selling and marketing salaries	64,588	63,440
Administration salaries	35,457	33,520
Directors' remuneration	77,031	62,254
Pension costs	18,100	13,200
	£461,695	£349,914

* Not disclosed in small company annual accounts.

This page does not form part of the statutory accounts.

Chapter 12 Example accounts

Registered number:
01715561200
England and Wales

SMALL COMPANY LIMITED
ABBREVIATED ACCOUNTS
30 SEPTEMBER 1997

Abbreviated accounts (small company) – These comprise: (a) special auditors' report; or independent accountants' report (on annual accounts) (if required, for audit-exempt accounts); (b) abbreviated balance sheet (Sch 8A CA 1985) (with directors' statements); and (c) notes to the abbreviated accounts.

Small Company Limited abbreviated accounts

AUDITORS' REPORT TO SMALL COMPANY LIMITED UNDER SECTION 247B OF THE COMPANIES ACT 1985

Page 1

We have examined the abbreviated accounts set out on pages 2 to 5, together with the full statutory accounts of the company for the year ended 30 September 1997 prepared under section 226 of the Companies Act 1985.

Respective responsibilities of directors and auditors

The directors are responsible for preparing the abbreviated accounts in accordance with section 246 of the Companies Act 1985. It is our responsibility to form an independent opinion as to whether the company is entitled to deliver abbreviated accounts prepared in accordance with sections 246(5) and (6) of the Act to the registrar of companies and whether the accounts to be delivered are properly prepared in accordance with those provisions and to report our opinion to you.

Basis of opinion

We have carried out the procedures we consider necessary to confirm, by reference to the accounts, that the company is entitled to deliver abbreviated accounts and that the abbreviated accounts to be delivered are properly prepared. The scope of our work for the purpose of this report did not include examining or dealing with events after the date of our report on the full statutory accounts.

Opinion

In our opinion the company is entitled to deliver abbreviated accounts prepared in accordance with sections 246(5) and (6) of the Companies Act 1985, and the abbreviated accounts on pages 2 to 5 are properly prepared in accordance with those provisions.

True & Fairview

TRUE & FAIRVIEW
Chartered Accountants and Registered Auditors

17 Queens Place
London EC4P 3BC

s236 CA 1985

3 March 1998

Sections 246(5) and (6) – *the above example assumes that the company has taken advantage of both sections 246(5) and 246(6). The reference should be included or amended according to the circumstances.*

Section 246(5) – essentially balance sheet complying with Sch 8A.

*Section 246(6) – disclosure exemptions (see **8.1**)*

Chapter 12 Example accounts

AUDITORS' REPORT TO SMALL COMPANY LIMITED UNDER SECTION 247B OF THE COMPANIES ACT 1985
[*QUALIFIED FULL AUDIT OPINION*]

Page 1

We have examined the abbreviated accounts set out on pages 2 to 5, together with the full statutory accounts of the company for the year ended 30 September 1997 prepared under section 226 of the Companies Act 1985.

Respective responsibilities of directors and auditors
The directors are responsible for preparing the abbreviated accounts in accordance with section 246 of the Companies Act 1985. It is our responsibility to form an independent opinion as to whether the company is entitled to deliver abbreviated accounts prepared in accordance with sections 246(5) and (6) of the Act to the registrar of companies and whether the accounts to be delivered are properly prepared in accordance with those provisions and to report our opinion to you.

Basis of opinion
We have carried out the procedures we consider necessary to confirm, by reference to the accounts, that the company is entitled to deliver abbreviated accounts and that the abbreviated accounts to be delivered are properly prepared. The scope of our work for the purpose of this report did not include examining or dealing with events after the date of our report on the full statutory accounts.

Opinion
In our opinion the company is entitled to deliver abbreviated accounts prepared in accordance with sections 246(5) and (6) of the Companies Act 1985, and the abbreviated accounts on pages 2 to 5 are properly prepared in accordance with those provisions.

Other information
On 3 March 1998 we reported as auditors to the shareholders of the company on the full statutory accounts prepared under section 226 of the Companies Act 1985 and our audit report *[under section 235 of the Companies Act 1985]* was as follows[/included the following statement/paragraph]:

[Qualified audit report under section 235 Companies Act 1985
or
Statements under section 237(2) [Inadequate accounting records] or section 237(3) [Failure to obtain necessary information]
or
Explanatory comment contained in Unqualified Audit Report under section 235 Companies Act 1985 concerning fundamental uncertainty

to be set out in full:]

True & Fairview

s236 CA 1985 TRUE & FAIRVIEW
Chartered Accountants and Registered Auditors

17 Queens Place
London EC4P 3BC

3 March 1998

Example of other information: explanatory paragraph

Going Concern
In forming our opinion, we have considered the adequacy of disclosures made in note 1 of the accounts concerning the uncertainty as to the continuation and renewal of the company's bank overdraft facility. In view of the significance of this uncertainty we consider that it should be drawn to your attention, but our opinion is not qualified in this respect.

Small Company Limited abbreviated accounts

AUDITORS' REPORT TO MEDIUM-SIZED COMPANY LIMITED UNDER SECTION 247B OF THE COMPANIES ACT 1985

Page [ ]

We have examined the abbreviated accounts set out on pages [to], together with the full statutory accounts of the company for the year ended 30 September 1997 prepared under section 226 of the Companies Act 1985.

Respective responsibilities of directors and auditors

The directors are responsible for preparing the abbreviated accounts in accordance with section 246A of the Companies Act 1985. It is our responsibility to form an independent opinion as to whether the company is entitled to deliver abbreviated accounts prepared in accordance with section 246A(3) of the Act to the registrar of companies and whether the accounts to be delivered are properly prepared in accordance with that provision and to report our opinion to you.

Basis of opinion

We have carried out the procedures we consider necessary to confirm, by reference to the accounts, that the company is entitled to deliver abbreviated accounts and that the abbreviated accounts to be delivered are properly prepared. The scope of our work for the purpose of this report did not include examining or dealing with events after the date of our report on the full statutory accounts.

Opinion

In our opinion the company is entitled to deliver abbreviated accounts prepared in accordance with section 246A(3) of the Companies Act 1985, and the abbreviated accounts on pages [to] are properly prepared in accordance with that provision.

True & Fairview

TRUE & FAIRVIEW
Chartered Accountants and Registered Auditors

17 Queens Place
London EC4P 3BC

3 March 1998

Medium-sized company – the above is an example of a special auditors' report on the abbreviated accounts of a medium-sized company.

SMALL COMPANY LIMITED
ABBREVIATED BALANCE SHEET – 30 SEPTEMBER 1997

	Notes	1997 £	1996 £
Fixed assets	2		
Intangible assets		22,065	18,846
Tangible assets		310,544	282,548
Investments		1,000	11,500
		333,609	312,894
Current assets			
Stocks		195,667	156,750
Debtors	3	251,531	146,237
Cash at bank and in hand		2,708	5,463
		449,906	308,450
Creditors: amounts falling due within one year	4	(233,191)	(251,924)
Net current assets		216,715	56,526
Total assets less current liabilities		550,324	369,420
Creditors: amounts falling due after more than one year	4	(66,667)	(10,500)
Net assets		£483,657	£358,920
Capital and reserves			
Called up share capital	5	75,000	50,000
Share premium account		10,000	10,000
Revaluation reserve		187,000	167,000
Profit and loss account		211,657	131,920
Shareholders' funds		£483,657	£358,920

> *Audit exemption only*
> For the financial year ended 30 September 1997, the company was entitled to exemption from audit under section 249A(1) [*total exemption*] [or 249A(2)] [*exemption with accountants' report*], [*as the case may be*] Companies Act 1985; and no notice has been deposited under section 249B(2) [*member or members requesting an audit*]. The directors acknowledge their responsibilities for ensuring that the company keeps accounting records which comply with section 221 [of the Act] and preparing accounts which give a true and fair view of the state of affairs of the company as at the end of the year and of its profit or loss for the financial year in accordance with the requirements of section 226 and which otherwise comply with the requirements of the Companies Act 1985, so far as applicable to the company.

The abbreviated accounts have been prepared in accordance with the special provisions of Part VII of the Companies Act 1985 relating to small [medium-sized] companies.

Signed on behalf of
the board of directors

C. Favell

CTG FAVELL
Director
Approved by the board: 28 February 1998

SMALL COMPANY LIMITED
NOTES TO THE ACCOUNTS – 30 SEPTEMBER 1997

1 Accounting policies

Basis of accounting
The accounts have been prepared under the historical cost convention as modified by the revaluation of certain fixed assets.

Consolidation
The company and its subsidiary comprise a small group. The company has therefore taken advantage of the exemption provided by section 248 of the Companies Act 1985 not to prepare group accounts.

Turnover
Turnover represents net invoiced sales of goods, excluding VAT.

Tangible fixed assets
Depreciation is provided, after taking account of any grants receivable, at the following annual rates in order to write off each asset over its estimated useful life:

Freehold buildings	–	2% on cost or revalued amounts
Plant and machinery	–	15% on cost
Fixtures and fittings	–	10% on cost
Motor vehicles	–	25% on cost

No depreciation is provided on freehold land.

Stocks
Stocks and work-in-progress are valued at the lower of cost and net realisable value, after making due allowance for obsolete and slow moving items. Cost includes all direct expenditure and an appropriate proportion of fixed and variable overheads.

Deferred taxation
Provision is made at current rates for taxation deferred in respect of all material timing differences except to the extent that, in the opinion of the directors, there is reasonable probability that the liability will not arise in the foreseeable future.

Research and development
Expenditure on research and development is written off in the year in which it is incurred.

Foreign currencies
Assets and liabilities in foreign currencies are translated into sterling at the rates of exchange ruling at the balance sheet date. Transactions in foreign currencies are translated into sterling at the rate of exchange ruling at the date of the transaction. Exchange differences are taken into account in arriving at the operating profit.

Disclosure of accounting policies
See comment on Small Company Limited Annual Report and Accounts, **example accounts page 7** (see p106). See also Schedule 8A.4 (Appendix **E**).

Chapter 12 Example accounts

SMALL COMPANY LIMITED Page 4
NOTES TO THE ACCOUNTS – 30 SEPTEMBER 1997

Leased assets
Rentals applicable to operating leases where substantially all of the benefits and risks of ownership remain with the lessor are charged against profit as incurred.

Assets held under finance leases and hire purchase contracts are capitalised and depreciated over their useful lives. The corresponding lease or hire purchase obligation is treated in the balance sheet as a liability. The interest element of rental obligations is charged to profit and loss account over the period of the lease at a constant proportion of the outstanding balance of capital repayments.

Pension costs
Contributions in respect of the company's defined contribution pension scheme are charged to the profit and loss account for the year in which they are payable to the scheme.

---

2 Fixed assets

	Intangible assets £	Tangible fixed assets £	Investments £	Total £
Cost or valuation				
At 1 October 1996	28,127	550,414	11,500	590,041
Additions	10,264	55,893	—	66,157
Revaluation	—	20,000	—	20,000
Disposals	(3,000)	(11,713)	(10,500)	(25,213)
At 30 September 1997	35,391	614,594	1,000	650,985
Depreciation				
At 1 October 1996	9,281	267,866	—	277,147
On disposals	(2,802)	(8,312)	—	(11,114)
Charge for year	6,847	44,496	—	51,343
At 30 September 1997	13,326	304,050	—	317,376
Net book values				
At 30 September 1997	£22,065	£310,544	£1,000	£333,609
At 30 September 1996	£18,846	£282,548	£11,500	£312,894

Investments
At 30 September 1997 investments comprise an investment in a subsidiary undertaking. The company's investment in its subsidiary company of £1,000 represents the cost of acquisition of the whole of the ordinary share capital of Smallsub Ltd which provides office design and consultancy services. At 30 September 1997, the aggregate amount of the share capital and reserves of Smallsub Limited amounted to £56,300 and the profit for the year to that date was £3,560.

3 Debtors
Debtors include an amount of £4,000 (1996 – £ nil) falling due after more than one year.

SMALL COMPANY LIMITED
NOTES TO THE ACCOUNTS – 30 SEPTEMBER 1997

4 Creditors

Creditors include the following:

	1997 £	1996 £
Bank loan not wholly repayable within five years		
– repayable within five years	62,500	—
– repayable after five years	12,500	—
	75,000	—
Bank overdraft	26,290	74,920
	£101,290	£74,920

The bank loan and overdraft are secured.

5 Called up share capital

	1997 £	1996 £
Authorised		
50,000 *10% (now 7% plus tax credit)*		
7% preference shares of £1 each	50,000	50,000
100,000 ordinary shares of £1 each	100,000	100,000
	£150,000	£150,000
Allotted, called up and fully paid		
10,000 7% preference shares of £1 each	10,000	10,000
65,000 (1996 – 40,000) ordinary shares of £1 each	65,000	40,000
	£75,000	£50,000

During the year 25,000 ordinary shares of £1 each were allotted and fully paid for cash at par.

6 Transactions with directors

Loan to director
During the year James Longslade was granted a short-term loan to facilitate the purchase of a house. Indebtedness on the loan was as follows:

Liability at 1 October 1996 £	Maximum liability during the year £	Liability at 30 September 1997 £
—	15,000	15,000

The loan is repayable on 31 August 1998. Interest, at the rate of 6% per annum, is payable upon repayment and at 30 September 1997 no interest was due and unpaid.

Material interests of directors
During the year the company purchased goods to the value of £312,100 (1996 – £197,000) from Medium Company (London) Limited, a company in which TL Bramshaw and CTG Favell are materially interested as shareholders. The purchases were made on a normal trading basis.

Chapter 12   Example accounts

**Registered number:
01715561212
England and Wales**

**DORMANT SMALL COMPANY LIMITED
ANNUAL REPORT AND UNAUDITED ACCOUNTS
YEAR ENDED 30 SEPTEMBER 1997**

Unaudited dormant company accounts – These accounts illustrate the accounts of a company which has been dormant (*within the meaning of section 250 of the Companies Act 1985*) throughout the financial year and which has agreed by special resolution not to appoint auditors (*see* **2.9**).

There is little benefit in preparing abbreviated dormant company accounts other than the omission of the directors' report and the profit and loss account. Abbreviated accounts will omit the boxed text but need to include the directors' statement.

Small Company Limited dormant company accounts

DORMANT SMALL COMPANY LIMITED

Report of the directors
Not required in abbreviated accounts

The directors present their annual report with the unaudited accounts of the company for the year ended 30 September 1997. The company is dormant and has not traded during the year.

RG Brown and CTG Favell were the directors of the company throughout the year. Their share interests in the ultimate parent company Small Company Limited, are shown in the report and accounts of that company.

Signed on behalf of the board of directors by

C. Favell

CGT FAVELL
Director/Secretary   Approved by the board: 3 March 1998

Profit and loss account for the year ended 30 September 1997
The company has not traded during the year or the preceding financial year. During these years, the company received no income and incurred no expenditure and therefore made neither profit nor loss.

BALANCE SHEET – 30 SEPTEMBER 1997

	1997 £	1996 £
CURRENT ASSETS		
Debtors		
Amounts owed by group undertakings – (Ultimate parent company – Small Company Limited)	100	100
TOTAL ASSETS LESS CURRENT LIABILITIES	£100	£100
CAPITAL AND RESERVES		
Called up share capital		
Authorised, allotted and fully paid 100 ordinary shares of £1	100	100
SHAREHOLDERS' FUNDS	£100	£100

The company was dormant (within the meaning of section 250 of the Companies Act 1985) throughout the year ended 30 September 1997.

Signed on behalf of the board of directors by

C. Favell

CGT FAVELL
Director   Approved by the board: 3 March 1998

Appendices

Appendix A   Company accounts sections

Companies Act 1985

Part VII 'Accounts and audit' and Schedules 4 to 10A to the Companies Act 1985 (as amended by the Companies Act 1989 and subsequent Regulations) are set out below. Sections amended or inserted by SI 1997 No. 220, SI 1997 No. 936 or SI 1997 No. 570 are indicated by an **emboldened** section or Schedule number.

CA 1985
Section

Accounting records
221   Duty to keep accounting records
222   Where and for how long records to be kept

A company's financial year and accounting reference periods
223   A company's financial year
224   Accounting reference periods and accounting reference date
225   Alteration of accounting reference date

Annual accounts
226   Duty to prepare individual company accounts
227   Duty to prepare group accounts
228   Exemption for parent companies included in accounts of larger group
229   Subsidiary undertakings included in the consolidation
230   Treatment of individual profit and loss account where group accounts prepared
231   Disclosure required in notes to accounts: related undertakings
232   Disclosure required in notes to accounts: emoluments and other benefits of directors and others

Approval and signing of accounts
233   Approval and signing of accounts

Directors' report
234   Duty to prepare directors' report
234A   Approval and signing of directors' report

Auditors' report
235   Auditors' report
236   Signature of auditors' report
237   Duties of auditors

Appendix A   Company accounts sections

Publication of accounts and reports
238   Persons entitled to receive copies of accounts and reports
239   Right to demand copies of accounts and reports
240   Requirements in connection with publication of accounts

Laying and delivering of accounts and reports
241   Accounts and reports to be laid before company in general meeting
242   Accounts and reports to be delivered to the Registrar
242A   Civil penalty for failure to deliver accounts
242B   Delivery and publication of accounts in ECUs
243   Accounts of subsidiary undertakings to be appended in certain cases
244   Period allowed for laying and delivering accounts and reports

Revision of defective accounts and reports
245   Voluntary revision of annual accounts or directors' report
245A   Secretary of State's notice in respect of annual accounts
245B   Application to court in respect of defective accounts
245C   Other persons authorised to apply to court

Small and medium-sized companies and groups
246   Special provisions for small companies
246A   Special provisions for medium-sized companies
247   Qualification of company as small or medium-sized
247A   Cases in which special provisions do not apply
247B   Special auditors' report
248   Exemption for small and medium-sized groups
248A   Group accounts prepared by small company
249   Qualification of group as small or medium-sized

Exemptions from audit for certain categories of small company
249A   Exemptions from audit
249B   Cases where exemptions not available
249C   The report required for the purposes of section 249A(2)
249D   The reporting accountant
249E   Effect of exemptions

Dormant companies
250   Resolution not to appoint auditors

Listed public companies
251   Provision of summary financial statement to shareholders

Private companies
252   Election to dispense with laying of accounts and reports before general meeting
253   Right of shareholder to require laying of accounts

Unlimited companies
254   Exemption from requirement to deliver accounts and reports

Banking and insurance companies and groups
255 Special provisions for banking and insurance companies
255A Special provisions for banking and insurance groups
255B Modification of disclosure requirements in relation to banking company or group
255D Power to apply provisions to banking partnerships

Accounting standards
256 Accounting standards

Power to alter accounting requirements
257 Power of Secretary of State to alter accounting requirements

Parent and subsidiary undertaking
258 Parent and subsidiary undertakings

Other interpretation provisions
259 Meaning of 'undertaking' and related expressions
260 Participating interests
261 Notes to the accounts
262 Minor definitions
262A Index of defined expressions

CA 1985
Schedule
4 Form and content of company accounts
4A Form and content of group accounts
5 Disclosure of information: related undertakings
6 Disclosure of information: emoluments and other benefits of directors and others
7 Matters to be included in directors' report
8 Form and content of accounts prepared by small companies
8A Form and content of abbreviated accounts of small companies delivered to Registrar
9 Special provisions for banking companies and groups
9A Special provisions for insurance companies and groups
10A Parent and subsidiary undertakings: supplementary provisions

© Crown copyright. Reproduced with the permission of the Controller of Her Majesty's Stationery Office.

Appendix B Statutory formats of accounts – Companies Act 1985 Schedules 4 and 8

This Appendix reproduces the formats contained in Schedule 4 Companies Act 1985 (Companies generally) and Schedule 8 (Small companies) ('The required formats for accounts').

For ease of reference, the 'notes following the formats' (Schedule 4 and Schedule 8) have been summarised and annotated against the format headings.

The formats for group accounts are as for individual companies in Schedule 4 CA 1985, amended for group circumstances by Schedule 4A.

Refer to Chapter 4 for use of the formats.

The formats are as follows:

Balance sheet formats (small companies – Schedule 8)
Balance sheet – Format 1
              Format 2

Balance sheet formats (full formats – Schedule 4)
Balance sheet – Format 1
              Format 2

Profit and loss account formats (all companies)
Profit and loss account – Format 1
                       Format 2
                       Format 3
                       Format 4

Abbreviated accounts
The formats may be further abbreviated in abbreviated accounts – see Chapter 8.

Appendix B Statutory formats of accounts

Small company balance sheet Format 1 (Sch 8)

The balance sheet format of a small company which adopts balance sheet Format 1 in accordance with CA 1985 Schedule 8 is as follows:

A Called up share capital not paid *Alternative position under C II 3 below*

B Fixed assets
   I Intangible assets
      1 Goodwill *Include only to the extent acquired for valuable consideration*
      2 Other intangible assets *Assets must have been acquired for valuable consideration or created by company itself (Note 1)*
   II Tangible assets
      1 Land and buildings
      2 Plant and machinery, etc.
   III Investments *(Note 2)*
      1 Shares in group undertakings and participating interests
      2 Loans to group undertakings and undertakings in which the company has a participating interest
      3 Other investments other than loans
      4 Others *Show the nominal value of own shares separately*

C Current assets
   I Stocks
      1 Stocks
      2 Payments on account
   II Debtors *(Note 3)*
      1 Trade debtors
      2 Amounts owed by group undertakings and undertakings in which the company has a participating interest
      3 Others
   III Investments
      1 Shares in group undertakings
      2 Other investments
   IV Cash at bank and in hand

D Prepayments and accrued income *Alternative position under C II 3 above*

E Creditors: amounts falling due within one year
      1 Bank loans and overdrafts
      2 Trade creditors
      3 Amounts owed to group undertakings and undertakings in which the company has a participating interest
      4 Other creditors *Show taxation and social security, and convertible loans separately*
         Include payments received on account of orders if not shown as deductions from stocks

F Net current assets (liabilities) *Take into account any prepayments and accrued income*

Small company balance sheet   Format 1 (Sch 8) (continued)

G Total assets less current liabilities

H Creditors: amounts falling due after more than one year
    1 Bank loans and overdrafts
    2 Trade creditors
    3 Amounts owed to group undertakings and undertakings in which the company has a participating interest
    4 Other creditors   *Show taxation and social security and convertible loans separately*
        Include payments received on account of orders if not shown as deductions from stocks

I Provisions liabilities and charges

J Accruals and deferred income   *Alternative position E4 or H4 as appropriate*

* **Minority interests**   *Group accounts – Alternative position below K*

K Capital and reserves
    I Called up share capital   *Show (a) allotted and (b) called up and paid up share capital separately*
    II Share premium account
    III Revaluation reserve
    IV Other reserves
    V Profit and loss account

* **Minority interests**   *Group accounts – Alternative position below J*

Notes
The italicised notes in the above formats are extracted from the notes on the balance sheet formats contained in Schedule 8 CA 1985. The following comments support the notes:

(1) Such assets comprise concessions, patents, licences, trade marks and similar rights and assets.

(2) In a consolidated balance sheet, the format for BIII 'Investments' (where a small company prepares small group accounts) is:

    1 Shares in group undertakings
    2 Interests in associated undertakings
    3 Other participating interests
    4 Loans to group undertakings and undertakings in which a participating interest is held
    5 Other investments other than loans
    6 Others.

(3) A small company must disclose the amount of 'debtors falling due after more than one year' for each item unless the aggregate amount of such debtors is disclosed in the notes to the accounts rather than in the balance sheet. ASB UITF abstract No. 4 requires disclosure in the balance sheet if it is material in the context of total net current assets.

* *Ascribed a letter in balance sheet formats*

Appendix B Statutory formats of accounts

Small company balance sheet   Format 2 (Sch 8)

ASSETS

A Called up share capital not paid *Alternative position under C II 3 below*

B Fixed assets
    I Intangible assets
       1 Goodwill   *Include only to the extent acquired for valuable consideration*
       2 Other intangible assets   *Concessions, patents, licences, trade marks and similar rights and assets must have been acquired for valuable consideration or created by company itself*
   II Tangible assets
       1 Land and buildings
       2 Plant and machinery, etc.
  III Investments
       1 Shares in group undertakings and participating interests
       2 Loans to group undertakings and undertakings in which the company has a participating interest
       3 Other investments other than loans
       4 Others   *Show the nominal value of own shares separately*

C Current assets
    I Stocks
       1 Stocks
       2 Payments on accounts
   II Debtors   *For each item show amounts falling due after more than one year unless aggregate is disclosed in the notes*
       1 Trade debtors
       2 Amounts owed by group undertakings and undertakings in which the company has a participating interest
       3 Others
  III Investments
       1 Shares in group undertakings
       2 Other investments
  IV Cash at bank and in hand

D Prepayments and accrued income *Alternative position under C II 3 above*

Small company balance sheet Format 2 (Sch 8) (continued)

LIABILITIES

Notes

A *Capital and reserves*
    I Called up share capital — *Show (a) allotted and (b) called up and paid up share capital separately*

    II Share premium account
    III Revaluation reserve
    IV Other reserves
    V Profit and loss account

* ***Minority interests*** — *Group accounts*

B *Provisions for liabilities and charges*

C *Creditors* — *Amounts falling due: 'within one year' and 'after one year' should be shown separately in aggregate and separately for each item of 'Creditors' unless the separate aggregate amounts are disclosed in the notes*

    1 Bank loans and overdrafts
    2 Trade creditors
    3 Amounts owed to group undertakings and undertakings in which the company has a participating interest
    4 Other creditors — *Show taxation and social security and convertible loans separately from other creditors. Include payments received on account of orders if not shown as deductions from stocks*
    5 Accruals and deferred income — *Alternative position D below*

D *Accruals and deferred income* — *Alternative position within C4 above*

* *Ascribed a letter in balance sheet formats*

Appendix B Statutory formats of accounts

Balance sheet   Format 1 (Sch 4)

Notes
(Extracted from the notes given with the formats in Schedule 4 CA 1985.)

A Called up share capital not paid   *Alternative position under C II 5*

B Fixed assets
    I Intangible assets
        1 Development costs
        2 Concessions, patents, licences, trade marks and similar rights and assets   *Assets must have been acquired for valuable consideration or created by company itself*
        3 Goodwill   *Goodwill must have been acquired for valuable consideration*
        4 Payments on account
    II Tangible assets
        1 Land and buildings
        2 Plant and machinery
        3 Fixtures, fittings, tools and equipment
        4 Payments on account and assets in course of construction
    III Investments
        1 Shares in group undertakings
        2 Loans to group undertakings
        3 Participating interests   *Take into account only the interests of the company. No requirement to show 'associated undertakings' separately*

        or (Group accounts):
        3 (a) Interests in associated undertakings
            (b) Other participating interests   *Include interests held by all group companies*
        4 Loans to undertakings in which the company has a participating interest   *Include interests held by all group companies*
        5 Other investments other than loans
        6 Other loans
        7 Own shares   *Show nominal value separately*

C Current assets
    I Stocks
        1 Raw materials and consumables
        2 Work-in-progress
        3 Finished goods and goods for resale
        4 Payments on account
    II Debtors   *For each item show amounts falling due after more than one year*
        1 Trade debtors
        2 Amounts owed by group undertakings
        3 Amounts owed by undertakings in which the company has a participating interest   *Include interests held by all group companies*
        4 Other debtors
        5 Called up share capital not paid   *Alternative position A*
        6 Prepayments and accrued income   *Alternative position D*
    III Investments
        1 Shares in group undertakings
        2 Own shares   *Show nominal value separately*
        3 Other investments
    IV Cash at bank and in hand

Balance sheet   Format 1 (Sch 4) (continued)

Notes

D Prepayments and accrued income   *Alternative position C II 6*

E Creditors: amounts falling due within one year
    1 Debenture loans   *Show amount of convertible loans separately*
    2 Bank loans and overdrafts
    3 Payments received on account   *If not shown as deduction from stocks*
    4 Trade creditors
    5 Bills of exchange payable
    6 Amounts owed to group undertakings
    7 Amounts owed to undertakings in which the company has a participating interest
    8 Other creditors including taxation and social security   *Show taxation and social security separately from other creditors*
    9 Accruals and deferred income   *Alternative position J*

F Net current assets (liabilities)   *Take into account D*

G Total assets less current liabilities

H Creditors: amounts falling due after more than one year
    1 Debenture loans   *Show amount of convertible loans separately*
    2 Bank loans and overdrafts
    3 Payments received on account   *If not shown as deduction from stocks*
    4 Trade creditors
    5 Bills of exchange payable
    6 Amounts owed to group undertakings
    7 Amounts owed to undertakings in which the company has a participating interest
    8 Other creditors including taxation and social security   *Show taxation and social security separately from other creditors*
    9 Accruals and deferred income   *Alternative position J*

I Provisions for liabilities and charges
    1 Pensions and similar obligations
    2 Taxation, including deferred taxation
    3 Other provisions

J Accruals and deferred income   *Alternative positions E9 and H9*

* Minority interests   *Group accounts – Alternative position below K*

K Capital and reserves
    I Called up share capital   *Show (a) allotted and (b) called up and paid up share capital separately*
    II Share premium account
    III Revaluation reserve
    IV Other reserves
        1 Capital redemption reserve
        2 Reserve for own shares
        3 Reserves provided for by the Articles of Association
        4 Other reserves
    V Profit and loss account

* Minority interests   *Group accounts – Alternative position below J*

* *Ascribed a letter in balance sheet formats*

Appendix B Statutory formats of accounts

Balance sheet   Format 2 (Sch 4)

Notes
(Extracted from the notes given with the formats in Schedule 4 CA 1985.)

ASSETS

A Called up share capital not paid   *Alternative position under C II 5 below*

B Fixed assets
    I Intangible assets
        1 Development costs
        2 Concessions, patents, licences, trade marks and similar rights and assets   *Assets must have been acquired for valuable consideration or created by company itself*
        3 Goodwill   *Goodwill must have been acquired for valuable consideration*
        4 Payments on account
    II Tangible assets
        1 Land and buildings
        2 Plant and machinery
        3 Fixtures, fittings, tools and equipment
        4 Payments on account and assets in course of construction
    III Investments
        1 Shares in group undertakings
        2 Loans to group undertakings
        3 Participating interests   *Take into account only the interests of the company. No requirement to show 'associated undertakings' separately*

        or (Group accounts):
        3 (a) Interests in associated undertakings   *Include interests held by all group companies*
            (b) Other participating interests
        4 Loans to undertakings in which the company has a participating interest   *Include interests held by all group companies*
        5 Other investments other than loans
        6 Other loans
        7 Own shares   *Show nominal value separately*

C Current assets
    I Stocks
        1 Raw materials and consumables
        2 Work-in-progress
        3 Finished goods and goods for resale
        4 Payments on account
    II Debtors   *For each item show amounts falling due after more than one year*
        1 Trade debtors
        2 Amounts owed by group undertakings
        3 Amounts owed by undertakings in which the company has a participating interest   *Include interests held by all group companies*
        4 Other debtors
        5 Called up share capital not paid   *Alternative position A above*
        6 Prepayments and accrued income   *Alternative position D below*
    III Investments
        1 Shares in group undertakings
        2 Own shares   *Show nominal value separately*
        3 Other investments
    IV Cash at bank and in hand

D Prepayments and accrued income   *Alternative position C II 6 above*

Balance sheet   Format 2 (Sch 4) (*continued*)

LIABILITIES   *Notes*

A   Capital and reserves
    I   Called up share capital   *Show (a) allotted and (b) called up and paid up share capital separately*

    II Share premium account
    III Revaluation reserve
    IV Other reserves
        1 Capital redemption reserve
        2 Reserve for own shares
        3 Reserves provided for by the Articles of Association
        4 Other reserves
    V   Profit and loss account

*   **Minority interests**   *Group accounts*

B   Provisions for liabilities and charges
    1 Pensions and similar obligations
    2 Taxation, including deferred taxation
    3 Other provisions

C   Creditors   *Amounts falling due: 'within one year' and 'after one year' should be shown separately in aggregate and separately for each item of 'Creditors'*

    1 Debenture loans   *Show amount of convertible loans separately*
    2 Bank loans and overdrafts
    3 Payments received on account   *If not shown as deduction from stocks*
    4 Trade creditors
    5 Bills of exchange payable
    6 Amounts owed to group undertakings
    7 Amounts owed to undertakings in which the company has a participating interest
    8 Other creditors including taxation and social security   *Show taxation and social security separately from other creditors*
    9 Accruals and deferred income   *Alternative position D below*

D   Accruals and deferred income   *Alternative position C9 above*

---

* *Ascribed a letter in balance sheet formats*

Appendix B   Statutory formats of accounts

Profit and loss account   Format 1

		Notes
1	Turnover	
2	Cost of sales	*Take into account any provision for depreciation or diminution of assets*
3	Gross profit or loss	
4	Distribution costs	*Take into account any provison for depreciation or diminution of assets*
5	Administrative expenses	*Take into account any provision for depreciation or diminution of assets*
6	Other operating income	
7	Income from shares in group undertakings	
8	Income from participating interests	
	or (Group accounts):	
8	(a) Income from interests in associated undertakings	*Include interests held by all group companies*
	(b) Income from other participating interests	
9	Income from other fixed asset investments	*Show group income separately*
10	Other interest receivable and similar income	*Show group income separately*
11	Amounts written off investments	
12	Interest payable and similar charges	*Show group interest separately*
13	Tax on profit or loss on ordinary activities	
14	Profit or loss on ordinary activities after taxation	
*	Minority interests	*Group accounts*
15	Extraordinary income	
16	Extraordinary charges	
17	Extraordinary profit or loss	
18	Tax on extraordinary profit or loss	
*	Minority interests	*Group accounts – Minority interests share in extraordinary items*
19	Other taxes not shown under the above items	
20	Profit or loss for the financial year	

Depreciation and other amounts written off tangible and intangible fixed assets must be disclosed in a note

* *Ascribed an arabic number in profit and loss account formats*

Profit and loss account   Format 2

Notes

1. Turnover
2. Change in stocks of finished goods and in work-in-progress
3. Own work capitalised
4. Other operating income
5. (a) Raw materials and consumables
   (b) Other external charges
6. Staff costs:
   (a) wages and salaries
   (b) social security costs
   (c) other pension costs
7. (a) Depreciation and other amounts written off tangible and intangible fixed assets
   (b) Exceptional amounts written off current assets
8. Other operating charges
9. Income from shares in group undertakings
10. Income from participating interests

or (Group accounts):

10. (a) Income from interests in associated undertakings   *Include interests held by all group companies*
    (b) Income from other participating interests
11. Income from other fixed asset investments   *Show group income separately*
12. Other interest receivable and similar income   *Show group income separately*
13. Amounts written off investments
14. Interest payable and similar charges   *Show group interest separately*
15. Tax on profit or loss on ordinary activities
16. Profit or loss on ordinary activities after taxation
* Minority interests   *Group accounts*
17. Extraordinary income
18. Extraordinary charges
19. Extraordinary profit or loss
20. Tax on extraordinary profit or loss
* Minority interests   *Group accounts – Minority interests share in extraordinary items*
21. Other taxes not shown under the above items
22. Profit or loss for the financial year

---

* *Ascribed an arabic number in profit and loss account formats*

Appendix B Statutory formats of accounts

Profit and loss account Format 3

Notes

A Charges
1. Cost of sales — *Take into account any provision for depreciation or diminution of assets*
2. Distribution costs — *Take into account any provison for depreciation or diminution of assets*
3. Administrative expenses — *Take into account any provision for depreciation or diminution of assets*
4. Amounts written off investments
5. Interest payable and similar charges — *Show group interest separately*
6. Tax on profit or loss on ordinary activities
7. Profit or loss on ordinary activities after taxation
* Minority interests — *Group accounts – Where minority interests share in loss*
8. Extraordinary charges
9. Tax on extraordinary profit or loss
* Minority interests — *Group accounts – Minority interests share in extraordinary items*
10. Other taxes not shown under the above items
11. Profit or loss for the financial year

B Income
1. Turnover
2. Other operating income
3. Income from shares in group undertakings
4. Income from participating interests

   or (Group accounts):

   4. (a) Income from interests in associated undertakings — *Include interests held by all group companies*
      (b) Income from other participating interests
5. Income from other fixed asset investments — *Show group income separately*
6. Other interest receivable and similar income — *Show group income separately*
7. Profit or loss on ordinary activities after taxation
* Minority interests — *Group accounts – Where minority interests share in loss*
8. Extraordinary income
* Minority interests — *Group accounts – Minority interests share in extraordinary items*
9. Profit or loss for the financial year

Depreciation and other amounts written off tangible and intangible fixed assets must be disclosed in a note

---

* *Ascribed an arabic number in profit and loss account formats*

Profit and loss account Format 4

Notes

A Charges
1. Reduction in stocks of finished goods and in work-in-progress
2. (a) Raw materials and consumables
   (b) Other external charges
3. Staff costs:
   (a) wages and salaries
   (b) social security costs
   (c) other pension costs
4. (a) Depreciation and other amounts written off tangible and intangible fixed assets
   (b) Exceptional amounts written off current assets
5. Other operating charges
6. Amounts written off investments
7. Interest payable and similar charges *Show group interest separately*
8. Tax on profit or loss on ordinary activities
9. Profit or loss on ordinary activities after taxation
* Minority interests *Group accounts – Where minority interests share in loss*
10. Extraordinary charges
11. Tax on extraordinary profit or loss
* Minority interests *Group accounts – Minority interests share in extraordinary items*
12. Other taxes not shown under the above items
13. Profit or loss for the financial year

B Income
1. Turnover
2. Increase in stocks of finished goods and in work-in-progress
3. Own work capitalised
4. Other operating income
5. Income from shares in group undertakings
6. Income from participating interests
   or (Group accounts):
6. (a) Income from interests in associated undertakings *Include interests held by all group companies*
   (b) Income from other participating interests
7. Income from other fixed asset investments *Show group income separately*
8. Other interest receivable and similar income *Show group income separately*
9. Profit or loss on ordinary activities after taxation
* Minority interests *Where minority interests share in profit*
10. Extraordinary income
* Minority interests *Minority interests share in extraordinary items*
11. Profit or loss for the financial year

* *Ascribed an arabic number in profit and loss account formats*

© Crown copyright. Reproduced with the permission of the Controller of Her Majesty's Stationery Office.

Appendix C Special accounting provisions for small and medium-sized companies – Companies Act 1985 sections 246 to 249

This Appendix reproduces sections 246 to 249 of the Companies Act 1985 as amended by SI 1996 No. 189, SI 1997 No. 220 and SI 1997 No. 570.

Special provisions for small companies

246.—(1) Subject to section 247A, this section applies where a company qualifies as a small company in relation to a financial year.

(2) If the company's individual accounts for the year—
  (a) comply with the provisions of Schedule 8, or
  (b) fail to comply with those provisions only in so far as they comply instead with one or more corresponding provisions of Schedule 4,

they need not comply with the provisions or, as the case may be, the remaining provisions of Schedule 4, and where advantage is taken of this subsection, references in section 226 to compliance with the provisions of Schedule 4 shall be construed accordingly.

(3) The company's individual accounts for the year—
  (a) may give the total of the aggregates required by paragraphs (a), (c) and (d) of paragraph 1(1) of Schedule 6 (emoluments and other benefits etc. of directors) instead of giving those aggregates individually; and
  (b) need not give the information required by—
    (i) paragraph 4 of Schedule 5 (financial years of subsidiary undertakings);
    (ii) paragraph 1(2)(b) of Schedule 6 (numbers of directors exercising share options and receiving shares under long-term incentive schemes);
    (iii) paragraph 2 of Schedule 6 (details of highest paid director's emoluments etc.); or
    (iv) paragraph 7 of Schedule 6 (excess retirement benefits of directors and past directors).

(4) The directors' report for the year need not give the information required by—
  (a) section 234(1)(a) and (b) (fair review of business and amount to be paid as dividend);
  (b) paragraph 1(2) of Schedule 7 (statement of market value of fixed assets where substantially different from balance sheet amount);
  (c) paragraph 6 of Schedule 7 (miscellaneous disclosures); or
  (d) paragraph 11 of Schedule 7 (employee involvement).

(5) Notwithstanding anything in section 242(1), the directors of the company need not deliver to the registrar any of the following, namely—
  (a) a copy of the company's profit and loss account for the year,
  (b) a copy of the directors' report for the year; and
  (c) if they deliver a copy of a balance sheet drawn up as at the last day of the year which complies with the requirements of Schedule 8A, a copy of the company's balance sheet drawn up as at that day.

(6) Neither a copy of the company's accounts for the year delivered to the registrar under section 242(1), nor a copy of a balance sheet delivered to the registrar under subsection (5)(c), need give the information required by—

Appendix C   Special accounting provisions for small and medium-sized companies

(a) paragraph 4 of Schedule 5 (financial years of subsidiary undertakings);
(b) paragraph 6 of Schedule 5 (shares of company held by subsidiary undertakings);
(c) Part I of Schedule 6 (directors' and chairman's emoluments, pensions and compensation for loss of office); or
(d) section 390A(3) (amount of auditors' remuneration).

(7) The provisions of section 233 as to the signing of the copy of the balance sheet delivered to the registrar apply to a copy of a balance sheet delivered under subsection (5)(c).

(8) Subject to subsection (9), each of the following, namely—
(a) accounts prepared in accordance with subsection (2) or (3),
(b) a report prepared in accordance with subsection (4), and
(c) a copy of accounts delivered to the registrar in accordance with subsection (5) or (6),

shall contain a statement in a prominent position on the balance sheet, in the report or, as the case may be, on the copy of the balance sheet, above the signature required by section 233, 234A or subsection (7), that they are prepared in accordance with the special provisions of this Part relating to small companies.

(9) Subsection (8) does not apply where the company is exempt by virtue of section 250 (dormant companies) from the obligation to appoint auditors.

Special provisions for medium-sized companies

246A.—(1) Subject to section 247A, this section applies where a company qualifies as a medium-sized company in relation to a financial year.

(2) The company's individual accounts for the year need not comply with the requirements of paragraph 36A of Schedule 4 (disclosure with respect to compliance with accounting standards).

(3) The company may deliver to the registrar a copy of the company's accounts for the year—
(a) which includes a profit and loss account in which the following items listed in the profit and loss account formats set out in Part I of Schedule 4 are combined as one item under the heading "gross profit or loss"—
Items 1, 2, 3 and 6 in Format 1;
Items 1 to 5 in Format 2;
Items A.1, B.1 and B.2 in Format 3;
Items A.1, A.2 and B.1 to B.4 in Format 4;
(b) which does not contain the information required by paragraph 55 of Schedule 4 (particulars of turnover).

(4) A copy of accounts delivered to the registrar in accordance with subsection (3) shall contain a statement in a prominent position on the copy of the balance sheet, above the signature required by section 233, that the accounts are prepared in accordance with the special provisions of this Part relating to medium-sized companies.

Qualification of company as small or medium-sized

247.—(1) A company qualifies as small or medium-sized in relation to a financial year if the qualifying conditions are met—
(a) in the case of the company's first financial year, in that year, and
(b) in the case of any subsequent financial year, in that year and the preceding year.

(2) A company shall be treated as qualifying as small or medium-sized in relation to a financial year—
(a) if it so qualified in relation to the previous financial year under subsection (1) above or was treated as so qualifying under paragraph (b) below; or
(b) if it was treated as so qualifying in relation to the previous year by virtue of paragraph (a) and the qualifying conditions are met in the year in question.

(3) The qualifying conditions are met by a company in a year in which it satisfies two or more of the following requirements—

Small company

1. Turnover   Not more than £2.8 million
2. Balance sheet total   Not more than £1.4 million
3. Number of employees   Not more than 50

Medium-sized company

1. Turnover   Not more than £11.2 million
2. Balance sheet total   Not more than £5.6 million
3. Number of employees   Not more than 250.

(4) For a period which is a company's financial year but not in fact a year the maximum figures for turnover shall be proportionately adjusted.

(5) The balance sheet total means—
   (a) where in the company's accounts Format 1 of the balance sheet formats set out in Part I of Schedule 4 or Part I of Schedule 8 is adopted, the aggregate of the amounts shown in the balance sheet under the headings corresponding to items A to D in that Format, and
   (b) where Format 2 is adopted, the aggregate of the amounts shown under the general heading "Assets".

(6) The number of employees means the average number of persons employed by the company in the year (determined on a monthly basis).

That number shall be determined by applying the method of calculation prescribed by paragraph 56(2) and (3) of Schedule 4 for determining the corresponding number required to be stated in a note to the company's accounts.

Cases in which special provisions do not apply

247A.—(1) Nothing in section 246 or 246A shall apply where—
   (a) the company is, or was at any time within the financial year to which the accounts relate—
      (i) a public company,
      (ii) a banking or insurance company, or
      (iii) an authorised person under the Financial Services Act 1986; or
   (b) the company is, or was at any time during that year, a member of an ineligible group.

(2) A group is ineligible if any of its members is—
   (a) a public company or a body corporate which (not being a company) has power under its constitution to offer its shares or debentures to the public and may lawfully exercise that power,
   (b) an authorised institution under the Banking Act 1987,
   (c) an insurance company to which Part II of the Insurance Companies Act 1982 applies, or
   (d) an authorised person under the Financial Services Act 1986.

(3) A parent company shall not be treated as qualifying as a small company in relation to a financial year unless the group headed by it qualifies as a small group, and shall not be treated as qualifying as a medium-sized company in relation to a financial year unless that group qualifies as a medium-sized group (see section 249).

Special auditors' report

247B.—(1) This section applies where—
   (a) the directors of a company propose to deliver to the registrar copies of accounts ("abbreviated accounts") prepared in accordance with section 246(5) or (6) or 246A(3) ("the relevant provision"),
   (b) the directors have not taken advantage of the exemption from audit conferred by section 249A(1) or (2), and

(c) the company is not exempt by virtue of section 250 from the obligation to appoint auditors.

(2) If abbreviated accounts prepared in accordance with the relevant provision are delivered to the registrar, they shall be accompanied by a copy of a special report of the auditors stating that in their opinion—
- (a) the company is entitled to deliver abbreviated accounts prepared in accordance with that provision, and
- (b) the abbreviated accounts to be delivered are properly prepared in accordance with that provision.

(3) In such a case a copy of the auditors' report under section 235 need not be delivered, but—
- (a) if that report was qualified, the special report shall set out that report in full together with any further material necessary to understand the qualification; and
- (b) if that report contained a statement under—
    - (i) section 237(2) (accounts, records or returns inadequate or accounts not agreeing with records and returns), or
    - (ii) section 237(3) (failure to obtain necessary information and explanations),

the special report shall set out that statement in full.

(4) Section 236 (signature of auditors' report) applies to a special report under this section as it applies to a report under section 235.

(5) If abbreviated accounts prepared in accordance with the relevant provision are delivered to the registrar, references in section 240 (requirements in connection with publication of accounts) to the auditors' report under section 235 shall be read as references to the special auditors' report under this section.

Exemption for small and medium-sized groups

248.—(1) A parent company need not prepare group accounts for a financial year in relation to which the group headed by that company qualifies as a small or medium-sized group and is not an ineligible group.

(2) A group is ineligible if any of its members is—
- (a) a public company or body corporate which (not being a company) has power under its constitution to offer its shares or debentures to the public and may lawfully exercise that power,
- (b) an authorised institution under the Banking Act 1987,
- (c) an insurance company to which Part II of the Insurance Companies Act 1982 applies, or
- (d) an authorised person under the Financial Services Act 1986.

(3) [Repealed]

(4) [Repealed]

Group accounts prepared by small company

248A.—(1) This section applies where a small company—
- (a) has prepared individual accounts for a financial year in accordance with section 246(2) or (3), and
- (b) is preparing group accounts in respect of the same year.

(2) If the group accounts—
- (a) comply with the provisions of Schedule 8, or
- (b) fail to comply with those provisions only in so far as they comply instead with one or more corresponding provisions of Schedule 4,

they need not comply with the provisions or, as the case may be, the remaining provisions of Schedule 4; and where advantage is taken of this subsection, references in Schedule 4A to compliance with the provisions of Schedule 4 shall be construed accordingly.

(3) For the purposes of this section, Schedule 8 shall have effect as if, in each balance sheet format set out in that Schedule, for item B.III there were substituted the following item—
"B.III Investments
1. Shares in group undertakings
2. Interests in associated undertakings
3. Other participating interests
4. Loans to group undertakings and undertakings in which a participating interest is held
5. Other investments other than loans
6. Others."

(4) The group accounts need not give the information required by the provisions specified in section 246(3).

(5) Group accounts prepared in accordance with this section shall contain a statement in a prominent position on the balance sheet, above the signature required by section 233, that they are prepared in accordance with the special provisions of this Part relating to small companies.

Qualification of group as small or medium-sized

249.—(1) A group qualifies as small or medium-sized in relation to a financial year if the qualifying conditions are met—
(a) in the case of the parent company's first financial year, in that year, and
(b) in the case of any subsequent financial year, in that year and the preceding year.

(2) A group shall be treated as qualifying as small or medium-sized in relation to a financial year—
(a) if it so qualified in relation to the previous financial year under subsection (1) above or was treated as so qualifying under paragraph (b) below; or
(b) if it was treated as so qualifying in relation to the previous year by virtue of paragraph (a) and the qualifying conditions are met in the year in question.

(3) The qualifying conditions are met by a group in a year in which it satisfies two or more of the following requirements—

Small group
1. Aggregate turnover   Not more than £2.8 million net (or £3.36 million gross)
2. Aggregate balance sheet total   Not more than £1.4 million net (or £1.68 million gross)
3. Aggregate number of employees   Not more than 50

Medium-sized group
1. Aggregate turnover   Not more than £11.2 million net (or £13.44 million gross)
2. Aggregate balance sheet total   Not more than £5.6 million net (or £6.72 million gross)
3. Aggregate number of employees   Not more than 250.

(4) The aggregate figures shall be ascertained by aggregating the relevant figures determined in accordance with section 247 for each member of the group.

In relation to the aggregate figures for turnover and balance sheet total, "net" means with the set-offs and other adjustments required by Schedule 4A in the case of group accounts and "gross" means without those set-offs and other adjustments; and a company may satisfy the relevant requirements on the basis of either the net or the gross figure.

(5) The figures for each subsidiary undertaking shall be those included in its accounts for the relevant financial year, that is—
(a) if its financial year ends with that of the parent company, that financial year, and
(b) if not, its financial year ending last before the end of the financial year of the parent company.

Appendix C   Special accounting provisions for small and medium-sized companies

(6) If those figures cannot be obtained without disproportionate expense or undue delay, the latest available figures shall be taken.

© Crown copyright. Reproduced with the permission of the Controller of Her Majesty's Stationery Office.

Appendix D Form and content of accounts prepared by small companies – Companies Act 1985 Schedule 8

This Appendix reproduces Schedule 8 to the Companies Act 1985 (Form and content of accounts prepared by small companies) as inserted by SI 1997 No. 220, which came into force on 1 March 1997.

Small company balance sheet and profit and loss account formats (and the notes thereto) are set out in Appendix **B**.

PART I

GENERAL RULES AND FORMATS

SECTION A

GENERAL RULES

1.—(1) Subject to the following provisions of this Schedule—
  (a) every balance sheet of a small company shall show the items listed in either of the balance sheet formats set out below in section B of this Part; and
  (b) every profit and loss account of a small company shall show the items listed in any one of the profit and loss account formats so set out;

in either case in the order and under the headings and sub-headings given in the format adopted.

(2) Sub-paragraph (1) above is not to be read as requiring the heading or sub-heading for any item to be distinguished by any letter or number assigned to that item in the format adopted.

2.—(1) Where in accordance with paragraph 1 a small company's balance sheet or profit and loss account for any financial year has been prepared by reference to one of the formats set out in section B below, the directors of the company shall adopt the same format in preparing the accounts for subsequent financial years of the company unless in their opinion there are special reasons for a change.

(2) Particulars of any change in the format adopted in preparing a small company's balance sheet or profit and loss account in accordance with paragraph 1 shall be disclosed, and the reasons for the change shall be explained, in a note to the accounts in which the new format is first adopted.

3.—(1) Any item required in accordance with paragraph 1 to be shown in a small company's balance sheet or profit and loss account may be shown in greater detail than required by the format adopted.

(2) A small company's balance sheet or profit and loss account may include an item representing or covering the amount of any asset or liability, income or expenditure not otherwise covered by any of the items listed in the format adopted, but the following shall not be treated as assets in any small company's balance sheet—
  (a) preliminary expenses;

(b) expenses of and commission on any issue of shares or debentures; and
(c) costs of research.

(3) In preparing a small company's balance sheet or profit and loss account the directors of the company shall adapt the arrangement and headings and sub-headings otherwise required by paragraph 1 in respect of items to which an Arabic number is assigned in the format adopted, in any case where the special nature of the company's business requires such adaptation.

(4) Items to which Arabic numbers are assigned in any of the formats set out in section B below may be combined in a small company's accounts for any financial year if either—
   (a) their individual amounts are not material to assessing the state of affairs or profit or loss of the company for that year; or
   (b) the combination facilitates that assessment;

but in a case within paragraph (b) the individual amounts of any items so combined shall be disclosed in a note to the accounts.

(5) Subject to paragraph 4(3) below, a heading or sub-heading corresponding to an item listed in the format adopted in preparing a small company's balance sheet or profit and loss account shall not be included if there is no amount to be shown for that item in respect of the financial year to which the balance sheet or profit and loss account relates.

(6) Every profit and loss account of a small company shall show the amount of the company's profit or loss on ordinary activities before taxation.

(7) Every profit and loss account of a small company shall show separately as additional items—
   (a) any amount set aside or proposed to be set aside to, or withdrawn or proposed to be withdrawn from, reserves;
   (b) the aggregate amount of any dividends paid and proposed.

4.—(1) In respect of every item shown in a small company's balance sheet or profit and loss account the corresponding amount for the financial year immediately preceding that to which the balance sheet or profit and loss account relates shall also be shown.

(2) Where the corresponding amount is not comparable with the amount to be shown for the item in question in respect of the financial year to which the balance sheet or profit and loss account relates, the former amount shall be adjusted and particulars of the adjustment and the reasons for it shall be disclosed in a note to the accounts.

(3) Paragraph 3(5) does not apply in any case where an amount can be shown for the item in question in respect of the financial year immediately preceding that to which the balance sheet or profit and loss account relates, and that amount shall be shown under the heading or sub-heading required by paragraph 1 for that item.

5. Amounts in respect of items representing assets or income may not be set off against amounts in respect of items representing liabilities or expenditure (as the case may be), or vice versa.

Section B

The Required Formats for Accounts

Preliminary

6. References in this Part of this Schedule to the items listed in any of the formats set out below are to those items read together with any of the notes following the formats which apply to any of those items, and the requirements imposed by paragraph 1 to show the items listed in any such format in the order adopted in the format is subject to any provision in those notes for alternative positions for any particular items.

7. [Not reproduced]

8. [Not reproduced]

Companies Act 1985 Schedule 8

Balance Sheet Formats

> Small company balance sheet formats are set out in Appendix **B** and in **7.8**

Profit and Loss Account Formats

> Small company profit and loss account formats, and notes thereto, are set out in Appendix **B**.

PART II

ACCOUNTING PRINCIPLES AND RULES

SECTION A

ACCOUNTING PRINCIPLES

Preliminary

9. Subject to paragraph 15 below, the amounts to be included in respect of all items shown in a small company's accounts shall be determined in accordance with the principles set out in paragraphs 10 to 14.

Accounting principles

10. The company shall be presumed to be carrying on business as a going concern.

11. Accounting policies shall be applied consistently within the same accounts and from one financial year to the next.

12. The amount of any item shall be determined on a prudent basis, and in particular—
    (a) only profits realised at the balance sheet date shall be included in the profit and loss account; and
    (b) all liabilities and losses which have arisen or are likely to arise in respect of the financial year to which the accounts relate or a previous financial year shall be taken into account, including those which only become apparent between the balance sheet date and the date on which it is signed on behalf of the board of directors in pursuance of section 233 of this Act.

13. All income and charges relating to the financial year to which the accounts relate shall be taken into account, without regard to the date of receipt or payment.

14. In determining the aggregate amount of any item the amount of each individual asset or liability that falls to be taken into account shall be determined separately.

Departure from the accounting principles

15. If it appears to the directors of a small company that there are special reasons for departing from any of the principles stated above in preparing the company's accounts in respect of any financial year they may do so, but particulars of the departure, the reasons for it and its effect shall be given in a note to the accounts.

SECTION B

HISTORICAL COST ACCOUNTING RULES

Preliminary

16. Subject to section C of this Part of this Schedule, the amounts to be included in respect of all items shown in a small company's accounts shall be determined in accordance with the rules set out in paragraphs 17 to 28.

155

Appendix D   Form and content of accounts prepared by small companies

Fixed assets

General rules

17. Subject to any provision for depreciation or diminution in value made in accordance with paragraph 18 or 19 the amount to be included in respect of any fixed asset shall be its purchase price or production cost.

18. In the case of any fixed asset which has a limited useful economic life, the amount of—
    (a) its purchase price or production cost; or
    (b) where it is estimated that any such asset will have a residual value at the end of the period of its useful economic life, its purchase price or production cost less that estimated residual value;

shall be reduced by provisions for depreciation calculated to write off that amount systematically over the period of the asset's useful economic life.

19.—(1) Where a fixed asset investment of a description falling to be included under item B.III of either of the balance sheet formats set out in Part I of this Schedule has diminished in value provisions for diminution in value may be made in respect of it and the amount to be included in respect of it may be reduced accordingly; and any such provisions which are not shown in the profit and loss account shall be disclosed (either separately or in aggregate) in a note to the accounts.

(2) Provisions for diminution in value shall be made in respect of any fixed asset which has diminished in value if the reduction in its value is expected to be permanent (whether its useful economic life is limited or not), and the amount to be included in respect of it shall be reduced accordingly; and any such provisions which are not shown in the profit and loss acount shall be disclosed (either separately or in aggregate) in a note to the accounts.

(3) Where the reasons for which any provision was made in accordance with sub-paragraph (1) or (2) have ceased to apply to any extent, that provision shall be written back to the extent that it is no longer necessary; and any amounts written back in accordance with this sub-paragraph which are not shown in the profit and loss account shall be disclosed (either separately or in aggregate) in a note to the accounts.

Rules for determining particular fixed asset items

20.—(1) Notwithstanding that an item in respect of "development costs" is included under "fixed assets" in the balance sheet formats set out in Part I of this Schedule, an amount may only be included in a small company's balance sheet in respect of development costs in special circumstances.

(2) If any amount is included in a small company's balance sheet in respect of development costs the following information shall be given in a note to the accounts—
    (a) the period over which the amount of those costs originally capitalised is being or is to be written off; and
    (b) the reasons for capitalising the development costs in question.

21.—(1) The application of paragraphs 17 to 19 in relation to goodwill (in any case where goodwill is treated as an asset) is subject to the following provisions of this paragraph.

(2) Subject to sub-paragraph (3) below, the amount of the consideration for any goodwill acquired by a small company shall be reduced by provisions for depreciation calculated to write off that amount systematically over a period chosen by the directors of the company.

(3) The period chosen shall not exceed the useful economic life of the goodwill in question.

(4) In any case where any goodwill acquired by a small company is shown or included as an asset in the company's balance sheet the period chosen for writing off the consideration for that goodwill and the reasons for choosing that period shall be disclosed in a note to the accounts.

Current assets

22. Subject to paragraph 23, the amount to be included in respect of any current asset shall be its purchase price or production cost.

23.—(1) If the net realisable value of any current asset is lower than its purchase price or production cost the amount to be included in respect of that asset shall be the net realisable value.

(2) Where the reasons for which any provision for diminution in value was made in accordance with sub-paragraph (1) have ceased to apply to any extent, that provision shall be written back to the extent that it is no longer necessary.

Miscellaneous and supplementary provisions

Excess of money owed over value received as an asset item

24.—(1) Where the amount repayable on any debt owed by a small company is greater than the value of the consideration received in the transaction giving rise to the debt, the amount of the difference may be treated as an asset.

(2) Where any such amount is so treated—
   (a) it shall be written off by reasonable amounts each year and must be completely written off before repayment of the debt; and
   (b) if the current amount is not shown as a separate item in the company's balance sheet it must be disclosed in a note to the accounts.

Assets included at a fixed amount

25.—(1) Subject to the following sub-paragraph, assets which fall to be included—
   (a) amongst the fixed assets of a small company under the item "tangible assets"; or
   (b) amongst the current assets of a small company under the item "raw materials and consumables",

may be included at a fixed quantity and value.

(2) Sub-paragraph (1) applies to assets of a kind which are constantly being replaced, where—
   (a) their overall value is not material to assessing the company's state of affairs; and
   (b) their quantity, value and composition are not subject to material variation.

Determination of purchase price or production cost

26.—(1) The purchase price of an asset shall be determined by adding to the actual price paid any expenses incidental to its acquisition.

(2) The production cost of an asset shall be determined by adding to the purchase price of the raw materials and consumables used the amount of the costs incurred by the company which are directly attributable to the production of that asset.

(3) In addition, there may be included in the production cost of an asset—
   (a) a reasonable proportion of the costs incurred by the company which are only indirectly attributable to the production of that asset, but only to the extent that they relate to the period of production; and
   (b) interest on capital borrowed to finance the production of that asset, to the extent that it accrues in respect of the period of production;

provided, however, in the case within paragraph (b) above, that the inclusion of the interest in determining the cost of that asset and the amount of the interest so included is disclosed in a note to the accounts.

(4) In the case of current assets distribution costs may not be included in production costs.

27.—(1) Subject to the qualification mentioned below, the purchase price or production cost of—

Appendix D Form and content of accounts prepared by small companies

(a) any assets which fall to be included under any item shown in a small company's balance sheet under the general item "stocks"; and
(b) any assets which are fungible assets (including investments);

may be determined by the application of any of the methods mentioned in sub-paragraph (2) below in relation to any such assets of the same class.

The method chosen must be one which appears to the directors to be appropriate in the circumstances of the company.

(2) Those methods are—
(a) the method known as "first in, first out" (FIFO);
(b) the method known as "last in, first out" (LIFO);
(c) a weighted average price; and
(d) any other method similar to any of the methods mentioned above.

(3) For the purposes of this pararaph, assets of any description shall be regarded as fungible if assets of that description are substantially indistinguishable one from another.

Substitution of original stated amount where price or cost unknown

28. Where there is no record of the purchase price or production cost of any asset of a small company or of any price, expenses or costs relevant for determining its purchase price or production cost in accordance with paragraph 26, or any such record cannot be obtained without unreasonable expense or delay, its purchase price or production cost shall be taken for the purposes of pararaphs 17 to 23 to be the value ascribed to it in the earliest available record of its value made on or after its acquisition or production by the company.

Section C

Alternative Accounting Rules

Preliminary

29.—(1) The rules set out in section B are referred to below in this Schedule as the historical cost accounting rules.

(2) Those rules, with the omission of paragraphs 16, 21 and 25 to 28, are referred to below in this Part of this Schedule as the depreciation rules; and references below in this Schedule to the historical cost accounting rules do not include the depreciation rules as they apply by virtue of paragraph 32.

30. Subject to paragraphs 32 to 34, the amounts to be included in respect of assets of any description mentioned in paragraph 31 may be determined on any basis so mentioned.

Alternative accounting rules

31.—(1) Intangible fixed assets, other than goodwill, may be included at their current cost.

(2) Tangible fixed assets may be included at a market value determined as at the date of their last valuation or at their current cost.

(3) Investments of any description falling to be included under item B.III of either of the balance sheet formats set out in Part I of this Schedule may be included either—
(a) at a market value determined as at the date of their last valuation; or
(b) at a value determined on any basis which appears to the directors to be appropriate in the circumstances of the company;

but in the latter case particulars of the method of valuation adopted and of the reasons for adopting it shall be disclosed in a note to the accounts.

(4) Investments of any description falling to be included under item C.III of either of the balance sheet formats set out in Part I of this Schedule may be included at their current cost.

(5) Stocks may be included at their current cost.

Application of the depreciation rules

32.—(1) Where the value of any asset of a small company is determined on any basis mentioned in paragraph 31, that value shall be, or (as the case may require) be the starting point for determining, the amount to be included in respect of that asset in the company's accounts, instead of its purchase price or production cost or any value previously so determined for that asset; and the depreciation rules shall apply accordingly in relation to any such asset with the substitution for any reference to its purchase price or production cost of a reference to the value most recently determined for that asset on any basis mentioned in paragraph 31.

(2) The amount of any provision for depreciation required in the case of any fixed asset by paragraph 18 or 19 as it applies by virtue of sub-paragraph (1) is referred to below in this paragraph as the adjusted amount, and the amount of any provision which would be required by that paragraph in the case of that asset according to the historical cost accounting rules is referred to as the historical cost amount.

(3) Where sub-paragraph (1) applies in the case of any fixed asset the amount of any provision for depreciation in respect of that asset—
- (a) included in any item shown in the profit and loss account in respect of amounts written off assets of the description in question; or
- (b) taken into account in stating any item so shown which is required by note *(11)* of the notes on the profit and loss account formats set out in Part I of this Schedule [*cost of sales, distribution costs, administrative expenses*] to be stated after taking into account any necessary provision for depreciation or diminution in value of assets included under it;

may be the historical cost amount instead of the adjusted amount, provided that the amount of any difference between the two is shown separately in the profit and loss account or in a note to the accounts.

Additional information to be provided in case of departure from historical cost accounting rules

33.—(1) This paragraph applies where the amounts to be included in respect of assets covered by any items shown in a small company's accounts have been determined on any basis mentioned in paragraph 31.

(2) The items affected and the basis of valuation adopted in determining the amounts of the assets in question in the case of each such item shall be disclosed in a note to the accounts.

(3) In the case of each balance sheet item affected (except stocks) either—
- (a) the comparable amounts determined according to the historical cost accounting rules; or
- (b) the difference between those amounts and the corresponding amounts actually shown in the balance sheet in respect of that item;

shall be shown separately in the balance sheet or in a note to the accounts.

(4) In sub-paragraph (3) above, references in relation to any item to the comparable amounts determined as there mentioned are references to—
- (a) the aggregate amount which would be required to be shown in respect of that item if the amounts to be included in respect of all the assets covered by that item were determined according to the historical cost accounting rules; and
- (b) the aggregate amount of the cumulative provisions for depreciation or diminution in value which would be permitted or required in determining those amounts according to those rules.

Revaluation reserve

34.—(1) With respect to any determination of the value of an asset of a small company on any basis mentioned in paragraph 31, the amount of any profit or loss arising from that

Appendix D Form and content of accounts prepared by small companies

determination (after allowing, where appropriate, for any provisions for depreciation or diminution in value made otherwise than by reference to the value so determined and any adjustments of any such provisions made in the light of that determination) shall be credited or (as the case may be) debited to a separate reserve ("the revaluation reserve").

(2) The amount of the revaluation reserve shall be shown in the company's balance sheet under a separate sub-heading in the position given for the item "revaluation reserve" in Format 1 or 2 of the balance sheet formats set out in Part I of this Schedule, but need not be shown under that name.

(3) An amount may be transferred—
  (a) from the revaluation reserve—
    (i) to the profit and loss account, if the amount was previously charged to that account or represents realised profit, or
    (ii) on capitalisation,
  (b) to or from the revaluation reserve in respect of the taxation relating to any profit or loss credited or debited to the reserve;

and the revaluation reserve shall be reduced to the extent that the amounts transferred to it are no longer necessary for the purposes of the valuation method used.

(4) In sub-paragraph (3)(a)(ii) "capitalisation", in relation to an amount standing to the credit of the revaluation reserve, means applying it in wholly or partly paying up unissued shares in the company to be allotted to members of the company as fully or partly paid shares.

(5) The revaluation reserve shall not be reduced except as mentioned in this paragraph.

(6) The treatment for taxation purposes of amounts credited or debited to the revaluation reserve shall be disclosed in a note to the accounts.

PART III

NOTES TO THE ACCOUNTS

Preliminary

35. Any information required in the case of any small company by the following provisions of this Part of this Schedule shall (if not given in the company's accounts) be given by way of a note to those accounts.

Disclosure of accounting policies

36. The accounting policies adopted by the company in determining the amounts to be included in respect of items shown in the balance sheet and in determining the profit or loss of the company shall be stated (including such policies with respect to the depreciation and diminution in value of assets).

Information supplementing the balance sheet

37. Paragraphs 38 to 47 require information which either supplements the information given with respect to any particular items shown in the balance sheet or is otherwise relevant to assessing the company's state of affairs in the light of the information so given.

Share capital and debentures
38.—(1) The following information shall be given with respect to the company's share capital—
  (a) the authorised share capital; and
  (b) where shares of more than one class have been allotted, the number and aggregate nominal value of shares of each class allotted.

(2) In the case of any part of the allotted share capital that consists of redeemable shares, the following information shall be given—

(a) the earliest and latest dates on which the company has power to redeem those shares;
(b) whether those shares must be redeemed in any event or are liable to be redeemed at the option of the company or of the shareholder; and
(c) whether any (and, if so, what) premium is payable on redemption.

39. If the company has allotted any shares during the financial year, the following information shall be given—
(a) the classes of shares allotted; and
(b) as respects each class of shares, the number allotted, their aggregate nominal value, and the consideration received by the company for the allotment.

Fixed assets

40.—(1) In respect of each item which is or would but for paragraph 3(4)(b) be shown under the general item "fixed assets" in the company's balance sheet the following information shall be given—
(a) the appropriate amounts in respect of that item as at the date of the beginning of the financial year and as at the balance sheet date respectively;
(b) the effect on any amount shown in the balance sheet in respect of that item of—
   (i) any revision of the amount in respect of any assets included under that item made during that year on any basis mentioned in paragraph 31;
   (ii) acquisitions during that year of any assets;
   (iii) disposals during that year of any assets; and
   (iv) any transfers of assets of the company to and from that item during that year.

(2) The reference in sub-paragraph (1)(a) to the appropriate amounts in respect of any item as at any date there mentioned is a reference to amounts representing the aggregate amounts determined, as at that date, in respect of assets falling to be included under that item on either of the following bases, that is to say—
(a) on the basis of purchase price or production cost (determined in accordance with paragraphs 26 and 27); or
(b) on any basis mentioned in paragraph 31,

(leaving out of account in either case any provisions for depreciation or diminution in value).

(3) In respect of each item within sub-paragraph (1)—
(a) the cumulative amount of provisions for depreciation or diminution in value of assets included under that item as at each date mentioned in sub-paragraph (1)(a);
(b) the amount of any such provisions made in respect of the financial year;
(c) the amount of any adjustments made in respect of any such provisions during that year in consequence of the disposal of any assets; and
(d) the amount of any other adjustments made in respect of any such provisions during that year;

shall also be stated.

41. Where any fixed assets of the company (other than listed investments) are included under any item shown in the company's balance sheet at an amount determined on any basis mentioned in paragraph 31, the following information shall be given—
(a) the years (so far as they are known to the directors) in which the assets were severally valued and the several values; and
(b) in the case of assets that have been valued during the financial year, the names of the persons who valued them or particulars of their qualifications for doing so and (whichever is stated) the bases of valuation used by them.

Investments

42.—(1) In respect of the amount of each item which is or would but for paragraph 3(4)(b) be shown in the company's balance sheet under the general item "investments" (whether as fixed assets or as current assets) there shall be stated how much of that amount is ascribable to listed investments.

(2) Where the amount of any listed investments is stated for any item in accordance with sub-paragraph (1), the following amounts shall also be stated—
   (a) the aggregate market value of those investments where it differs from the amount so stated; and
   (b) both the market value and the stock exchange value of any investments of which the former value is, for the purposes of the accounts, taken as being higher than the latter.

Reserves and provisions

43.—(1) Where any amount is transferred—
   (a) to or from any reserves; or
   (b) to any provisions for liabilities and charges; or
   (c) from any provision for liabilities and charges otherwise than for the purpose for which the provisions was established;

and the reserves or provisions are or would but for paragraph 3(4)(b) be shown as separate items in the company's balance sheet, the information mentioned in the following sub-paragraph shall be given in respect of the aggregate of reserves or provisions included in the same item.

(2) That information is—
   (a) the amount of the reserves or provisions as at the date of the beginning of the financial year and as at the balance sheet date respectively;
   (b) any amounts transferred to or from the reserves or provisions during that year; and
   (c) the source and application respectively of any amounts so transferred.

(3) Particulars shall be given of each provision included in the item "other provisions" in the company's balance sheet in any case where the amount of that provision is material.

Details of indebtedness

44.—(1) For the aggregate of all items shown under "creditors" in the company's balance sheet there shall be stated the aggregate of the following amounts, that is to say—
   (a) the amount of any debts included under "creditors" which are payable or repayable otherwise than by instalments and fall due for payment or repayment after the end of the period of five years beginning with the day next following the end of the financial year; and
   (b) in the case of any debts so included which are payable or repayable by instalments, the amount of any instalments which fall due for payment after the end of that period.

(2) In respect of each item shown under "creditors" in the company's balance sheet there shall be stated the aggregate amount of any debts included under that item in respect of which any security has been given by the company.

(3) References above in this paragraph to an item shown under "creditors" in the company's balance sheet include references, where amounts falling due to creditors within one year and after more than one year are distinguished in the balance sheet—
   (a) in a case within sub-paragraph (1), to an item shown under the latter of those categories; and
   (b) in a case within sub-paragraph (2), to an item shown under either of those categories;

and references to items shown under "creditors" include references to items which would but for pararaph 3(4)(b) be shown under that heading.

45. If any fixed cumulative dividends on the company's shares are in arrear, there shall be stated—
   (a) the amount of the arrears; and
   (b) the period for which the dividends or, if there is more than one class, each class of them are in arrear.

Guarantees and other financial commitments

46.—(1) Particulars shall be given of any charge on the assets of the company to secure the liabilities of any other person, including, where practicable, the amount secured.

(2) The following information shall be given with respect to any other contingent liability not provided for—
- (a) the amount or estimated amount of that liability;
- (b) its legal nature; and
- (c) whether any valuable security has been provided by the company in connection with that liability and if so, what.

(3) There shall be stated, where practicable, the aggregate amount or estimated amount of contracts for capital expenditure, so far as not provided for.

(4) Particulars shall be given of—
- (a) any pension commitments included under any provision shown in the company's balance sheet; and
- (b) any such commitments for which no provision has been made;

and where any such commitment relates wholly or partly to pensions payable to past directors of the company separate particulars shall be given of that commitment so far as it relates to such pensions.

(5) Particulars shall also be given of any other financial commitments which—
- (a) have not been provided for; and
- (b) are relevant to assessing the company's state of affairs.

(6) Commitments within any of sub-paragrahs (1) to (5) which are undertaken on behalf of or for the benefit of—
- (a) any parent undertaking or fellow subsidiary undertaking, or
- (b) any subsidiary undertaking of the company,

shall be stated separately from the other commitments within that sub-paragraph, and commitments within paragraph (a) shall also be stated separately from those within paragraph (b).

Miscellaneous matters

47. Particulars shall be given of any case where the purchase price or production cost of any asset is for the first time determined under paragraph 28.

Information supplementing the profit and loss account

48. Paragraphs 49 and 50 require information which either supplements the information given with respect to any particular items shown in the profit and loss account or otherwise provides particulars of income or expenditure of the company or of circumstances affecting the items shown in the profit and loss account.

Particulars of turnover

49.—(1) If the company has supplied geographical markets outside the United Kingdom during the financial year in question, there shall be stated the percentage of its turnover that, in the opinion of the directors, is attributable to those markets.

(2) In analysing for the purposes of this paragraph the source of turnover, the directors of the company shall have regard to the manner in which the company's activities are organised.

Miscellaneous matters

50.—(1) Where any amount relating to any preceding financial year is included in any item in the profit and loss account, the effect shall be stated.

(2) Particulars shall be given of any extraordinary income or charges arising in the financial year.

(3) The effect shall be stated of any transactions that are exceptional by virtue of size or incidence though they fall within the ordinary activities of the company.

General

51.—(1) Where sums originally denominated in foreign currencies have been brought into account under any items shown in the balance sheet or profit and loss account, the basis on which those sums have been translated into sterling shall be stated.

(2) Subject to the following sub-paragraph, in respect of every item stated in a note to the accounts the corresponding amount for the financial year immediately preceding that to which the accounts relate shall also be stated and where the corresponding amount is not comparable, it shall be adjusted and particulars of the adjustment and the reasons for it shall be given.

(3) Sub-paragraph (2) does not apply in relation to any amounts stated by virtue of any of the following provisions of this Act—
    (a) pararaph 13 of Schedule 4A (details of accounting treatment of acquisitions),
    (b) paragraphs 2, 8(3), 16, 21(1)(d), 22(4) and (5), 24(3) and (4) and 27(3) and (4) of Schedule 5 (shareholdings in other undertakings),
    (c) Parts II and III of Schedule 6 (loans and other dealings in favour of directors and others), and
    (d) paragraphs 40 and 43 above (fixed assets and reserves and provisions).

PART IV

INTERPRETATION OF SCHEDULE

52. The following paragraphs apply for the purposes of this Schedule and its interpretation.

Historical cost accounting rules
53. References to the historical cost accounting rules shall be read in accordance with paragraph 29.

Listed investments
54. "Listed investment" means an investment as respects which there has been granted a listing on a recognised investment exchange other than an overseas investment exchange within the meaning of the Financial Services Act 1986 or on any stock exchange of repute outside Great Britain.

Loans
55. A loan is treated as falling due for repayment, and an instalment of a loan is treated as falling due for payment, on the earliest date on which the lender could require repayment or (as the case may be) payment, if he exercised all options and rights available to him.

Materiality
56. Amounts which in the particular context of any provision of this Schedule are not material may be disregarded for the purposes of that provision.

Provisions
57.—(1) References to provisions for depreciation or diminution in value of assets are to any amount written off by way of providing for depreciation or diminution in value of assets.

(2) Any reference in the profit and loss account formats set out in Part I of this Schedule to the depreciation of, or amounts written off, assets of any description is to any provision for depreciation or diminution in value of assets of that description.

58. References to provisions for liabilities or charges are to any amount retained as reasonably necessary for the purpose of providing for any liability or loss which is either likely to be incurred, or certain to be incurred but uncertain as to amount or as to the date on which it will arise.

59.—(1) "Social security costs" means any contributions by the company to any state social security or pension scheme, fund or arrangement.

(2) "Pension costs" includes any costs incurred by the company in respect of any pension scheme established for the purpose of providing pensions for persons currently or formerly employed by the company, any sums set aside for the future payment of pensions directly by the company to current or former employees and any pensions paid directly to such persons without having first been set aside.

(3) Any amount stated in respect of the item "social security costs" or in respect of the item "wages and salaries" in the company's profit and loss account shall be determined by reference to payments made or costs incurred in respect of all persons employed by the company during the financial year under contracts of service.

© Crown copyright. Reproduced with the permission of the Controller of Her Majesty's Stationery Office.

Appendix E Form and content of abbreviated accounts of small companies delivered to Registrar – Companies Act 1985 Schedule 8A

This Appendix reproduces Schedule 8A to the Companies Act 1985 (Form and content of abbreviated accounts of small companies delivered to Registrar) as inserted by SI 1997 No. 220 which came into force on 1 March 1997.

PART I

BALANCE SHEET FORMATS

1. A small company may deliver to the registrar a copy of the balance sheet showing the items listed in either of the balance sheet formats set out in paragraph 2 below in the order and under the headings and sub-headings given in the format adopted, but in other respects corresponding to the full balance sheet.

2. The formats referred to in paragraph 1 are as follows—

Balance sheet formats

Format 1

A. Called up share capital not paid
B. Fixed assets
    I Intangible assets
    II Tangible assets
    III Investments
C. Current assets
    I Stocks
    II Debtors *(1)*
    III Investments
    IV Cash at bank and in hand
D. Prepayments and accrued income
E. Creditors: amounts falling due within one year
F. Net current assets (liabilities)
G. Total assets less current liabilities
H. Creditors: amounts falling due after more than one year
I. Provisions for liabilities and charges
J. Accruals and deferred income
K. Capital and reserves
    I Called up share capital
    II Share premium account
    III Revaluation reserve
    IV Other reserves
    V Profit and loss account

Format 2

ASSETS
A. Called up share capital not paid
B. Fixed assets
    I Intangible assets
    II Tangible assets
    III Investments
C. Current assets
    I Stocks
    II Debtors *(1)*
    III Investments
    IV Cash at bank and in hand
D. Prepayments and accrued income

LIABILITIES
A. Capital and reserves
    I Called up share capital
    II Share premium account
    III Revaluation reserve
    IV Other reserves
    V Profit and loss account
B. Provisions for liabilities and charges
C. Creditors *(2)*
D. Accruals and deferred income

Notes on the balance sheet formats

(1) Debtors
(Formats 1 and 2, item C.II.)

The aggregate amount of debtors falling due after more than one year shall be shown separately, unless it is disclosed in the notes to the accounts.

(2) Creditors
(Format 2, Liabilities item C.)

The aggregate amount of creditors falling due within one year and of creditors falling due after more than one year shall be shown separately, unless it is disclosed in the notes to the accounts.

PART II

NOTES TO THE ACCOUNTS

Preliminary

3. Any information required in the case of any small company by the following provisions of this Part of this Schedule shall (if not given in the company's accounts) be given by way of a note to those accounts.

Disclosure of accounting policies

4. The accounting policies adopted by the company in determining the amounts to be included in respect of items shown in the balance sheet and in determining the profit or loss of the company shall be stated (including such policies with respect to the depreciation and diminution in value of assets).

Information supplementing the balance sheet

Share capital and debentures

5.—(1) The following information shall be given with respect to the company's share capital—
   (a) the authorised share capital; and
   (b) where shares of more than one class have been allotted, the number and aggregate nominal value of shares of each class allotted.

(2) In the case of any part of the allotted share capital that consists of redeemable shares, the following information shall be given—
   (a) the earliest and latest dates on which the company has power to redeem those shares;
   (b) whether those shares must be redeemed in any event or are liable to be redeemed at the option of the company or of the shareholder; and
   (c) whether any (and, if so, what) premium is payable on redemption.

6. If the company has allotted any shares during the financial year, the following information shall be given—
   (a) the classes of shares allotted; and
   (b) as respects each class of shares, the number allotted, their aggregate nominal value, and the consideration received by the company for the allotment.

Fixed assets

7.—(1) In respect of each item to which a letter or Roman number is assigned under the general item "fixed assets" in the company's balance sheet the following information shall be given—
   (a) the appropriate amounts in respect of that item as at the date of the beginning of the financial year and as at the balance sheet date respectively;

(b) the effect on any amount shown in the balance sheet in respect of that item of—
  (i) any revision of the amount in respect of any assets included under that item made during that year on any basis mentioned in paragraph 31 of Schedule 8;
  (ii) acquisitions during that year of any assets;
  (iii) disposals during that year of any assets; and
  (iv) any transfers of assets of the company to and from that item during that year.

(2) The reference in sub-paragraph (1)(a) to the appropriate amounts in respect of any item as at any date there mentioned is a reference to amounts representing the aggregate amounts determined, as at that date, in respect of assets falling to be included under that item on either of the following bases, that is to say—
  (a) on the basis of purchase price or production cost (determined in accordance with paragraphs 26 and 27 of Schedule 8); or
  (b) on any basis mentioned in paragraph 31 of that Schedule,

(leaving out of account in either case any provisions for depreciation or diminution in value).

(3) In respect of each item within sub-paragraph (1)—
  (a) the cumulative amount of provisions for depreciation or diminution in value of assets included under that item as at each date mentioned in sub-paragrah (1)(a);
  (b) the amount of any such provisions made in respect of the financial year;
  (c) the amount of any adjustments made in respect of any such provisions during that year in consequence of the disposal of any assets; and
  (d) the amount of any other adjustments made in respect of any such provisions during that year;

shall also be stated.

Details of indebtedness

8.—(1) For the aggregate of all items shown under "creditors" in the company's balance sheet there shall be stated the aggregate of the following amounts, that is to say—
  (a) the amount of any debts included under "creditors" which are payable or repayable otherwise than by instalments and fall due for payment or repayment after the end of the period of five years beginning with the day next following the end of the financial year; and
  (b) in the case of any debts so included which are payable or repayable by instalments, the amount of any instalments which fall due for payment after the end of that period.

(2) In respect of each item shown under "creditors" in the company's balance sheet there shall be stated the aggregate amount of any debts included under that item, in respect of which any security has been given by the company.

General

9.—(1) Where sums originally denominated in foreign currencies have been brought into account under any items shown in the balance sheet or profit and loss account, the basis on which those sums have been translated into sterling shall be stated.

(2) Subject to the following sub-paragraph, in respect of every item required to be stated in a note to the accounts by or under any provision of this Act, the corresponding amount for the financial year immediately preceding that to which the accounts relate shall also be stated and where the corresponding amount is not comparable, it shall be adjusted and particulars of the adjustment and the reasons for it shall be given.

(3) Sub-paragraph (2) does not apply in relation to any amounts stated by virtue of any of the following provisions of this Act—
  (a) paragraph 13 of Schedule 4A (details of accounting treatment of acquisitions),
  (b) paragraphs 2, 8(3), 16, 21(1)(d), 22(4) and (5), 24(3) and (4) and 27(3) and (4) of Schedule 5 (shareholdings in other undertakings),

Appendix E Form and content of abbreviated accounts of small companies delivered to Registrar

    (c) Parts II and III of Schedule 6 (loans and other dealings in favour of directors and others), and
    (d) paragraph 7 above (fixed assets).

© Crown copyright. Reproduced with the permission of the Controller of Her Majesty's Stationery Office.

Appendix F Exemptions from audit for certain categories of small company – Companies Act 1985 sections 249A to 249E

This Appendix reproduces sections 249A to 249E of the Companies Act 1985.

Exemptions from audit for certain categories of small company

Exemptions from audit
249A.—(1) Subject to section 249B, a company which meets the total exemption conditions set out below in respect of a financial year is exempt from the provisions of this Part relating to the audit of accounts in respect of that year.

(2) Subject to section 249B, a company which is a charity and which meets the report conditions set out below in respect of a financial year is exempt from the provisions of this Part relating to the audit of accounts in respect of that year if the directors cause a report in respect of the company's individual accounts for that year to be prepared in accordance with section 249C and made to the company's members.

(3) The total exemption conditions are met by a company in respect of a financial year if—
  (a) it qualifies as a small company in relation to that year for the purposes of section 246,
  (b) its turnover in that year is not more than £350,000, and
  (c) its balance sheet total for that year is not more than £1.4 million.

(3A) In relation to any company which is a charity, subsection (3)(b) shall have effect with the substitution—
  (a) for the reference to turnover of a reference to gross income, and
  (b) for the reference to £350,000 of a reference to £90,000.

(4) The report conditions are met by a company which is a charity in respect of a financial year if—
  (a) it qualifies as a small company in relation to that year for the purposes of section 246,
  (b) its gross income in that year is more than £90,000 but not more than £250,000, and
  (c) its balance sheet total for that year is not more than £1.4 million.

(5) [Repealed]

(6) For a period which is a company's financial year but not in fact a year the maximum figures for turnover or gross income shall be proportionately adjusted.

(6A) A company is entitled to the exemption conferred by subsection (1) or (2) notwithstanding that it falls within paragraph (a) or (b) of section 250(1).

(7) In this section—
"balance sheet total" has the meaning given by section 247(5), and
"gross income" means the company's income from all sources, as shown in the company's income and expenditure account.

Cases where exemptions not available

249B.—(1) Subject to subsections (1A) to (1C), a company is not entitled to the exemption conferred by subsection (1) or (2) of section 249A in respect of a financial year if at any time within that year—
  (a) it was a public company,

Appendix F Exemptions from audit for certain categories of small company

  (b) it was a banking or insurance company,
  (c) it was enrolled in the list maintained by the Insurance Brokers Registration Council under section 4 of the Insurance Brokers (Registration) Act 1977,
  (d) it was an authorised person or an appointed representative under the Financial Services Act 1986,
  (e) it was a special register body as defined in section 117(1) of the Trade Union and Labour Relations (Consolidation) Act 1992 or an employers' association as defined in section 122 of that Act, or
  (f) it was a parent company or a subsidiary undertaking.

(1A) A company which, apart from this subsection, would fall within subsection (1)(f) by virtue of its being a subsidiary undertaking for any period within a financial year shall not be treated as so falling if it is dormant (within the meaning of section 250) throughout that period.

(1B) A company which, apart from this subsection, would fall within subsection (1)(f) by virtue of its being a parent company or a subsidiary undertaking for any period within a financial year shall not be treated as so falling if throughout that period it was a member of a group meeting the conditions set out in subsection (1C).

(1C) The conditions referred to in subsection (1B) are—
  (a) that the group qualifies as a small group, in relation to the financial year within which the period falls, for the purposes of section 249 and is not, and was not at any time within that year, an ineligible group within the meaning of section 248(2),
  (b) that the group's aggregate turnover in that year (calculated in accordance with section 249) is not more than £350,000 net (or £420,000 gross), and
  (c) that the group's aggregate balance sheet total for that year (calculated in accordance with section 249) is not more than £1.4 million net (or £1.68 million gross).

(2) Any member or members holding not less in the aggregate than 10 per cent in nominal value of the company's issued share capital or any class of it or, if the company does not have a share capital, not less than 10 per cent in number of the members of the company, may, by notice in writing deposited at the registered office of the company during a financial year but not later than one month before the end of that year, require the company to obtain an audit of its accounts for that year.

(3) Where a notice has been deposited under subsection (2), the company is not entitled to the exemption conferred by subsection (1) or (2) of section 249A in respect of the financial year to which the notice relates.

(4) A company is not entitled to the exemption conferred by subsection (1) or (2) of section 249A unless its balance sheet contains a statement by the directors—
  (a) to the effect that for the year in question the company was entitled to exemption under subsection (1) or (2) (as the case may be) of section 249A,
  (b) to the effect that no notice has been deposited under subsection (2) of this section in relation to its accounts for the financial year, and
  (c) to the effect that the directors acknowledge their responsibilities for—
    (i) ensuring that the company keeps accounting records which comply with section 221, and
    (ii) preparing accounts which give a true and fair view of the state of affairs of the company as at the end of the financial year and of its profit or loss for the financial year in accordance with the requirements of section 226, and which otherwise comply with the requirements of this Act relating to accounts, so far as applicable to the company.

(5) The statement required by subsection (4) shall appear in the balance sheet above the signature required by section 233.

The report required for the purposes of section 249A(2)

249C.—(1) The report required for the purposes of section 249A(2) shall be prepared by a person (referred to in this Part as "the reporting accountant") who is eligible under section 249D.

(2) The report shall state whether in the opinion of the reporting accountant making it—
- (a) the accounts of the company for the financial year in question are in agreement with the accounting records kept by the company under section 221, and
- (b) having regard only to, and on the basis of, the information contained in those accounting records, those accounts have been drawn up in a manner consistent with the provisions of this Act specified in subsection (6), so far as applicable to the company.

(3) The report shall also state that in the opinion of the reporting accountant, having regard only to, and on the basis of, the information contained in the accounting records kept by the company under section 221, the company satisfied the requirements of subsection (4) of section 249A (or, where the company is a charity, of that subsection as modified by subsection (5) of that section) for the financial year in question, and did not fall within section 249B(1)(a) to (f) at any time within that financial year.

(4) The report shall state the name of the reporting accountant and be signed by him.

(5) Where the reporting accountant is a body corporate or partnership, any reference to signature of the report, or any copy of the report, by the reporting accountant is a reference to signature in the name of the body corporate or partnership by a person authorised to sign on its behalf.

(6) The provisions referred to in subsection (2)(b) are—
- (a) section 226(3) and Schedule 4,
- (b) section 231 and paragraphs 7 to 9A and 13(1), (3) and (4) of Schedule 5, and
- (c) section 232 and Schedule 6,

where appropriate as modified by section 246(2) and (3).

The reporting accountant

249D.—(1) The reporting accountant shall be either—
- (a) any member of a body listed in subsection (3) who, under the rules of the body—
  - (i) is entitled to engage in public practice, and
  - (ii) is not ineligible for appointment as a reporting accountant, or
- (b) any person (whether or not a member of any such body) who—
  - (i) is subject to the rules of any such body in seeking appointment or acting as auditor under Chapter V of Part XI, and
  - (ii) under those rules, is eligible for appointment as auditor under that Chapter.

(1A) In subsection (1), references to the rules of a body listed in subsection (3) are to the rules (whether or not laid down by the body itself) which the body has power to enforce and which are relevant for the purposes of Part II of the Companies Act 1989 or this section.

This includes rules relating to the admission and expulsion of members of the body, so far as relevant for the purposes of that Part or this section.

(2) An individual, a body corporate or a partnership may be appointed as a reporting accountant, and section 26 of the Companies Act 1989 (effect of appointment of partnership) shall apply to the appointment as reporting accountant of a partnership constituted under the law of England and Wales or Northern Ireland, or under the law of any other country or territory in which a partnership is not a legal person.

(3) The bodies referred to in subsections (1) and (1A) are—
- (a) the Institute of Chartered Accountants in England and Wales,
- (b) the Institute of Chartered Accountants of Scotland,
- (c) the Institute of Chartered Accountants in Ireland,
- (d) the Association of Chartered Certified Accountants,
- (e) the Association of Authorised Public Accountants,
- (f) the Association of Accounting Technicians,
- (g) the Association of International Accountants, and
- (h) the Chartered Institute of Management Accountants.

Appendix F   Exemptions from audit for certain categories of small company

(4) A person is ineligible for appointment by a company as reporting accountant if he would be ineligible for appointment as an auditor of that company under section 27 of the Companies Act 1989 (ineligibility on ground of lack of independence).

Effect of exemptions

249E.—(1) Where the directors of a company have taken advantage of the exemption conferred by section 249A(1)—
- (a) sections 238 and 239 (right to receive or demand copies of accounts and reports) shall have effect with the omission of references to the auditors' report;
- (b) no copy of an auditors' report need be delivered to the registrar or laid before the company in general meeting;
- (c) subsections (3) to (5) of section 271 (accounts by reference to which distribution to be justified) shall not apply.

(2) Where the directors of a company have taken advantage of the exemption conferred by section 249A(2)—
- (a) subsections (2) to (4) of section 236 (which require copies of the auditors' report to state the names of the auditors) shall have effect with the substitution for references to the auditors and the auditors' report of references to the reporting accountant and the report made for the purposes of section 249A(2) respectively;
- (b) sections 238 and 239 (right to receive or demand copies of accounts and reports), section 241 (accounts and reports to be laid before company in general meeting) and section 242 (accounts and reports to be delivered to the registrar) shall have effect with the substitution for references to the auditors' report of references to the report made for the purposes of section 249A(2);
- (c) subsections (3) to (5) of section 271 (accounts by reference to which distribution to be justified) shall not apply;
- (d) section 389A(1) and (2) (rights to information) shall have effect with the substitution for references to the auditors of references to the reporting accountant.

© Crown copyright. Reproduced with the permission of the Controller of Her Majesty's Stationery Office.

Appendix G Dormant companies – Companies Act 1985 section 250

This Appendix reproduces section 250 of the Companies Act 1985 as amended by SI 1996 No. 189 and SI 1997 No. 220.

Resolution not to appoint auditors

250.—(1) A company may by special resolution make itself exempt from the provisions of this Part relating to the audit of accounts in the following cases—
    (a) if the company has been dormant from the time of its formation;
    (b) if the company has been dormant since the end of the previous financial year and—
        (i) is entitled in respect of its individual accounts for that year to prepare accounts in accordance with section 246(2), or would be so entitled but for the application of subsection (1)(a)(i) or (b) of section 247A, and
        (ii) is not required to prepared group accounts for that year,

by a special resolution passed at a general meeting of the company at any time after copies of the annual accounts and reports for that year have been sent out in accordance with section 238(1).

(2) A company may not pass such a resolution if it is—
    (a) a banking or insurance company, or
    (b) an authorised person under the Financial Services Act 1986.

(3) A company is "dormant" during a period in which no significant accounting transaction occurs, that is, no transaction which is required by section 221 to be entered in the company's accounting records; and a company ceases to be dormant on the occurrence of such a transaction.

For this purpose there shall be disregarded any transaction arising from the taking of shares in the company by a subscriber to the memorandum in pursuance of an undertaking of his in the memorandum.

(4) Where a company is, at the end of a financial year, exempt by virtue of this section from the provisions of this Part relating to the audit of accounts—
    (a) sections 238 and 239 (right to receive or demand copies of accounts and reports) have effect with the omission of references to the auditors' report;
    (b) no copies of an auditors' report need be laid before the company in general meeting;
    (c) no copy of an auditors' report need be delivered to the registrar, and if none is delivered, the copy of the balance sheet so delivered shall contain a statement by the directors, in a position above the signature required by section 233(4), to the effect that the company was dormant throughout the financial year, and
    (d) the company shall be treated as a company entitled to prepare accounts in accordance with section 246(2) notwithstanding that it is a member of an ineligible group.

(5) Where a company which is exempt by virtue of this section from the provisions of this Part relating to the audit of accounts—
    (a) ceases to be dormant, or

Appendix G   Dormant companies

(b) would no longer qualify (for any other reason) to make itself exempt by passing a resolution under this section),

it shall thereupon cease to be so exempt.

© Crown copyright. Reproduced with the permission of the Controller of Her Majesty's Stationery Office.

Appendix H Disclosure of information: related undertakings – Companies Act 1985 Schedule 5

Companies not required to prepare group accounts

Schedule 5 to the Companies Act 1985 (Part I) (as amended by SI 1996 No. 189) specifies the information to be given in notes to a company's annual accounts in relation to related undertakings, where group accounts are not required, as follows:

With certain exceptions, exemption from disclosure may be granted by the Secretary of State in respect of certain foreign undertakings carrying on business outside the UK where: s231(3)
(a) *the results or financial position of which principally affect the figures in the accounts, and*
(b) *the undertakings are excluded from consolidation under s229(3) or (4).*   s231(5)

Subsidiary undertakings
(a) The name of each subsidiary undertaking.
(b) With respect to each subsidiary undertaking:
   (i) the country in which it is incorporated (if it is incorporated outside Great Britain);
   (ii) ~~whether it is registered in England and Wales or in Scotland (if it is incorporated in Great Britain);~~ [repealed]
   (iii) the address of its principal place of business (if it is unincorporated).
(c) The reason why the company is not required to prepare group accounts. If the reason is that all subsidiary undertakings fall within the exclusions provided for in s229 CA 1985 the exclusion applicable to each subsidiary undertaking shall be stated.

The above information shall be given where, at the end of the financial year, the company has subsidiary undertakings.

Holdings in subsidiary undertakings
In relation to shares of each class held by the company in a subsidiary undertaking:

(a) the identity of the class; and
(b) the proportion of the nominal value of the shares of that class represented by those shares.

The shares held by or on behalf of the company itself shall be distinguished from those attributed to the company which are held by or on behalf of a subsidiary undertaking.

Financial information about subsidiary undertakings
With respect to each subsidiary undertaking:

(a) the aggregate amount of its capital and reserves as at the end of its relevant financial year; and
(b) its profit or loss for that year.

This information need not be given if:

(a) the company is exempt by virtue of s228 CA 1985 from the requirement to prepare group accounts (Parent company included in accounts of larger group);
(b) the company's investment in the subsidiary undertaking is included in the company's accounts by way of the equity method of valuation;

Appendix H Disclosure of information: related undertakings

(c) the subsidiary undertaking is not required to deliver or publish its balance sheet in Great Britain or elsewhere; and
the company's holding is less than 50 per cent of the nominal value of the shares in the undertaking; or
(d) the information is not material.

If this information is given where a subsidiary undertaking's financial year does not end with that of the company, in relation to each undertaking the following disclosure is required:

(a) ~~the reasons why the company's directors consider that its financial year should not end with that of the company; and~~ [repealed]
(b) the date on which its last financial year ended (last before the end of the company's financial year).

Shares and debentures of company held by subsidiary undertakings

The number, description and amount of the shares in the company held by, or on behalf of, its subsidiary undertakings. *Does not apply in relation to shares held as personal representative or (in certain circumstances) as trustee.*

Significant holdings in undertakings other than subsidiary undertakings

A holding is significant for this purpose if:

(a) it amounts to 20 per cent or more of the nominal value of any class of shares in the undertaking; or
(b) the amount of the holding (as stated or included in the company's accounts) exceeds one-fifth of the amount (as so stated) of the company's assets.

The following information must be supplied:

(a) The name of the undertaking and:
   (i) the country in which it is incorporated (if the undertaking is incorporated outside Great Britain);
   (ii) ~~whether it is registered in England and Wales or in Scotland (if it is incorporated in Great Britain);~~ [repealed]
   (iii) the address of its principal place of business (if it is unincorporated).
(b) (i) The identity of each class of shares in the undertaking held by the company; and
   (ii) the proportion of the nominal value of the shares of that class represented by those shares.
(c) (i) The aggregate amount of the capital and reserves of the undertaking as at the end of its relevant financial year; and
   (ii) its profit or loss for that year.

Need not be given if:

(a) the company is exempt by virtue of s228 CA 1985 from the requirement to prepare group accounts (Parent company included in accounts of larger group), and
the investment of the company in all such undertakings is shown, in aggregate, in the notes to the accounts by way of the equity method of valuation; or
(b) the information otherwise required is not material.

Membership of certain undertakings

Information to be given, if material, where the company is subject to the Partnerships and Unlimited Companies (Accounts) Regulations 1993 (SI 1993 No. 1820).

Unless the notes to the company's accounts disclose that advantage has been taken of exemption conferred by Regulation 7 of SI 1993 No. 1820, where the company is a member of a qualifying partnership (company) it must disclose:

- its name and legal form; and
- the address of its registered or head office.

In addition, the accounts of the qualifying partnership must state:

- that its accounts have been or will be appended to the company's accounts delivered to the Registrar of Companies; and
- the name of the body corporate in whose group accounts the partnership has been or will be consolidated.

Parent undertaking drawing up accounts for larger group (where the company is a subsidiary undertaking)
The following information shall be given with respect to the parent undertakings of:

(a) the largest group of undertakings for which group accounts are drawn up and of which the company is a member; and
(b) the smallest such group of undertakings.

(a) The name of the parent undertaking and:
(b) (i) the country in which it is incorporated (if the undertaking is incorporated outside Great Britain);
~~(ii) whether it is registered in England and Wales or in Scotland (if it is incorporated in Great Britain);~~ [repealed]
(iii) the address of its principal place of business (if it is unincorporated);
(c) the addresses from which copies of group accounts can be obtained if available to the public.

Identification of ultimate parent company (where the company is a subsidiary undertaking)
(a) The name of the company (if any) (including any body corporate) regarded by the directors as being the company's ultimate parent company.
(b) The country in which it is incorporated (if incorporated outside Great Britain).
~~(c) Whether it is registered in England and Wales or in Scotland (if it is incorporated in Great Britain).~~ [repealed]

Disclosure of information: related undertakings
Companies required to prepare group accounts

In many respects the disclosure requirements are identical to those identified above in Appendix H and are not set out here. The detailed requirements are provided by Part II of Schedule 5 to the Companies Act 1985 (Sch 3 CA 1989) 'Companies required to prepare group accounts'.

In addition to the above disclosure requirements, disclosure is required for:

(a) subsidiary undertakings not included in the consolidation;
(b) joint ventures;
(c) associated undertakings.

Appendix I 'Accounting Simplifications' and SI 1996 No. 189

Following a DTI consultative paper of May 1995 on 'Accounting Simplifications', modifications to the Companies Act 1985 have been made in SI 1996 No. 189 The Companies Act 1985 (Miscellaneous Accounting Amendments) Regulations 1996. Modifications included:

- simplifications (reductions) of accounts disclosures;
- amendment to the audit exemption regulations affecting 'off the shelf' companies; and
- requirement to disclose policy on payment to creditors (public companies and large private companies).

Many of the changes are deletions of disclosure requirements, corrections of minor anomalies or simple textual changes.

Unless otherwise stated, the changes apply to all companies and came into effect for accounting periods ended on or after 2 February 1996.

This Appendix summarises the main changes. Sections of legislation repealed are stated in italics.

Directors' report requirements

Directors' reports need no longer state:

- *Amounts, if any, proposed to be transferred to reserves.*   s234
- *Particulars of significant changes in fixed assets.*   Sch 7.1(1) repealed
- *Statement of insurance purchased or maintained for officers or auditors against liabilities in relation to the company.*   Sch 7.5A repealed
- *Arrangements for securing the health, safety and welfare of employees (regulations never came into operation).*   Sch 7.10 repealed

Amendments to requirement are:

- The disclosure of the difference in market value of interests in land from the amount at which they are stated as fixed assets in the balance sheet is now to refer to fixed assets of subsidiary undertakings as well as the company itself.   Sch 7.1(2)
- Statement of policy on payment of creditors – [not small companies]. New requirements for public companies or large private companies within a group headed by a public company are for the directors' report to disclose the company's policy in relation to the payment of creditors.   Sch 7.12

Directors' statements

Statements by the directors on the balance sheet and director's reports concerning:

- small company accounts entitlement [following SI 1992 No. 2452];   s246(8)
- abbreviated accounts;   s246(8)
- directors' report;   s246(8)

Appendix I 'Accounting Simplifications' and SI 1996 No. 189

s249B(4) and (5)
s250(4)(c)
- audit exemption; and
- dormant company audit exemption,

s246(8) must be above (but not necessarily immediately above) the directors' signatures (required by section 233 or section 234A) but need no longer be literal transcriptions of the text of the Act but a précis 'to the effect that...' instead.

Section 246(8) requires the accounts or directors' report to contain a statement *in a prominent position* on the balance sheet above the directors' signature(s) that the accounts 'are prepared in accordance with the special provisions [contained in section 246] relating to small companies'.

Accounting reference date

s224(3A) The accounting reference date for all companies after 1 April 1996 is now the last day of the month in which the anniversary of incorporation falls.

s225 Companies now have a general right to change the accounting reference date of either the current or previous accounting period provided only one extension may be made within a five-year period (except in respect of EEA group undertakings).

Condition for exemption from requirement to prepare group accounts

s228 (2)(d)(ii) repealed

A company is no longer required to state in its individual accounts whether its GB parent undertaking (i.e., incorporated in Great Britain) is registered in England and Wales or Scotland in order to be entitled to exemption from the requirement to prepare group accounts. It is still required to disclose:

- its entitlement to exemption; and
- the name of its parent undertaking.

Auditors

s237(4A) Where advantage is taken of section 248 exemption (from preparing small or medium-sized group accounts) but in the auditors' opinion there is no such entitlement, the auditors must state the fact in their audit report.

s248(3), (4) repealed

Auditors no longer have a duty to provide a report confirming entitlement to section 248 exemption.

Audit exemption

s249B(1A) A subsidiary undertaking that is dormant (within meaning of section 250 CA 1985) throughout the period it was a subsidiary, is entitled to audit exemption, providing other criteria are met. 'Off the shelf' companies in their first period following incorporation are thus entitled to exemption.

Disclosure amendments

Form and content of accounts (Schedule 4)
Disclosure items contained within CA 1985 Schedule 4 amended or no longer required are as follows:

- Transfers may be made to or from a revaluation reserve in respect of taxation relating to the profit or loss credited or debited to the reserve. A provision for deferred tax on a revaluation surplus can, therefore, now be set against the revaluation reserve.   *Sch 4.34(3)(b)*
- *The reason for making an allotment of shares or issue of debentures during the financial year – no longer required.*   *Sch 4.39(a)* / *Sch 4.41(1)(a) repealed*
- *Particulars of any redeemed debentures which company has power to reissue – no longer required.*   *Sch 4.41(2) repealed*
- *Analysis of listed investments between UK and overseas stock exchanges – no longer required.*   *Sch 4.45(1)(b) repealed*
- *Analysis of debts due (for each item of creditors) after more than five years between those repayable by instalments and otherwise – no longer required.*   *Sch 4.48(1)(b) repealed*
- *Capital commitments – aggregate amount or estimated amount of capital expenditure authorised by the directors which has not been contracted for – no longer required.*   *Sch 4.50(3) repealed*
- *Aggregate amount of dividend recommended – no longer required.*   *Sch 4.51(3) repealed*
- Interest payable is now only required to be analysed between that in respect of: *Sch 4.53(2)*
  (i) bank loans and overdrafts; and
  (ii) loans of any other kind.

Other disclosures no longer required are:

- *Amounts set aside for redemption of share capital and for redemption of loans.*   *Sch 4.53(3) repealed*
- *Amount of income from listed investments.*   *Sch 4.53(4) repealed*
- *Amount of rents from land.*   *Sch 4.53(5) repealed*
- *Charges in respect of hire of plant and machinery.*   *Sch 4.53(6) repealed*
- *Basis on which the charge for UK corporation tax and income tax is computed.*   *Sch 4.54(1) repealed*
- *Pre-tax profit or loss attributable to classes of turnover.*   *Sch 4.55(1)(b) repealed*
- *For group companies, balances with parent and fellow subsidiaries, or with subsidiaries respectively.*   *Sch 4.59 repealed*

Group accounts
Auditors' remuneration disclosed in group accounts must now include remuneration of all auditors of all undertakings included in the consolidation.   *Sch 4A.1(1)*

Pre-acquisition profit or loss of an acquired undertaking for the year of acquisition and the previous financial year – disclosure no longer required.   *Sch 4A.13(4) repealed*

Cumulative goodwill written off is required to be disclosed only where it has not been written off previously in the consolidated profit and loss account.   *Sch 4A.14(1)*

Numerous amendments and deletions of disclosure requirements (reflected in Appendix H).   *Sch 5*

Appendix I *'Accounting Simplifications' and SI 1996 No. 189*

Profit and loss account
Changes to disclosure requirements are:

s247(6)
Sch 4.56(2), (3)
- The calculation of the number of employees (used for the purposes of qualifying conditions for company size (section 247 CA 1985) and for determining the average number of employees (Schedule 4.56 CA 1985) is now to be made on a monthly rather than weekly basis.

Sch 4.3(7)
- The aggregate amount of any dividends proposed – if not shown in the notes to the accounts – is to be shown in the profit and loss account (this is in addition to the requirement to disclose the aggregate amount of any dividends paid *and* proposed).

Appendix J Abbreviated accounts checklist

Introduction

Checklist for the preparation of abbreviated accounts
The checklist in this Appendix is a guide to the appropriate disclosure requirements in producing 'abbreviated accounts' for delivery to the Registrar of Companies. This checklist therefore does not purport to be a complete checklist, detailing the disclosure requirements applicable where individual full accounts are prepared. For this purpose one of the accounts checklists suggested in Appendix **K** should be used.

Special provisions may apply where a company is a 'dormant company' under the Companies Act 1985 section 250 (see **2.9**).

References in this checklist to 'full accounts' include simplified 'small company accounts' (in accordance with Schedule 8 – see **7.1**).

A company which qualifies as small or medium-sized is entitled to deliver abbreviated accounts to the Registrar of Companies.

Company classification   *s246*
1. Complete the following information:

	19 £	19 £	19 £
Turnover			
Balance sheet total	£	£	£
Employees			

Refer to 'Decision chart to determine size qualification' (Diagram 6.1).

Two of the following three criteria must be met:

		Small company	Medium-sized company
Turnover	Under	£2.8m	£11.2m
Balance sheet total (gross assets before deducting liabilities, i.e., A–D (Format 1) or total of 'Assets' (Format 2))	Under	£1.4m	£5.6m
Employees (average number)	Under	50	250

s247

Public companies, members of public groups, authorised persons (FSA 1986), banking or insurance companies are ineligible, i.e., not entitled to prepare abbreviated accounts.

A parent company is not treated as small or medium-sized unless the group headed by it is small or medium-sized respectively.

Appendix J   Abbreviated accounts checklist

	Are abbreviated accounts appropriate?	✓ or N/A
	2. Based on the above information (a) The company qualifies as: 　　(i) small　　　　(if so, answer 3 to 11)　　⎱ abbreviated 　　　　　　　　　　　　　　　　　　　　　　　⎰ accounts 　　(ii) medium-sized　(if so, answer 3 to 7 and 12)　may be prepared (b) The company is: 　　(i) ineligible　　　　　　　　　　　　　　　⎱ if so, abbreviated 　　　or　　　　　　　　　　　　　　　　　　　⎰ accounts *not* 　　(ii) large (i.e., neither 'small' nor 'medium-sized')　appropriate	
s246(9)	*Directors' statements and signature* (Not applicable where 'dormant company' under CA 1985 s250 see 5 below) 3. Where advantage is taken of audit exemption, the directors are required to confirm or acknowledge: (a) company's entitlement to audit exemption (b) no notice requesting an audit received (c) duty to keep accounting records (s221 CA 1985) (d) duty to prepare true and fair view accounts (s226 CA 1985).	
s246(8)	4. Directors are required to state in a prominent position above approval signature on the balance sheet that the accounts are prepared in accordance with the special provisions of Part VII CA 1985 relating to small companies.	
s250	5. If the company is dormant, and is exempted from the need to appoint auditors, instead of 3 and 4 above, a statement is required that the company was dormant throughout the financial year.	
s246 s233	6. Abbreviated balance sheet (small company) or full balance sheet (medium-sized company) must be signed by a director (in accordance with CA 1985 s233) on behalf of the board.	
s247B(1)	*Special auditors' report* (Not applicable where 'dormant company' under CA 1985 s250 or advantage taken of audit exemption but see 13 below)	
s247B(2)	7. Where abbreviated accounts are filed, the special auditors' report is required to state that in the auditors' opinion: (a) the company is entitled to deliver abbreviated accounts prepared in accordance with the relevant provision (s246(5) or (6) [small companies] or s246A(3) [medium-sized companies]); (b) the accounts are properly prepared in accordance with that relevant provision.	
s247B(3)	If the auditors' report on the full shareholders' accounts was qualified, the special report must reproduce the text in full (with further material necessary to understand a qualification).	
s247B(3)	The special auditors' report must also reproduce any statement contained in the full auditors' report under s237(2) or (3) (proper accounting records or failure to obtain necessary information etc.).	

Checklist for the preparation of abbreviated accounts

Small company *Note: Small company accounts exceeding the basic Schedule 8 minimum requirements may be presented as abbreviated accounts.*		*s246(5)* *s246(2)(b)*
8. No directors' report.		
9. No profit and loss account.		*s246(5)*
10. Balance sheet – abbreviated version		
(a) Only format headings with letter or roman number need be shown (in the order and presentation of Sch 8A).		*Sch 8A*

(b) For debtors *and* creditors, show aggregate amounts falling due:
       (i) within one year;
       (ii) after more than one year,
    (unless shown in notes).
		Sch 8A

(c) The signature of a director (see 6 above).		*s246(7)*
11. Notes – show only:		*Sch 8A.3*
(a) Accounting policies adopted.		*Sch 8A.4*
(b) Share capital:		*Sch 8A.5*

(i) authorised share capital;
       (ii) number and aggregate nominal value of allotted shares of each class;
       (iii) share allotments during the year – state classes allotted and reason for allotment and for each class of shares, the number allotted, their aggregate nominal value and the consideration received by the company;
       (iv) redeemable shares – redemption dates and option details.
		Sch 8A.6

(c) Fixed assets movements – only format headings with letter or roman number (i.e., movements in tangible fixed assets, intangible fixed assets, and fixed asset investments for the categories in total) need be shown, including cost or valuation and accumulated depreciation at beginning and end of year; additions, disposals, revaluations, and depreciation provisions.		*Sch 8A.7*
(d) Creditors and indebtedness (i) liabilities repayable in more than five years		*Sch 8A.8*
(1) amount due for repayment, other than by instalments, after more than five years from the balance sheet date;		
(2) amount repayable by instalments, after more than five years;		
(ii) aggregate amount of *secured* liabilities.		*Sch 8A.8(2)*
(e) Foreign currencies – basis for translating foreign currencies.		*Sch 8A.9(1)*
(f) Comparative figures except in respect of directors' loans (Sch 6), shareholdings in other undertakings (Sch 5), accounting treatment of acquisitions (Sch 4A) and fixed assets: where corresponding amounts are not comparable, adjust and give particulars of and reasons for adjustment.		*Sch 8A.9(2)*
(g) Particulars of holdings in undertakings (other than subsidiary undertakings) where holdings exceed 20 per cent. (For disclosure details see Appendix **H**.)		*Sch 5.7*
(h) Loans and transactions involving directors and officers. (Certain comparatives not required – see Sch 6.)		*Sch 6*
(i) Particulars of subsidiary undertakings. (For disclosure details see Appendix **H**.)		*Sch 5*

Appendix J Abbreviated accounts checklist

Sch 5	(j) Parent undertakings (name and country of incorporation or principal business address if unincorporated).	
Sch 5	(k) Ultimate parent company.	
s246A	*Medium-sized company* 12. Full shareholders' accounts including directors' report, should be reproduced as abbreviated accounts *except*:	

s246A(3)(a)	(a) Profit and loss account may commence with 'Gross profit or loss'.
	
	'Gross profit or loss' is achieved by combining
	    items 1, 2, 3 *and* 6 (Format 1)
	    items 1 to 5 (Format 2)
	    items A1, B1 and B2 (Format 3)
	    items A1, A2 and B1 to B4 (Format 4)	

s246A(3)(b)	(b) Notes may omit information required by Sch 4.55: turnover analysis by class of business and geographical market.	
s242(1) s249E(2)(b)	*Accountants' report – abbreviated accounts* 13. Where abbreviated accounts are prepared based on unaudited full individual accounts, the accountants' report prepared for the purposes of s249A(2) on those accounts (if required) should be filed with the Registrar of Companies (see **10.12**).	

Appendix K Selected reading

This Appendix provides a selection of the literature to which this book might form a companion.

British Companies Legislation		CCH Editions
Company Law Handbook	K Walmsley (Editor)	Butterworths
(Both texts contain full (amended and up-to-date) company law statutes, statutory instruments and European legislation. It is best to use 1997 and subsequent editions.)		
The Companies Act 1985 and 1989 – Accounting and Related Requirements (1996)	J Aldis and A Bogie	Accountancy Books
Companies' Accounts Checklists (Accountants Digest 363)	S Hastie and R Rhodes	Accountancy Books
Financial Reporting and Accounting Manual (4th ed. 1994)	Touche Ross	Butterworths
Financial Statements for Smaller Companies: A Guide to Practice and the FRSSE	M Lennon and I Sharp	Accountancy Books
Reporting Requirements for the Smaller Company (July 1993) (Accountants Digest 302) (due to be updated in late 1997)	R Bryant	Accountancy Books
Company Accounts Disclosure Checklist (vol 3 of The Practitioner's Audit Service)	SWAT Ltd	Accountancy Books

Index

Abbreviated accounts, 1.1, 1.7.1, *Tables 1.1–1.3*, 7.1, 8.1–8.8, *Tables 8.1–8.5*
  accountants' reports, 8.2, *Table 8.2*, Appendix J
  additional costs of, 8.8
  auditors' reports, 1.7.1, 2.8, 8.2, *Table 8.2*, 8.9, 10.7, Appendix C, Appendix J
  audit exemptions, 10.5, *Table 10.1*, 10.12
  checklist, Appendix J
  contents, 8.2, *Table 8.2*
  definition, 8.2
  example, Small Company Ltd, 12.2 (pp95, 117–25)
  format of, 4.4, 8.1–8.6, *Tables 8.2–8.5*, Appendix E, Appendix J
  guidelines and definitions, 5.2.3–5.2.4
  notes to the accounts, 8.2, 8.5, *Tables 8.2, 8.4*, Appendix E
  Registrar of Companies, 8.1, Appendix J
Accountants' reports
  abbreviated accounts, 8.2, *Table 8.2*, Appendix J
  approval and signature, 2.12
  audit exemptions, 7.9, 10.7, 10.10–10.12, Appendix F
Accounting
  alternative bases of, 5.9, *Tables 5.1, 7.1*, Appendix D
  disclosure of policies, Appendix D
  guidelines and definitions, 5.1–5.11, *Table 5.1*
  historical cost, *Table 7.1*, Appendix D
  principles, 2.5, 3.3, Appendix D
    FRSSE, 11.2, *Table 11.1*
  recognised bodies, 10.11, Appendix F
  simplifications, 1.5.1, 1.6.1, Appendix I
  standards, 1.2, 3.1–3.7, *Table 3.2*
    ASB, 3.1–3.7, *Table 3.2*
    cash flow statements, 3.4
    Companies Act 1985, 3.1–3.7, *Table 3.2*, Appendix A
    financial statements, 3.1
    FRSSE, 11.1–11.4, *Tables 11.1, 11.2*
    GAAP, 3.3
    primary statements, 3.2, *Table 3.1*
    transactions, substance of, 3.5
Accounting Standards Board (ASB)
  FRS, 1.6.3
  standards, 1.2, 3.1–3.7, *Table 3.2*
  Urgent Issues Task Force (UITF), 3.3
    FRSSE, 11.1
    UITF, acounting standards, *Table 3.2*
    UITF 7, true and fair view, 5.1
Accounting standards table, 3.6, *Table 3.2*
Accounts
  see also **abbreviated accounts; accounting; group accounts**
  annual, 5.2.2–5.2.3, Appendix A
  approval and signature, 2.12, Appendix A
  audit exemption, 1.6.4
  classifications, 6.1, Appendix J
  defects, Appendix A
  EC Fourth Directive, 1.3
  ECUs, 1.5.1
  examples
    abbreviated accounts, Small Company Ltd, 12.2 (pp95, 117–25)
    accounts, Small Company Ltd, 12.1 (pp95, 97–117)
    auditors' reports, 12.4 (pp96, 99, 103, 117–19)
    unaudited accounts, Dormant Small Company Ltd, 12.3 (pp96, 124–5)
  format of, 2.4, 4.1–4.6, *Tables 4.1–4.6*, 7.2, 8.3
    format headings, 4.2, *Table 4.1*
    FRS 3, effect of, 4.5, *Tables 4.4–4.5*
    FRS 4, effect of, 4.6, *Table 4.4*
    smaller companies, 7.1–7.10, *Tables 7.1–7.3*, 8.1–8.6, *Tables 8.2–8.5*
    statutory format options, 4.1, Appendix B
  guidelines and definitions, 5.1–5.11, *Table 5.1*
  interpretations, Appendix A
  laying and delivering, 2.2, 8.1, *Table 8.1*, Appendix A
  periods of, Appendix A, Appendix I
  primary statements, 3.2, *Table 3.1*
  provisions, Companies Act 1985, 2.1–2.12
  publication, 2.10, Appendix A
  records, Companies Act 1985, Appendix A
  requirements, 2.2, 2.8, 10.1
  Secretary of State powers, Appendix A
  special provisions, 1.6.2, 1.6.4, *Tables 1.1–1.2*, 6.1–6.4, 7.1–7.10, *Tables 7.1–7.3*
  statutory, 5.2.3
  true and fair view, 2.3, 5.1, 7.9, 10.1
    FRSSE, 11.1.1, *Table 11.1*
  variety of, 1.8, *Table 1.3*
Accruals
  balance sheets formats, Appendix B
  concept, accounting principles, 2.5
  creditors, 5.5.2
Accruals and deferred income
  abbreviated accounts format, Appendix E
Acquisitions, 5.3.17
Administrative expenses, 5.3.4
  profit and loss accounts, Appendix B
Annual reports *see* **Directors' reports**
ASB *see* **Accounting Standards Board**
Assets
  abbreviated accounts, 8.4, *Tables 8.3, 8.4*
  balance sheet restrictions, 2.4

current
  abbreviated accounts format, Appendix E
  balance sheets, 5.4.5, Appendix B
  rules, Appendix D
depreciation, FRSSE, 11.2, *Table 11.1*
disposal of, 5.3.23, 5.4.1
fixed, 5.4.1
  abbreviated accounts formats, Appendix E
  balance sheets formats, Appendix B
  notes to the accounts, Appendix D
  rules, Appendix D
format of, Appendix B, Appendix D
securitised, 5.11
tangible, balance sheets, 5.4.3

Associated company
SSAP 1, definition, 5.4.6

Audits
auditors' remuneration, profit and loss accounts, 5.3.13
auditors' reports
  abbreviated accounts, 2.8, 8.2, *Table 8.2*, 10.7, Appendix C
  approval and signature, 2.12
  Companies Act 1985, 2.8, Appendix A, Appendix C
  directors' reports, 5.8, Appendix I
  disclosure requirements checklist, Appendix J
  examples, Small Company Ltd, 12.4 (pp96, 99, 102, 117–18)
  group accounts exemptions, 9.5, Appendix C
  special provisions, 1.7.1, *Table 1.1*, Appendix C
  statutory accounts, 5.2.3
exemptions, 2.8, *Table 1.3*, 10.1–10.12, *Tables 10.1–10.2*, Appendix A
  abbreviated accounts, 10.5, 10.12, *Table 10.1*
  accountants' reports, 10.7, 10.10–10.12, *Example 10.2*, Appendix F
  charities, 10.6, 10.8, 10.12, *Table 10.1*, *Example 10.1*
  directors' statements, 10.6, 10.9, *Example 10.1*, Appendix F, Appendix I
  dormant companies, Appendix I
  ineligibility, 10.3, 10.4, *Table 10.1*, Appendix F
  'off the shelf' companies, Appendix I
  qualifying conditions, 1.5.2, 10.5, 10.6, *Table 10.1*, Appendix F
  report conditions, 10.8
  smaller companies, 1.6.4, 6.4, 7.1, 7.9, Appendix F
group accounts' exemptions, Appendix I
shareholders powers to require, 10.4, 10.6, *Table 10.1*
true and fair view, 7.9

Balance sheet events
post FRSSE, 11.2, *Table 11.1*

Balance sheets
abbreviated accounts, 5.2.4, 8.2, *Table 8.2*, Appendix E, Appendix J
  format of, 8.4, *Table 8.3*
audit exemptions, 10.5, 10.6, *Table 10.1*
directors' statements, 10.9, *Example 10.1*
'report conditions', 10.8
dormant company, example, 12.2 (p125)
elements, 5.4–5.6, Appendix B, Appendix E
example, Small Company Ltd, 12.1 (p104)
format of, 7.1–7.3, 7.6.1, 7.8, *Tables 7.1, 7.2*, Appendix C, Appendix D
  options, 2.4, 4.1.2, 4.2, *Tables 4.1–4.2, 7.2*, Appendix B, Appendix D, Appendix E
FRSSE, 11.2, *Table 11.1*
group accounts' exemptions, 9.4, *Diagram 9.1*, Appendix C
guidelines and definitions, 5.4
primary statements, 3.2, *Table 3.1*
smaller companies qualifier, 6.2, Appendix C, Appendix J

Banking and insurance companies, Appendix A

Capital
see also **shareholders; shares**
abbreviated accounts format, Appendix E
balance sheets formats, Appendix B
instruments
  equity shares, 5.6.4
  FRS 4 requirements, 4.6, *Table 4.6*
  FRSSE, 11.2, *Table 11.1*
  guidelines and definitions, 5.6
  liabilities, 5.6.6, 5.6.7
  non-equity shares, 5.6.5
  shareholder's funds, 5.6.2
  shares, 5.6.3

Cash
abbreviated accounts format, Appendix E
balance sheets, 5.4.4

Cash flow statements
abbreviated accounts, 8.2, *Table 8.2*
accounts' standards, 3.4
exemptions, 3.4, 3.6, *Table 3.2*
primary statements, 3.2, *Table 3.1*

Charitable companies (charities) *see* **Audits**, exemptions

Companies
see also **smaller companies; unlimited companies**
banking and insurance, Appendix A
dormant, 2.9, Appendix A, Appendix G
  audit exemptions, Appendix I
listed public, Appendix A

Companies Act 1981
EC Fourth Directive, 1.3

Companies Act 1985
abbreviated accounts, Appendix E, Appendix J
accounting simplifications, Appendix I
audit exemptions, Appendix F
disclosures, Appendix H
dormant companies, Appendix G
form and content of accounts, Appendix D
general background, 1.3
special provisions, Appendix C
statutory formats, Appendix B

Index

Companies Act 1989
group accounts, exemptions, 1.4, 2.11, 9.1–9.7, *Diagram 9.1*
Companies acts
interpretation difficulties, 1.2
Consistency concept
accounting principles, 2.5
Consolidated accounts
FRSSE, 11.2, *Table 11.1*
group accounts, 2.11, 9.1–9.7, *Diagram 9.1*
Contingencies
FRSSE, 11.2, *Table 11.1*
Continuing operations, 5.3.16
Cost of sales, 5.3.2, Appendix B
abbreviated accounts, 8.6, *Table 8.5*
Creditors
abbreviated accounts format, Appendix E
balance sheets, 5.5.2
balance sheets formats, Appendix B
notes to the accounts, 7.5, Appendix D

Debtors
abbreviated accounts format, Appendix E
balance sheets, 5.5.1
example, Small Company Ltd, 12.1 (p117)
Debts
factoring of, 5.11, 11.2, *Table 11.1*
Decision chart
smaller companies qualification, 6.4
Depreciation
FRSSE, Appendix B, 11.2, *Table 11.1*
profit and loss accounts, 4.1, *Table 4.3*
rules, Companies Act 1985, Appendix D
Directors' reports, 2.7, 5.7, 7.6.2, 7.11, *Table 7.6*, Appendix A, Appendix I
abbreviated accounts, 8.2, *Table 8.2*
approval and signature, 2.12
auditors' reports, 5.8, Appendix I
disclosure, emoluments, 7.10.2, *Table 7.5*
events since the end of the year, 5.7.4
example, Small Company Ltd, 12.1 (pp95, 97–115)
future developments, 5.7.3
guidelines and definitions, 5.2.1, 5.7
research and development, 5.7.5
review of business, 5.7.2
statutory accounts, 5.2.3
Directors' statements, 7.6, Appendix I
abbreviated accounts, 8.3
audit exemptions, 10.6, 10.9, *Example 10.1*, Appendix F, Appendix I
disclosure requirements checklist, Appendix J
Disclosures, 7.1, *Table 7.2*, Appendix H
abbreviated accounts, checklists, Appendix J
accounting policies, Appendix D, Appendix E
amendments, Appendix I
Companies Act 1985, 2.6, Appendix H
directors' emoluments, 7.10.2, *Table 7.5*
example, Small Company Ltd, 12.2 (p121)
FRSSE requirements, related parties 11.4
group accounts exemptions, Appendix H
smaller company concessions, 7.10, *Table 7.4*
turnover, 5.3.5
Discontinued operations, 5.3.18
Disposal of assets, 5.3.23, 5.4.1
Distribution costs
profit and loss accounts, 5.3.3, Appendix B
Dividends
creditors, 5.5.2
FRS 4 requirements, 4.6
non-equity shares, 4.6
profit and loss accounts, 4.1, *Table 4.3*, Appendix I
Dormant companies, 1.8, 2.9, *Table 1.3*, Appendix A, Appendix G
audit exemptions, Appendix I
example, Dormant Small Company Ltd, 12.3 (pp96, 124–25)
smaller companies qualification, 6.4.1

ECUs
accounts in, 1.5.1
European Community (EC)
Fourth Directive, 1.3
Events since the end of the year
directors' reports, 5.7.4
Example accounts, 12.1–12.4 (pp95–125)
Exceptional items, Appendix B
FRS 3 format requirements, 4.5.1
FRSSE, 11.3, *Table 11.2*
profit and loss accounts, 5.3.19
Extraordinary items, Appendix B
FRS 3 format requirements, 4.5.2
FRSSE, 11.3, *Table 11.2*
profit and loss accounts, 5.3.20

Factoring of debts, 5.11, 11.2, *Table 11.1*
Financial Reporting Standard (FRS)
accounting standards, 3.3
ASB, 1.6.3
FRSs, accounting standards table, 3.6, *Table 3.2*
FRS 1
cash, 5.4.4
cash flow statements, 3.4, 3.6, *Tables 3.1, 3.2*
FRS 2
accounting principles, 2.5
group accounts, 2.11
participating interest, 5.4.6
FRS 3
format of accounts, 4.5, *Tables 4.4–4.5*
FRSSE, 11.3, *Table 11.2*
profit and loss accounts, 5.3.15–5.3.23
statement of gains and losses, 3.2, *Table 3.1*
FRS 4
capital instruments, 5.6
format of accounts, 4.6, *Table 4.6*
liabilities, 4.6, *Table 4.1*
FRS 5, substance of transactions, 3.5, 5.11
Financial Reporting Standard for Smaller Entities (FRSSE), 11.1–11.4, *Tables 11.1, 11.2*
accounting principles, 11.2, *Table 11.1*
accounting standards, 3.3

193

background, 1.6.3
balance sheets, 11.2, *Table 11.1*
capital instruments, 11.2, *Table 11.1*
consolidated financial statements, 11.2, *Table 11.1*
contingencies, 11.2, *Table 11.1*
debt factoring, 11.2, *Table 11.1*
depreciation, 11.2, *Table 11.1*
exceptional items, 11.3, *Table 11.2*
extraordinary items, 11.3, *Table 11.2*
foreign currency translation, 11.2, *Table 11.1*, 11.5
FRS 3, 11.3, *Table 11.2*
goodwill, 11.2, *Table 11.1*
government grants, 11.2, *Table 11.1*
investment properties, 11.2, *Table 11.1*
leases, 11.2, *Table 11.1*
long-term contracts, 11.2, *Table 11.1*
pensions, 11.2, *Table 11.1*
post balance sheet events, 11.2, *Table 11.1*
profit and loss accounts, 11.2, 11.3, *Tables 11.1, 11.2*
qualifying conditions, 11.1
related parties, 11.2, *Table 11.1*, 11.4
research and development, 11.2, *Table 11.1*
SSAPs, 1.6.3, 11.1
statement of gains and losses, 11.2, 11.3, *Tables 11.1, 11.2*
stocks, 11.2, *Table 11.1*
taxation, 11.2, 11.3, *Tables 11.1, 11.2*
true and fair view, 11.1.1, *Table 11.1*
UITF, 11.1

Financial statements
objectives, 3.1
Foreign currency translation, 11.2, *Table 11.1*, 11.5
FRS *see* **Financial Reporting Standard**
FRSSE *see* **Financial Reporting Standard for Smaller Entities**
Future developments
directors' reports, 5.7.3

GAAP *see* **Generally Accepted Accounting Principles**
Generally Accepted Accounting Principles (GAAP), 3.3
Going concern concept
accounting principles, 2.5
Goodwill
balance sheets, 5.4.2
FRSSE, 11.2, *Table 11.1*
Government grants, 11.2, *Table 11.1*
Gross profit or loss, 4.1.1, 8.6, *Tables 4.3, 8.5*, Appendix B, Appendix J
Group accounts, 6.3, 7.7, Appendix A
abbreviated accounts, 8.7
annual accounts, 5.2.2, Appendix A
consolidated accounts, 2.11, 9.1–9.7, *Diagram 9.1*
disclosures, Appendix I
exemptions, 9.1–9.7, *Diagram 9.1*, Appendix C
auditors' reports, 9.5, Appendix C
Companies Act 1989, 1.4, 2.11, 9.3, Appendix C
disclosures required, Appendix H
qualifying conditions, 9.2–9.4, 9.7, *Diagram 9.1*, Appendix C, Appendix I
format, 4.3, Appendix B
income from shares, 5.3.11, Appendix B
parent undertakings, 5.10
requirements, 9.1
subsidiary undertakings, 5.10
Guarantees, notes to the accounts, 7.5, Appendix D

Income
group undertakings, 5.3.11, Appendix B
participating interests, 5.3.12, Appendix B
Income and expenditure accounts, 5.2.2
Individual determination concept
accounting principles, 2.5
Interest payable and similar charges, 5.3.14, Appendix B
Investment properties
FRSSE, 11.2, *Table 11.1*
Investments
abbreviated accounts format, Appendix E
notes to the accounts, Appendix D

Joint ventures, 5.10

Leases
FRSSE, 11.2, *Table 11.1*
Liabilities
abbreviated accounts, 8.4, *Tables 8.3, 8.4*
balance sheets formats, Appendix B
capital instruments, 5.6.6, 5.6.7
FRS 4 requirements, 4.6, *Table 4.1*
Listed public companies
Companies Act 1985, Appendix A
Loan transfers, 5.11
Long-term contracts
FRSSE, 11.2, *Table 11.1*

Medium-sized companies *see* **Smaller companies**
Minority interests
balance sheets formats, Appendix B
Modified accounts *see* **Abbreviated accounts**

Net current assets
abbreviated accounts format, Appendix E
balance sheet formats, Appendix B
Netting concept
accounting principles, 2.5
Notes to the accounts, 5.2.2, 7.5, *Table 7.1*, Appendix D
abbreviated accounts, 8.2, 8.5, *Tables 8.2, 8.4*, Appendix E, Appendix J
concessions, 7.10, *Table 7.4*
example, Small Company Ltd, 12.1 (pp106–12)

Ordinary activities, 5.3.15
Other external charges, 5.3.8, 5.3.9

Index

Other interest receivable, Appendix B
Other operating charges, 5.3.9, Appendix B
Other operating income, 5.3.6, Appendix B
   abbreviated accounts, 8.6, *Table 8.5*
Own work capitalised, 5.3.7

Parent companies *see* Group accounts
Participating interest, 5.4.6
Pensions
   FRSSE, 11.2, *Table 11.1*
Post balance sheet events
   FRSSE, 11.2, *Table 11.1*
Prepayments, Appendix B, Appendix E
   see also accruals
   debtors, 5.5.1
Primary statements, 3.2, *Table 3.1*
Prior period adjustments, 5.3.21
Private companies
   Companies Act 1985, Appendix A
Production cost
   alternative bases of accounting, 5.9.2
Profit and loss accounts
   abbreviated accounts, 8.2, 8.6, *Tables 8.2, 8.5*, Appendix J
   disclosures, amendments, Appendix I
   elements, 4.1, 5.3, *Table 4.3*, Appendix B
   example, Small Company Ltd, 12.1, (pp103, 113–15)
   format, 2.4, Appendix B, Appendix D
   FRS 3 format requirements, 4.5.4, *Tables 4.4–4.5*
   FRSSE, 11.2, 11.3, *Tables 11.1, 11.2*
   guidelines and definitions, 5.3
   notes to the accounts, Companies Act 1985, Appendix D
   options format, 4.1, 4.2, 5.3.1, *Table 4.3*
   primary statements, 3.2, *Table 3.1*
   realised profits, 2.5
   smaller company formats, 7.4, *Table 7.2*
Profit or loss on disposal, 5.3.23
Properties
   investment, 11.2, *Table 11.1*
Provisions
   balance sheets formats, Appendix B
   liabilities
      abbreviated accounts, Appendix E
      balance sheets, 5.4.8
   notes to the accounts, Appendix D
Prudence concept
   accounting principles, 2.5
Purchase price
   alternative bases of accounting, 5.9.1

Quasi-subsiduaries
   substance of transactions, 5.11

Realised profits, 2.5
Registrar of Companies
   abbreviated accounts, 8.1, Appendix J
      special auditors' report, 8.9
   delivery of accounts, 2.2, Appendix A
   requirements, 10.1

statutory accounts, 5.2.3
Related parties
   FRSSE, 11.2, *Table 11.1*, 11.4
Research and development
   directors' reports, 5.7.5
   FRSSE, 11.2, *Table 11.1*
Reserves
   abbreviated accounts format, Appendix E
   balance sheet formats, Appendix B
   notes to the accounts, Companies Act 1985, 7.5, Appendix D
   profit and loss accounts, 4.1, *Table 4.3*
   revaluation, alternative bases of accounting, 5.9.3, Appendix D
Revaluation reserves
   alternative bases of accounting, 5.9.3
Review of business, directors' reports, 5.7.2

Sale and repurchase agreements
   substance of transactions, 5.11
Selling and distribution costs *see* Distribution costs
Shareholders
   capital instruments, 5.6.2
   funds' requirements, 4.6, *Table 4.4*
   powers to require audit, 10.4, 10.6, *Table 10.1*
Shares, 7.5
   abbreviated accounts, 8.4, *Tables 8.3, 8.4*
   capital
      abbreviated accounts format, Appendix E
      balance sheet formats, Appendix B
      example, Small Company Ltd, 12.1 (p118)
      capital instruments, 5.6.3
   equity
      capital instruments, 4.6, 5.6.4
   non-equity
      capital instruments, 5.6.5
      dividends, 4.6
   undertakings, 5.10
Smaller companies
   audit exemption, 1.6.4
   balance sheet formats, 7.6.1, 7.8, *Tables 7.1, 7.3*
   classifications, 6.1, Appendix J
   directors' emoluments disclosure, 7.10.2, *Table 7.5*
   disclosure concessions, 7.10, *Table 7.4*
   example, auditors' reports, 12.4 (pp117–19)
   profit and loss account formats, 7.4, *Table 7.2*
   qualifying conditions, 6.1, 6.2, Appendix A, Appendix C, Appendix J
      balance sheet total, 6.2, Appendix C, Appendix J
      decision chart, 6.4, *Diagram 6.1*, Appendix J
      ineligible companies, 6.1, 6.4.1, Appendix C, Appendix J
      staff count, 6.2, Appendix C, Appendix I, Appendix J
      turnover, 6.2, Appendix C, Appendix J
   special accounting provisions, 1.7.1
Social security
   creditors, 5.5.2

Index

Special auditors' report, 8.9
Special circumstances
　true and fair view, 5.1
SSAP *see* **Statement of Standard Accounting Practice**
Staff
　costs, 5.3.10, Appendix B
　count
　　group accounts exemptions, 9.4, *Diagram 9.1*, Appendix C
　　smaller companies qualifier, 6.2, Appendix I
Statement of Standard Accounting Practice (SSAP)
　accounting standards, 3.3, *Table 3.2*
　FRSSE, 1.6.3, 11.1
　SSAPs, accounting standards table, *Table 3.2*
　SSAP 1
　　associated company, 5.4.6
　　income, participating interests, 5.3.12
　SSAP 2, accounting principles, 2.5
　SSAP 13
　　fixed assets, 5.4.1
　　research and development, 5.7.5
　SSAP 17, directors' reports, 5.7.4
Statement of total recognised gains and losses
　example, Small Company Ltd, 12.1 (p105)
　FRSSE, 11.2, 11.3, *Tables 11.1, 11.2*
　primary statements, 3.2, *Table 3.1*
Stocks
　consignment, 5.11
　FRSSE, 11.2, *Table 11.1*
　valuation, balance sheets, 5.4.7
Substance of transactions, 3.5, 5.11
Supplementary notes
　FRS 3 format requirements, 4.5.3, *Table 4.5*

Taxation
　balance sheets, 5.4.9
　creditors, 5.5.2
　FRSSE, 11.2, 11.3, *Tables 11.1, 11.2*
Total recognised gains and losses, 5.3.22
Transactions
　example, directors, 12.2 (p123)
　substance of
　　accounts standards, 3.5
　　guidelines and definitions, 5.11
True and fair view, 2.3, 10.1
　audits, 7.9
　FRSSE, 11.1.1, *Table 11.1*
　guidelines and definitions, 5.1
Turnover
　abbreviated accounts, 8.6, *Table 8.5*, Appendix B
　audit exemptions, 10.5, 10.6, 10.8, *Table 10.1*, Appendix F
　group accounts' exemptions, 9.4, *Diagram 9.1*, Appendix C
　notes to the accounts, 7.5, Appendix D
　profit and loss accounts, 5.3.5
　smaller companies qualifier, 6.2, Appendix C, Appendix J

UITF *see* **Accounting Standards Board**, Urgent Issues Task Force
Undertakings
　Companies Act 1985, Appendix H
　guidelines and definitions, 5.10
　shares, 5.10
Unlimited companies, 10.1, Appendix A

Variety of accounts, 1.8, *Table 1.3*